FREAK PERFORMANCES

Freak Performances

DISSIDENCE IN LATIN AMERICAN THEATER

Analola Santana

UNIVERSITY OF MICHIGAN PRESS

Ann Arbor

Published in the United States of America by
the University of Michigan Press
Manufactured in the United States of America
Printed on acid-free paper

First published October 2018

Library of Congress Cataloging-in-Publication Data

Names: Santana, Analola, author.
Title: Freak performances : dissidence in Latin American theater / Analola
  Santana.
Description: Ann Arbor : University of Michigan Press, 2018. | Includes
  bibliographical references and index.
Identifiers: LCCN 2018022519 (print) | LCCN 2018028980 (ebook) | ISBN
  9780472124077 (E-book) | ISBN 9780472073917 (hardback) | ISBN
  9780472053919 (paper)
Subjects: LCSH: Theater--Political aspects—Latin America. | Theater and
  society—Latin America. | Monsters in the theater. | Other (Philosophy) in
  the performing arts | Postcolonialism—Social aspects—Latin America. |
  BISAC: PERFORMING ARTS / Theater / General.
Classification: LCC PN2445 (ebook) | LCC PN2445 .S26 2018 (print) | DDC
  792.098—dc23
LC record available at https://lccn.loc.gov/2018022519

*Para mi hijo Sebastián, para mi padre Arturo,
mis maestros de siempre.*

Acknowledgments

This book is the result of many years of research and writing, as well as ongoing dialogues with generous colleagues. The process of writing has been made more compelling through the many comments and conversations I am fortunate enough to have had with these kind individuals. First and foremost, I owe a debt of gratitude to Laura Edmondson, Jean Graham-Jones, Eng-Beng Lim, Alberto Sandoval-Sánchez, and Silvia Spitta, whose generous guidance and suggestions transformed my manuscript. I would not have been able to complete this book without the support of my writing group: Annelle Curulla, Dominick Grundy, Scott Sanders, and Karen Santos Da Silva. Writing is truly conceived in collaboration, and the bimonthly meetings of our group transformed the way I think about my own writing process. I am forever grateful to Rosemarie Garland-Thomson, who has proven to be an invaluable source of knowledge and advice. Her words inspired my own research and continue to motivate my work.

I would especially like to thank all the artists whose work is discussed in the pages of this book for their fearless aesthetics and profound work: Claudio Valdés Kuri, Miguel Rubio, Romina Paula, Roxana Ávila, Regina José Galindo, Violeta Luna, Arístides Vargas, Charo Francés, Katia Tirado, Suely Machado, Norman Brisky, Juan Carlos Zagal, Ana Correa, and Rodolfo Rodríguez. I am grateful for their generosity in sharing their time, materials, and conversations. In addition, I am grateful to the Instituto Nacional de Bellas Artes (INBA) and the Centro de Investigación Teatral Rodolfo Usigli (CITRU) in Mexico City, which allowed me access to its archives and provided invaluable information.

Discussions with many interlocutors over the years have informed and changed my thinking. These include Josefina Alcazar, Efraín Barradas, Roger Bartra, Debra Castillo, Jorge Dubatti, Paola Hernández, Jorge Huerta, Heather Nathans, Rosalina Perales, Lola Proaño-Gómez, Beatriz Rizk, Diana Taylor, Claudia Villegas, and Juan Villegas. I have no words with which to thank Jimmy Noriega, a best friend like no other, who has patiently listened to my ideas, coerced me into writing, appeased my fears, corrected my English, and, more than anything, given me the peace of mind that you can only get when you know that someone is unconditionally willing to pick up the phone and support you in this academic life. Jimmy, you preserve my sanity.

My family, especially my son Sebastian, gives me love and affection. Without them, the years spent writing this book would have been very lonely. I am so appreciative of their unfailing encouragement. My sisters and mother helped me with their warm spirit and reminders that there is life outside of work. I am eternally thankful for their laughter and phone calls. Most of all, I'm forever grateful to my partner in life, Alejandro, whose love and patience throughout the years have brought me inspiration and indescribable support and care.

Teaching constantly tests your ideas, and I have to thank my students at Dartmouth College, especially in the fall 2014 and winter 2017 seminars, who contributed to this project through their critical readings and discussions of several texts analyzed in this book. I would also like to thank Barbara Will, Associate Dean of Arts and Humanities at Dartmouth, for generously supporting this project through funds for a manuscript revision, which helped prepare it for publication. I want to thank my colleagues at Dartmouth, especially Sara Muñoz, Jill Baron, and Carlos Cortez Minchillo, who not only provided meaningful conversations about the subject of this book but gave me support and *convivencia* in the mountains of New Hampshire.

LeAnn Fields, my editor at the University of Michigan Press, has been an incredible inspiration. Her unwavering support for this manuscript through all its different stages motivated me to no end.

I also want to thank those who have given me the opportunity to share some of my work in progress with a wider audience. Some small parts of the "Introduction" and chapter 3 have been part of articles that appeared in *Theatre Topics* and *Lateral: Journal of the Cultural Studies Association* ("Between Pen and Sweat: An Account of an Experience between a Director and a Dramaturg," *Theatre Topics* 26.1 [March 2016]: 131–40; and "Circuits of Invisibility: Performance, Violence, and Sexuality," *Lateral: Journal of the Cultural Studies Association* 5.2 [Fall 2016]).

Contents

Aquí todos somos deformes
y nos resistimos a usar uniforme.
Lo más feo de la flor es el tallo
la belleza se alimenta de fallos.

Cómo nos vemos curiosos,
ponemos a los lindos nerviosos.
Que toda la gente nos señale,
lo que no es igual, sobresale.

Original, no lo pueden copiar.
Lo que es impuro no se puede duplicar.
La raza se arregla cuando se daña.
¡Somos de la tribu que con sucio se baña!

Here we are all deformed
and we refuse to use a uniform.
The ugliest part of the flower is the stem
beauty feeds on mistakes.

Since we look curious,
we get the pretty ones nervous.
Let everyone point to us
all that is different stands out.

Original, you can't copy it.
The things that are impure can't be multiplied.
Race gets better when it's damaged.
We are the tribe who clean themselves with dirt!

| The Freak Onstage

From Colonialism to Neoliberalism

Puerto Rican hip-hop artist Residente raps these lyrics in the song "Somos anormales" (We Are Abnormal), which debuted in January 2017. An aggressive affirmation of those perceived as imperfect and deformed, Residente continues, "We give birth to strange creatures / Like us, but with different features / Our gene pool, an endless maze / We're the same in different ways."[1] Residente (whose real name is René Pérez Joglar), the former lead singer in Puerto Rican hip-hop/reggaeton duo Calle 13 (13th Street), is known for his political activism as well as his provocative lyrics and videos.[2] In his song, Residente depicts the birth of humanity and focuses on imperfections as the core of human characteristics. In the accompanying video, all sorts of human types (different races, different sizes, different genders, a person with one eye, a dwarf, and even actor John Leguizamo) are birthed from the vagina (a giant simulated vagina) of one African woman who has just hatched from an egg. In an interview, Residente states, "The usage of the word 'abnormal' allowed me to break the negative connotation of the word and make it into an inclusive term." Although this is a simplification of the historical use of the marker *abnormal*, the way in which the singer conceives of it is quite innovative. The video shows the newborn adults devolving into chaos as they fight for the one piece of fruit available in the vast desert landscape (an apple, of course). The men and women split into opposing groups, an act described by Residente in the following manner: "We divide ourselves into two big social groups: the clean ones or the ones who have the power and the dirty ones that don't have a lot. Everything was born out of a fight and from then on the struggle has continued."[3] By dividing the humans in the video into the clean versus the dirty ones, the song acknowledges a history of stigma imposed on those who constitute the marginal sectors of society. Residente's lyrics offer a sociopolitical commentary and solidarity with a worldwide underclass.

Even though *Freak Performances* is about theater and performance, I can't help but use this song and video as an entry point precisely because they address some of the main issues that I investigate. Residente, a Puerto Rican rapper, exposes the historical construction of difference as dirt and reappropriates the trope of the freak (as an exaltation of difference) to produce an instance of political dissidence. The significance of Puerto Rico as a US colony should not be dismissed either; its continuing history of colonization is an example of the lasting effects of colonial power on subjectivity and culture. This legacy of colonialism is embedded in a history that has traditionally placed native Latin Americans in the position of "dirt"—they are the savage, the cannibal, and the monstrous other. Nevertheless, in the video difference triumphs; it is a condition to be admired and emulated. Residente's song and video show a process of self-enfreakment as an act that contests the Anglo-European hegemonic and imperialist gaze.[4] Similarly, in the plays that I analyze throughout this book, the actors onstage are not identified as physical freaks. Instead they embody an aesthetic of otherness through a process of self-enfreakment (whether through makeup, costume, movement, gesture, dialogue, or other theatrical means). In order to understand the significance of the freak in Latin American theatrical practices, I propose that the performances in this book function as allegories of the freak for the purpose of denouncing a racist, hegemonic construction of Latin American identity that began with colonization and continues into the present.

Residente's music video shares the concerns that I address in this book. In particular, *Freak Performances* demonstrates how mass culture has appropriated and disseminated the racial implication of difference as a point of contention in the western gaze's problematic construction of otherness as a stigmatized category. Mass media have promulgated a mythology of racialized bodies as criminal through a rhetoric that maintains that these individuals are out of control, a threat to the white citizen (particularly white women), and an evil to be banished. Historically, mass media, through their antagonistic portrayals of brown bodies, have confirmed white, privileged discourses about the other. The connecting theme in the reappropriation of these images by Latin American artists is an attempt to rewrite the stories of others as complicated human beings—as something other than the visceral image of criminality, menace, and threat that the mass media have associated with the racialized body. I begin *Freak Performances* with a reference to this video and then as an example of contestatory representations of otherness in contemporary mass culture.

In addition, the video has appeared precisely at a historical moment when the world is extremely divided by issues of immigration. Framed in a xenophobic discourse, the political Far Right has insisted on categorizing nonwhite identity as a threat to the economic, capitalist system of domination. Thus, the notion of the abnormal has acquired such cultural significance that even the most obvious forms of mass culture (such as the music video) have taken over the term as an example of dissidence and denunciation. This embrace of difference by mass culture builds on the assertions of Guy Debord: "The society which carries the spectacle does not dominate the underdeveloped regions by its economic hegemony alone. It dominates them *as the society of the spectacle.*"[5] If the mass media oppresses the underdeveloped, those considered outsiders can also fight through the reappropriation of this medium. In other words, even though the freak has continually been a part of mass culture, it has traditionally been a fixture that intends to promote the marginalization and control of different identities. The fact that popular musicians are using this figure as an instance of defiance indicates that it has transcended the limitations of its initial representations. Identity construction is embedded in popular culture and I recognize its role in the (self-)construction of subjectivities. In the face of global hegemonic discourses that condemn difference as deviance, even the commercial arts recognize the impact of reformulating and reappropriating the image of the freak as a defiant position that is not inherently negative. Instead, the representation of the freak in these forms of mass media is celebrated because of its ability to persist *as* a category of uniqueness — celebrating and claiming the very labels that seek to constrain them. Residente's video shows how images of the freak as a figure of political dissidence have acquired commercial value through popular music that seeks to present political activism regardless of commercial success.

I move from this focus on mass culture to theatrical production to demonstrate how contemporary Latin American theater grapples with these same issues. The fundamental question of *Freak Performances* is, in other words, how do we examine the role of the freak on the Latin American stage? To answer this question, I examine the images of unruly bodies as performances of protest. Rather than analyzing commercial theater, I focus on the images of the freak that have persisted in Latin American experimental theater because these are the stages that present dissident discourses. The performances I investigate are a rich symbol of the power inequities and normative constructions that continue to challenge identity politics in the region to this day.

Notions of any different body (by this I mean the freak in all its connotations — the grotesque, the deformed, the disabled, the visually/morally/socially excluded, the prostitute, the beggar, the terrorist, the antihero, and the homosexual, among many other types) as monstrous and freakish and representations of absolute otherness have become a common trope in many Latin American performative practices. I find this predominance to be connected to the political changes that have taken place in the last few decades, as globalization has forced different nations to question their role as modern states. Jesús Martín-Barbero defines this break as a reformulation of the construction and definition of difference.

> To think of *difference* in Latin America has ceased to mean the search for that authenticity in which a form of being is preserved in its original purity to become the inquiry into the *deviant* and *decentered* way of our inclusion in, and our appropriation of, modernity: that of a difference that cannot be digested or expelled, otherness that resists from within the very project of universality that modernity implies.[6]

The freak onstage symbolizes the recognition of the different body as a political issue, social construction, individual difference, and category of inquiry. It examines reconceptions of the body as a tool for dissidence and considers how the body can be transformed and mutated to reflect deeper social and political acts of resistance. The aim of *Freak Performances* is to question the dominant discourses that present freak bodies and behaviors as stigmatized narratives that validate the free-market system. These narratives are questioned through the performances themselves, which appear as dissident accounts of the freak body as a symbol of resistance. *Freak Performances* combines disability studies and freak studies with the various performance practices of Latin America. Through these intersections, I am interested in the fundamental meanings behind the act of transforming the body onstage and, in turn, how this "marks" the body as politically illegitimate.

Throughout this book, I address the categorization of human difference in terms of abnormal/normal. This binary has had a continued impact on the globalized discourses that have developed through the establishment of a neoliberal order in a vast part of Latin America. For the purposes of this book I look at a variety of countries: Costa Rica, Peru, Mexico, Argentina, Chile, Brazil, Ecuador, and Guatemala. The neoliberal order, as it has extended throughout Latin America, has shaped a particular understanding of the role of the body as part of a political economy. The freak acquires greater significance in a globalized community that defines the "normal" person as useful and docile, while the "abnormal" person demonstrates an inability to conform mentally, physically, or emotionally and thus is implicitly disqualified from citizenship. Early colonial practices linked "monstrousness" to a refusal to embrace Christianity, and indigenous peoples were disqualified as citizens based on their unwillingness to conform to particular performances of normative culture. In today's neoliberal world order the freak is the one who is unable, or unwilling, to follow the economic and cultural norms of the institutions in power. In order to understand this phenomenon in the present, we must first look back to the construction of difference in the colonial era.

UNDERSTANDING THE MONSTER: MAPPING THE TRACES OF COLONIALITY

As I traveled throughout different countries of Latin America, I kept seeing a pattern in the theater: a representation of characters that I could only describe as "freaks." Many of these performances dealt with characters that violated normative physical representations of the body, as well as behavioral representations. At first I understood these performances in relation to mass culture and its focus on creating images for consumption, which is the subject of my first book. But the more I delved into the topic, the more I saw it as an example of political dissidence against the identity categorizations of Latin American subjectivity. The freaks on these stages were reconfigured as instances of beauty, agency, even social change, not as the horrific and abject spectacle that hegemonic culture presents. I saw the different embodiments of freak identity as a reaction to the ways in which we, as Latin Americans, have been formatted as a body that does not fit the imperialist imaginary of normalcy.

There are two figures that permeate this book: the freak and the monster. These terms are meant to be rhetorical representations of the Latin American other. Whenever there is an epistemic break, different elements of society attempt to define what constitutes the "normal" human; all else remains beyond those limits of representation. I am interested in the freak as an allegory of Latin American identity because it is a figure that invites us to look at ourselves and consider what is unusual and odd about our own identity. In addition, the freak in Latin America is a representation of perseverance. This is an idea that follows Diane Arbus's suggestion that freaks have already been "through it" and have come out at the other end. Freaks, then, as a theatrical representation, offer a characterization of resilience in relation to their capacity to transform the normative and thus survive and cope in a hegemonic society.

I agree with theater and performance scholar Alberto Sandoval-Sánchez's argument that the concepts of the monster and the freak border on the notion of abjection.[7] As he explains, this means a return to Julia Kristeva's theorization in *Powers of Horror: An Essay on Abjection*, where she creates a theoretical framework from which to approach the different body and its subjectivity.

> [W]hat is abject . . . the jettisoned object, is radically excluded and draws me toward the place where meaning collapses. A certain "ego" that merged with its master, a superego, has flatly driven it away. . . . And yet, from its place of banishment, the abject does not cease challenging its master. . . . Not me. Not that. But not nothing, either. . . . On the edge of nonexistence and hallucination, of a reality that, if I acknowledge it, annihilates me. There, abject and abjection are my safeguards. The primers of my culture.[8]

What constitutes this being "on the edge," then, is that interstitial zone between the "not me," the "not that," and the "but not nothing either," where the abject subject is contrasted with a clean and proper body. Continuing with Sandoval's analysis, the body that is under the threat of abjection matters because it constitutes the outside zone of the social order, the positionality of a subject as proposed by Judith Butler, who writes, "[T]he abject designates . . . those 'unlivable' and 'uninhabitable' zones of social life which are nevertheless densely populated by those who do not enjoy the status of the subject, but whose living under the sign of the 'unlivable' is required to circumscribe the domain of the subject."[9] As a whole, the monster and the freak exist within these "uninhabitable" parameters but function as different perceptions of otherness. These two figures have different meanings and require different approaches: they are both abject but not in the same way.

I will not dwell on the historical trajectory of these terms in this introduction because I address the genealogy of these two tropes in the first chapter of this book. What needs to be emphasized here about the monster and the freak, however, is that the monster of antiquity embodied an almost divine identity. There is a rich corpus on the study of the monster in antiquity, from the biological works of Aristotle to works of divination (best exemplified by Cicero in *De Divinatione*). The recurring categories for identifying monstrosity in antiquity were by means of excess, defect, or hybridity. It is important to highlight these identity markers because they remain the standard by which difference is understood throughout history. In addition, the ethnic connotations of monstrosity were inherently found in the depiction of mythical otherness as the western mind explored and conquered the inhabitants of other lands. In chapter 1, I also consider how the characteristics of the monstrous races of antiquity were transposed onto the inhabitants of the Americas and how the other is reimagined in an intertextuality with the monstrous races of the Middle Ages. The indigenous inhabitants of the "New World" were captured as specimens to be placed on public display and were often considered soulless creatures. For these reasons, it is necessary to consider the history of the racialization of the monstrous body as it pertains to the construction of Latin American subjectivities and the theatricality that accompanied the exhibition of these "exotic creatures" as a means of establishing cultural dominion over other lands.

It is also important to understand the Eurocentric framing of Latin America as the abject other. This can be seen in early maps of the globe (after the "discovery" of the Americas): the maps where women represented particular values imposed by a European colonial mind-set on the "discovered" lands. These maps often included additional illustrations that served as worldviews and allegories for the different continents. The visual tropes that depicted the Americas as a land of cannibals and savages aimed to naturalize colonization and legitimize the violent practices that decimated the native populations. Latin America, as an idea, is culturally constructed, and the images that have been associated with this region are strongly linked to cartography.[10] A great example is found in Abraham Ortelius's influential *Theatrum orbis terrarum* of 1570—the world's first atlas. On the title page, Europe is represented as the empress, holding a scepter, dressed in glorious robes, and enthroned at the top of the world (as on a theatrical stage), ready to exert her domination. America, placed at the bottom of the stage, is also allegorized as a woman, but she is naked and looking down at the floor while holding a severed human head, with arrows below her legs. These allegorical representations of the continents reinforced the myth of the Americas as a land of cannibals and savagery (an idea that began with the voyages of Columbus).[11]

The basic subdivision of the continents into four (Asia, Africa, America, and Europe) established a set of conditions that was explicitly hierarchical for the purpose of creating a geopolitical structure imposed on them by an imperial discourse that has persevered for the past five hundred years. I am interested in this "perspective of coloniality," as proposed by Walter Mignolo. He describes the way in which colonial history has shaped the idea of the Americas, stating that "both people and continents outside of Europe were overly present as 'objects,' but they were absent as subjects and, in a

Fig. 1. Title page from Abraham Ortelius's *Theatrum orbis terrarum* (Antver-
piae: Apud Aegid. Coppenium Diesth, 1570). Courtesy of the Library of
Congress, American Memory Website.

way, out of history."[12] He continues to view this narrative as one of modernity. The colonial subjects were reduced to oversimplified categories ("Indians," "blacks") that also embodied negative values and classifications: primitive, savage, and monstrous. For these reasons, the notion of coloniality permeates the analysis of freak identity within the Latin American realm throughout this book, because

> Coloniality names the experiences and view of the world and history of those whom Fanon called *les damnés de la terre* ("the wretched of the earth," those who have been and continue to be, subjected to the standards of modernity). The wretched are defined by the *colonial wound*, and the colonial wound, physical and/or psychological, is a consequence of *racism*, the hegemonic discourse that questions the humanity of all those who do not belong to the locus of enunciation (and the geo-politics of knowledge) of those who assign the standards of classification and assign to themselves the right to classify.[13]

The construction of Latin American identity as freak is the embodiment of this "colonial wound," which aims to marginalize the multiple possibilities of individual existence into a threatening other, simplified by the abjection into which this identity category is placed. This racist othering has continued into an age of paranoid nationalism, which has often rendered entire bodies of performance in Latin American worlds as a monstrous body of surveillance in the theaters of everyday life. Achille Mbembe highlights the close relationship between geopolitical power and identity construction: "Violence and sovereignty, in this case, claim a divine foundation: peoplehood itself is forged by the worship of one deity, and national identity is imagined as an identity against the Other, other deities. History, geography, cartography, and archaeology are supposed to back these claims, thereby closely binding identity and topography."[14] Perhaps more than ever, Latin American bodies onstage (and off) have to negotiate an existence in a particularly hostile public sphere.

Thus, within the discourse of coloniality, Latin American subjectivity has historically been formatted within the domain of abjection; these are bodies that threaten the expansion of a project of colonization in the name of modernization. In order to justify a system of imperial domination, Latin America had to be condensed into a single, homogeneous identity. In the beginning, these undesirable subjects were generalized categories such as the indigenous native, the black slave, the peasant, and the woman. In contemporary society they now include the lower classes, the political dissident, the immigrant, and the queer. These bodies have been made into a spectacle of difference exhibited as the monstrous and the freak, that which will destroy the social order if not controlled. Recognizing enfreakment as one more form of colonial violence imposed on Latin American subjects may put a decontextualized concept to good use. In the hands of Latin American artists that deconstruct a European gaze to unveil its workings, appropriating the concept of the freak may be one more way to resist the Eurocentric stare that turns Latin Americans first into monsters, then freaks, while refusing to acknowledge or address their histories and individual stories.

THE RISE OF THE FREAK

The movement from monster to freak is first established when the study of monstrosity becomes a science and the basis of study moves from wonder to scientific curiosity. The monstrous, by the seventeenth-century, was no longer a divine warning but a specimen that required careful categorization. For example, Carl Linnaeus, considered the father of modern taxonomy, placed humans into different categories. In the tenth edition of his *Systema Naturae per Regna Tria Naturae* (1758) he marks a distinction between *Homo sapiens* and *Homo sapiens monstrosus*, a division that was primarily based on physical and racial difference. By the nineteenth century, the natural philosopher Etienne Geoffroy de Saint-Hilaire had conducted exhaustive studies on prenatal anomalies, coining the term *teratology* for the study and definition of the monstrous in terms of excess, lack, or displacement of the fetus's organs. With the advent of the Enlightenment, the monster of religious thought—supernatural and symbolic—became progressively abstract and lay and began to be interpreted through two normative systems, the medical and the juridical.[15] In that way, the monster became the freak through a language that stigmatized deviance and distanced those who fit into those categories from the rest of "normal" humanity. Accordingly, what was once a prodigious monster became something abnormal and intolerable in modernity, requiring either its normalization or annihilation. In any case, the monstrous was relegated to the category of pathological specimen.[16]

As far as the trope *freak* itself is concerned, as Robert Bogdan has established, it is a term that was used throughout the nineteenth century to represent people with physical, mental, or behavioral anomalies in order to attract paying customers (a domain of abject bodies in Butler's terminology), which leads one to question whether this renders bodies legible or livable. The freak came into being from this disruption in perception and the fascination that nineteenth-century Europe had with all forms of bodily and behavioral difference. This is obvious in the gothic literature of the time, which provided a space from which to explore all phenomena that existed on the verge of "normal" human identity and culture—phenomena such as madness, criminality, barbarism, perversion, and degeneration, both physical and moral. In the introduction to his book *Staging Stigma: A Critical Examination of the American Freak Show*, Michael Chemers provides a complete history of the use of the term *freak*. He details how the word entered into common usage in the late eighteenth century in reference to the performance of human abnormality that developed from the tradition of the Cabinets of Curiosities exhibits.[17] This collective exhibition of living human bodies that differed from the norm eventually became known as the freak show.

Consequently, the nineteenth century gave rise to the exhibition of human anomalies as a cultural and consumer product. P. T. Barnum began his career with "The Greatest Show on Earth" (the Barnum and Bailey Circus) in 1835 when he "acquired" Joice Heth, an enslaved African American woman who was blind. He advertised her to the public as George Washington's 161-year-old nursemaid. Between 1841 and 1868, Barnum expanded and exhibited his collection of human oddities, which included albinos, giants, dwarves, fat people, bearded ladies, and exotic people from around the world. In this manner, the freak show imploded the imperialist stereotypes of ethnic and racial otherness and Latin American identity was implicitly exploited to the benefit of these showmen. The story of Julia Pastrana (addressed in the second chapter of this book) is a perfect example of this: a Mexican woman who suffered from physical deformities and hirsuteness and was purchased and exhibited throughout the world as an example of exotic difference. Susan Antebi calls our attention to the point that "the freak show functions as ethnographic spectacle, and betrays its intimate ties to ongoing colonialist practices."[18] The freak is a contemporary critical approach toward the different body. What changed were not the bodies that were observed but the ways of seeing this other as hegemonic discourses redefined what was human and what was not. This is a reminder of what Tobin Siebers explains, that all bodies are socially constructed and social attitudes and institutions determine, far more than biological fact, the social perception of the body.[19] Stigmatized bodies presuppose the existence of the able-bodied as a corporeal standard. Disability theory has illustrated how all bodies are in perpetual transition, always suffering modifications, decline, or failure, just like any other matter, whether organic or inorganic, human or nonhuman. "Able-bodiedness is a temporary identity at best," claims Siebers, meaning that disability is never static or fixed.[20] As Rosemarie Garland-Thomson has proclaimed, the discourse of freak construction follows a trajectory that moves from a narrative of wonder to a narrative of deviance.[21]

In modern times, the pathological deviance of difference moved further to become a product for consumption and entertainment, generating awe and terror. *Freak* continued to be a pejorative term that signaled deviation from the norm. "The most common use of 'freak' since the 1940s in English slang refers to anything that appears in contrast to expectations," explains Chemers, but this changed with the counterculture of the 1960s, whose members "appropriated [and] flaunted convention by letting their 'freak flags' fly."[22] This reappropriation of the term continues in popular culture as a term that references a "positive, desirable context, a context that moreover has nothing to do with disability or performance, but one that is capitalized upon by the postmodern performance of freakery."[23] That is, the modern concept of the term *freak* has shifted from its original meaning and been embraced by individuals who want to emphasize their positionality against the established norm. The freak is used as a counternarrative that questions authority and power. This, of course, is a reappropriation of the term as a self-classification that opposes the imposition of an idea of difference on a body.

Within the Latin American context, the term *freak* has no translation in Spanish. The most widely used synonyms are *anormal* (abnormal), *fenómeno* (phenomenon), *criatura* (creature), and *raro* (weird), which is more of an adjective. When Latin Americans talk about the freak, they use the adopted word in English: *lo freak* or *lo friqui*. As Antebi explains, "The question of freakishness and freaks in Latin American contexts is fraught from the beginning by its decontextualized and translated quality; it is an imposition, even when embraced."[24] Nevertheless, it is a term whose history is embedded with Latin American identity as a site of exotic otherness that has permeated a lasting tradition of ethnographic spectacle, from the traditional freak shows of the nineteenth century to the immigration raids of the Barack Obama and Donald Trump administrations. The use of the term *freak* in Latin American culture constitutes a semantic shift aimed at denouncing the categorizational imposition of exclusion.

Freak Performances is an attempt to provide a counternarrative in which all incarnations of these negotiation strategies are recognized and valued. I examine the continuing effects of colonialism on modern Latin American identities, with a particular focus on the way it has constructed the body of the other through performance. Colonialism creates an inescapable legacy. Even in the twentieth and twenty-first centuries Latin America has been unable to move beyond a colonial gaze that marks certain bodies as undesirable others in the eyes of imperialist powers. The most obvious examples include the figures of the indigenous body and the proletariat, which are often perceived as threats to modern power and relegated to the margins of society. Following the work of Rosi Braidotti, I also question the western logic of binary opposition, which "treats difference as that which is other-than the accepted norm. The question then becomes: Can we free difference from these normative connotations? Can we learn to think differently about difference?"[25] I am interested in interrogating the multiple ways in which theater and performances in different Latin American countries use the freak as an allegory of otherness. I probe the ways in which an "ordinary" body becomes "extraordinary" in performance through processes of representation.

THE NEOLIBERAL FREAK

The objectification of the Latin American body through discursive constructions of otherness based on race, ethnicity, class, and gender has existed since the colonial era and extends to the imperialist endeavors of the United States in the modern era. This means that the freak in Latin America today is constructed through the lens of neoliberal practices that aim to produce a "normal" and productive body that benefits the political and economic systems of dominance. Neoliberal policies have created new cartographies that establish distinct allegories of monstrosity and enfreakment, which are exemplified in the performances analyzed in this book. In order to understand the trope of the freak in the context of neoliberalism, it is important to first clarify the implementation of these political practices in Latin America. Over the past four decades, Latin America has experienced significant and dramatic changes that have transformed virtually all areas of its political, economic, and social reality. In the 1970s, with its inauguration through the Chilean experiment, neoliberal capitalism introduced new mythologies about the benefits of the open markets and assumed an automatic economic growth that would guarantee financial stability.[26] Chile was the perfect stage for the practice of these theories. The government of Salvador Allende and the Unidad Popular party proposed socialism as an alternative to the capitalist world and its cycles of crisis, propaganda, and destabilization. This all came to an end with the military overthrow of his government with the backing of the United States, which was fueled by economic interests at local and international levels.[27] Augusto Pinochet's fierce dictatorship, the executor of this coup, came in a moment of great economic instability at the global level. He needed an economic-political project in order to cement his power.[28] This created the perfect ground on which the interests of an even more radical capitalism (a "savage" capitalism) could demonize the state as the cause of all problems and propose the absolute freedom of the market. Nevertheless, more than solving the economic crisis, this only guaranteed extreme profits for a few.

The consequences for Chile and other Latin American countries were not long in coming as these reforms fueled the establishment of authoritarian dictatorships across the continent. Pinochet's dictatorship was the first experiment in neoliberal utopia and the elimination of socialist possibility.[29] Countries were economically and politically weakened to meet the demands of integration into the world economy through the intervention of foreign capital. Added to this was the subjugation of these economies to the provisions of international financial institutions (The World Bank and the International Monetary Fund [IMF]), which complicated their inclusion in the world economy with impossible exigencies that led to increased dependence on foreign capital. The combination of the power held by the interests of the oligarchic elites, transnational market policies, and local corruption made up a devastating grouping through which Latin America was first introduced to neoliberal globalization.[30]

Taking into account the inability of many Latin American countries to pay their external debts, the second stage of the development of neoliberalism in the area continued in the 1980s. This meant the implementation of programs for stabilization and adjustment, which further facilitated the entry of the international market through privatization and the weakening of the state. This led to the development of new rules in the economic-political arena, exacerbated by the Washington Consensus, which aimed to control the economies of the countries and guarantee the payment of debts.[31] Economist Joseph E. Stiglitz explains the effects of these policies.

> As countries like Argentina adopted the Washington Consensus policies, praise was heaped upon them. When price stability was restored and growth resumed, the World Bank and the IMF claimed credit for the success; the case for the Washington Consensus had been made. But, as it turned out, the growth was not sustainable. It was based on heavy borrowing from abroad and on privatizations, which sold off national assets to foreigners—the proceeds from which were not invested. There was a consumption boom.[32]

The results were major crises in the principal economies of Latin America and an almost permanent recession due to the unfairness of the policies that were carried out.

Although many countries have questioned the economic policies of neoliberalism, in no way has this resulted in the abandonment of its programs. This is made obvious through market liberalization, financial and investment programs, new trade agreements such as the Free Trade Agreements (FTAs) and international agreements such as that of the Organization for Economic Cooperation and Development (OECD) for the creation of a Multilateral Agreement on Investment (MAI). The widespread disillusionment, though, is reflected in the election of leftist governments in Brazil, Venezuela, and Bolivia with the advent of the twenty-first century (which was followed by a return to the extreme right in Brazil). Nevertheless, the policies of neoliberalism continue to be implemented in contexts of extreme violence, and its doctrines have greatly influenced the development and growth of other clandestine markets such as narcotics trafficking and even human trafficking.

The purpose of *Freak Performances*, then, is to question what happens in a neoliberal era when the monsters of the past become the freaks of the present, as they are deemed incapable of fitting into a mercantile "body" politic. How does neoliberalism create tropes of enfreakment and monstrosity? How do they differ from traditional ways of seeing the other? Through the use of movement, gesture, behavior, wardrobe, makeup, and so on, the actor in each of the plays that comprise *Freak Performances* becomes the other. Simply put, global imperialism has transformed the monsters from the realm of the imagination and the divine into an observable spectacle of bodily and behavioral aberration (the freak), ready to be consumed as entertainment or constrained as a threat. Because theater is a medium that works primarily with the body, it allows the spectator to engage with the immediate political and social issues that impact society's understanding of identity. The freak has always been a part of the Latin American imaginary as perceived by the western gaze, from the letters that Columbus wrote about his encounters with dog-faced people to Shakespeare's Caliban and Donald Trump's "Mexican rapists." Theater questions the representations of these bodies, as it allows for the empowerment of the silenced other. Thus, the freak that was constructed through the colonial gaze and presented as a spectacle of otherness finds in modern performance an opportunity for reappropriation by artists resisting the dominant authority.

Freak Performances takes on the figure of the freak as an allegory that captures the dynamics of neoliberal accumulation and the extreme objectification of the subject from this paradigm in Latin America. This allegory stands out for its powerful visual impact, inscribing in the body extreme violence as the ultimate consequence of these economic, political, and cultural changes in the new millennium. Through these images it is possible to understand the human mercantilization of otherness, its evolution, and its consequences. Theater, then, becomes the medium through which to question the norms established by this system; or, as Lara Nielsen asks, "But is not the performer (talent) adept at reporting codes of interiority and exteriority to reveal the fictitious domains of rules, as world-making endeavors?"[33] By focusing on Latin American performance culture from the 1990s to the present, I consider theatrical practices that have used the freak as a medium through which to explore underlying myths of national identity. Throughout this book I use an array of theatrical and performance pieces to explore the challenges of forming a coherent reality due to the fragmented identity that is produced through the implementation of a globalized Latin American culture. The strange bodies that appear onstage often find themselves isolated, doubled, fragmented, or removed completely from a social order that privileges the free market system over the rights of the individual.

THE DRAMATURGICAL EYE

The analyses of the different performances and plays in *Freak Performances* draws directly from my own experience as a professional dramaturg with the theater company Teatro de Ciertos Habitantes. Since 2010 I have worked with this company from Mexico City, and my analysis of the different plays in this book (including one by Teatro de Ciertos Habitantes) intersects with my experience as a dramaturg outside the United States. I mention this because in Latin American theater most assume that the theatrical creative work takes place between the director and the actors. While others may also work on staging a play—for example, sometimes a playwright works on the text with the director and actors—it is unusual to discuss the relationship between these artists and the figure of the dramaturg. This role is uncommon in the world of Latin American theater. While dramaturgy is a widespread profession in European theater, especially in Germany, it has not earned professional status in Latin America. However, this does *not* mean that there have not been, and continue to be, people who conduct this type of work in Latin American theater. What exactly is the work of a dramaturg? As many have discussed, this role encompasses many possible duties. Mark Bly defines it simply as the person who "serves as a resource and active collaborator during the planning stages of a production and throughout the rehearsal period," as well as the artist "who functions in a multifaceted manner helping the director and other artists to interpret and shape the sociological, textual, acting, directing and design values."[34] Based on this definition, Latin America's long-standing tradition of *creación colectiva* (collective creation) has always maintained the figure of the dramaturg, even if the person occupying this position was not labeled as such.

Within US scholarship, the history of *creación colectiva* (often simplified by the term *devised theater*) is an underrecognized contribution of Latin American theatrical practice. Additionally, as theater scholar and director Jimmy Noriega says of the words *devised* and *devising*, "[T]hese descriptors carry with them a history and set of values forged from a colonial gaze that often sees the Global South as a receptor for European and US artistic innovation rather than as a joint creator/innovator in theatrical practice and theory."[35] Throughout Latin America, many theater companies have used *creación colectiva* to forge new texts and performance pieces based, for the most part, on ethnographic materials collected by members of the troupes. Some of these groups include individuals and companies such as Augusto Boal's Theatre of the Oppressed, Enrique Buenaventura and the Teatro Experimental de Cali (founded in 1955 in Colombia), Teatro La Candelaria (1966, Colombia), Teatro Escambray (1968, Cuba), Teatro de los Andes (1991, Bolivia), Teatro Malayerba (1980, Ecuador), Grupo Cultural Yuyachkani (1971, Peru), and many others that base their methods on a collective practice. Even though *creación colectiva* encompasses many different possibilities in the rehearsal space, at its core it's a rigorous investigation process for the basis of stage representation. According to Buenaventura, who is credited with the formalization and theorization of the process of collective creation in Latin America, the aim was to overcome the authoritative figure of the director as the sole voice in the creation of a piece. Instead, the creative process must "fill the void left in the conceptions of the director. Thus, the analytical stage of this method came to be and it evolved, in the following pieces, as the most objective way— meaning the most collective possibility—of analyzing a text."[36] In Latin America the traditional work of the dramaturg, as defined by Bly, became connected to the essence of risk taking as these companies based their work on a dynamic exchange of ideas that removed the limitations imposed by hierarchical stage creation.

The innovative work started by these troupes, especially during the

1960s, had a common objective: "to expose the mechanisms and dynamics determining general and specific social phenomena and the class character of economic relations, and to demystify the various strategies for manufacturing consensus among different social classes."[37] These first instances of *creación colectiva* utilized the knowledge of each member of the company in order to benefit the creative process. And so, along with the figure of the director, there were often secondary collaborators (many times the actors themselves) who conducted research and interviews that influenced the themes that were explored in the pieces. We could say that they were implicitly following Hana Worthen's call for a dramaturg who "impels a searching inquiry into the material conditions and cultural work of theater animating each production," bringing together *that which must be thought* to rupture the rationalized political and aesthetic consensus, to contest what the dominant discourses assert as the illusion of the unthinkable" (emphasis in original).[38] Therefore, in the process of creating pieces that broke away from traditional theatrical practices, Latin American theater utilized Worthen's "skeptical dramaturg." In other words, one could argue that the work of the dramaturg has been an integral part of most creative processes in Latin American theater, even as the embodied individual may not have existed in title. The contributions established by these founding companies continue to guide the artistic processes of theater companies in Latin America today. As such, dramaturgy continues to maintain a central role in theatrical exploration and evolves in these productions, although under different auspices than those found in the US and European theater communities.

Now, I find my own work as a dramaturg to fit into this history as I "skeptically" consider the themes and forms that comprise the characterization of enfreakment on the Latin American stage and expose the creative processes that question the dynamics of difference. The considerations that guide my analysis in this book are embedded in the same concerns and questions that guide my work as a dramaturg: primarily a consideration of the period and context (social, cultural, political) that concern the dramatic work and its performance, the implicit recognition of the value that must be placed on the enacted text, a close analysis of the textual work (when available), the relationship between artistic framing and audience reception, the possibility of multiple interpretations, and the consideration of the artistic goals of the different artists that compose a single performance. My methodology is further informed by the opportunity to engage directly with the artists whose work I study. *Freak Performances* is informed by original interviews with playwrights, directors, performers, and cultural critics. The inclusion of artists' voices is a valuable element in this study, and, moreover, their perspectives and artistic intentions are integral to the analysis of the performances and my own scholarly opinions about each dramatic work. I was able to interview most of the artists featured in this book, and I use their thoughts and visions as tools to strengthen the analysis and interpretation of their works.

My analyses of the performances in this book are influenced by a number of factors, including my own politics of location, the time and context of a text's production, and my decision to analyze these particular texts alongside one another. I offer my thoughts as contributions to a critical archive of analysis and inquiry as a new frame for the study of Latin American identity construction while also bringing together plays and performances that are not often grouped together in scholarly discourse. It is through these lenses that *Freak Performances* examines the artistic use of freakery in Latin American theater and performance in the late twentieth and early twenty-first centuries. Particularly, I examine how artists use the freak body as a tool for exploring problematic social attitudes about race, class, and gender. In many cases, the freak emerges as an alternative of the self—one that recognizes and embraces bodies and behaviors that deviate from the norm.

OVERVIEW OF CHAPTERS

In this book I examine the aesthetics of freakery in order to further understand the ways in which Latin American bodies have been constructed through a discourse of difference and how performance utilizes these same markers to make a political statement about imperialist powers that seek to dominate and deform Latin American identity politics. The chapters are organized as case studies that have to do with the distinct constructions of Latin America as freak: an unstable category that has permeated theatrical representations of difference as an allegory. These case studies traverse four main instances of freak identity as categories of marginality: the historical construction of the freak, the medical classification of abnormality, the associations brought on by gender and class, and the removal of citizenship through violence. The methodological styles exhibited in each chapter suitably differ, thereby reflecting the specifics of the various genres in question, as well as the distinctive lines of inquiry that propel each chapter's investigation.

Chapter 1 provides a detailed genealogy of the freak in Latin American discourse as the figure has evolved throughout history: from the colonial gaze to the technological frame, from the divine imagination to the economic spectacle. Through the analysis of three performances I explore bodies rendered as freak by a legacy of colonial economies of power. *De monstruos y prodigios* (Of Monsters and Prodigies, Teatro de Ciertos Habitantes, Mexico, 2000) is a dramatized conference presented by conjoined twins, a surgeon and an opera columnist, which takes the audience on a three-century journey through the rise and fall of an Italian castrato. The play is a reflection on the value society places on beauty and the predictable collapse of this category with each historical change. *Hecho en Perú* (Made in Peru, Yuyachkani, Peru, 2001), a performance installation, consists of a series of *vitrinas* (small stages) where different aspects of Peruvian cultural and social identity are exhibited in a freak show that seeks to challenge the past and present history of Peru. *Fauna* (Romina Paula, Argentina, 2012) tells the story of a documentary filmmaker who goes into the jungles of Argentina to find what he believes to be an Amazonian woman, who takes on the identity of a man to attend the university. In this chapter, the focus of analysis follows the reformulations and reconsiderations of corporeal difference as we move from a perspective of the abject (the monster) to one of deviance (the freak). The purpose of this chapter is to reveal the practices and cultural logic that construct certain corporeal variations and assign them meaning.

Similarly inspired by the hegemonic imposition of the idea of normalcy, chapter 2 deals with the discourses of science and medicine as a hegemonic political gaze that categorizes certain modes of behavior and corporality as difference, providing cultural meaning to certain moral and bodily traits deemed to be submissive before a hierarchy of privilege and power. It is through these lenses (science and medicine) that I look at three performances that highlight power struggles in Latin America. *Vacío* (Emptiness, Teatro Abya Yala, Costa Rica, 2010), is an experimental piece that combines music, dance, and text to tell stories of women in a mental institution who have been rendered as insane because of their inability to perform the socially dictated roles of womanhood. This performance expresses the formation of a pathologized body through the institutionalization of women. *De un suave color blanco* (Of a Soft White Color, Teatro Malayerba, Ecuador, 2010) is grounded in the work of the Ecuadorian writer Pablo Palacio and consists of a series of vignettes that explore issues of cannibalism, insanity, murder, and desire. Through this play I examine the further deformation of the pathologized body by means of the reinforcement of the scientific discourse in a neoliberal world order that seeks to exploit that which it deems different. *NK 603: Acción para performer & E-Maíz* (NK 603: Action for a Performer & E-Corn, Violeta Luna, Mexico/United States, 2009) is a performance art piece that focuses on the effects of transgenic corn on Latin American society. This piece shows how the category of normalcy is further muddled in the modern globalized world of genetic experimentation so that the idea of freakery as an identity category expands and doubles through the mutation of the natural environment. These performances allow me to trace culture-bound categories of difference through the spectrum of deviance and as social stigmas that require institutions of power to step in and restrain/contain such individuals in order to maintain the status quo.

Chapter 3 takes up the rhetorical queries in the construction of normalcy and further emphasizes the importance of gender and class as fundamental categories of difference. These artists treat gender as an unstable category that is culturally constructed without any essential traits so as to define masculinity or femininity, especially as they relate to class consciousness. With this in mind, I approach the work of Brazilian theatrical dance troupe Primeiro Ato and its performance *Geraldas e Avencas* (2008), which takes on the standardization of beauty as a form of aesthetic dictatorship that seeks to erase all forms of difference. I then turn to the work of Mexican performance artist Katia Tirado as a way of further focusing on issues of class. Her piece, *El brillo en la negrura de sobrevivir* (The Brightness in the Darkness of Survival, 2015), is a site-specific performance that can take up to eight hours to complete. In it Tirado narrates to two tattoo artists the personal histories of the cleaning staff, security guards, cooks, and other "blue-collar" workers of the space in which the performance takes place. The tattoo artists then turn these into visual microstories that they tattoo on pigskins, which, in the end, are fried and eaten as *chicharrón*. I close the chapter with the performance piece *Piedra* (Stone, 2013) by Guatemalan artist Regina José Galindo. Another site-specific piece, Galindo takes on the violence inflicted on women by a society that devalues their bodies, especially those of women marginalized by poverty in an industrial economic complex that seeks to benefit from their work and their bodies. Through these performances I signal the ways in which class and sexuality (as well as race, though that category permeates the entire book) have become entangled with notions of the normal and the perverse.

Chapter 4 enters a conceptual terrain that is one of the most studied aspects of Latin American studies: the authoritarian dictatorships and genocides that aimed to eliminate all bodies that did not fit into the category of citizenship in the modern state. This chapter examines connections between enfreakment and social and political violence. For the purpose of understanding this social dynamic, I focus on performances that consider these forms of violence as they pertain to the histories of the military dictatorships in their respective countries (Chile, Argentina, and Peru) during the late twentieth century. I analyze three plays, starting with Norman Briski's *El barro se subleva* (The Mud Revolts, Argentina, 2013), a play about one man who wants to change the world by any means possible, even if that means violence. *Gemelos* (Twins, Teatro Cinema, Chile, 1999) is an adaptation of a short novel by Agota Kristof about two boys who feel and think in identical ways. After a fictional war begins, they are abandoned and forced to survive through a process of reeducation that will allow them to deal with the horrors and violence of war. *Halcón de oro: Q'orihuaman* (Golden Falcon: Q'orihuaman, Ana Correa and Rodolfo Rodríguez, Peru, 1995) tells the story of an encounter between an Andean priest and a young ex-military man who has been sent to an insane asylum to face his own demons. These three performances deal with state violence and offer a new interpretation of the periods in question for each nation. In them freakness becomes something more than stigma, as it leads to the removal of the individual from society and leaves a lasting impact on future generations that have been violently taught the price of not fitting in.

Together the chapters in this book wrestle with performances that decenter a national neoliberal discourse. My aim is to introduce the reader to a number of performances that they are unlikely to see. *Freak Performances* deals with figures of stigma and marginality. This acquires even more urgency because of the history of exploitation that has framed Latin America. For this reason, the freak becomes a powerful trope. The figure of the freak also reveals a moment of redemption as it gains agency and intervenes historically through the enactment and inversion of colonial representation. The aim of this book is to deconstruct notions of privilege, purity, and normalcy while complicating the perception of an abject figure that has permeated the historical configuration of identity as perceived and constructed by a legacy of imperialist domination. These artistic representations force the audience (and the reader) to take notice of their own complicated relationship with configurations of the self and the different other. In this way, the freak on these stages is an identity for survival in an institutionalized reality that attempts to impose normativity.

| # From Monster to Freak

A Latin American Genealogy of Corporeal Difference

Most scholars often think of marginal figures in terms of race, gender, or cultural beliefs, and, as explained in the introduction to this book, those elements play an integral part in our examination of the "freak" in Latin American theatrical discourses. Yet I find it necessary to begin this chapter with the most common way of understanding freak subjectivity: through the physical aspect. Thus, I analyze the performances that comprise this chapter through multiple conceptualizations of the different body so as to create a genealogy of this subject through the lens of Latin American identity politics. This is an effort to consider the deterritorialization that occurs when the concept of the freak is applied to a Latin American perspective, an issue already tackled by Susan Antebi when she warns, "The question of freakishness and freaks in Latin American contexts is fraught from the beginning by its decontextualized and translated quality; it is an imposition, even when embraced. To study freakishness in Latin America, or just to pay attention to it, necessarily involves an awkward back-and-forth movement, between apologizing for radical decontextualization, and reclaiming the notion by distancing oneself from possible misunderstandings."[1] In order to reclaim and translate the applicability of the freak to Latin American theatrical production, this chapter traces the construction of otherness, focusing on its physical dimensions, in three performances from Mexico, Peru, and Argentina.

As Leslie Fiedler clearly stated in his groundbreaking book *Freaks: Myths and Images of the Secret Self* (1978), the strangely formed body has always represented absolute otherness in our collective imaginations, regardless of time or place. To quote the notable freak studies scholar Rosemarie Garland-Thomson, "People who are visually different have always provoked the imaginations of their fellow human beings. Those of us who have been known since antiquity as 'monsters' and more recently as 'freaks' defy the ordinary and mock the predictable, exciting both anxiety and speculation among our more banal brethren."[2] Humanity has always exhibited an interest in difference, and when this is related to the body it allows for a further fascination, as we compare our own realities (through our bodies) to the unknown. This complicated notion motivates this chapter's discussions. Are our bodies our realities or do we construct reality through bodily experience? Through the use of freak discourses that focus on bodily abnormalities and extend to the cultural exercise of agency through bodily alteration, I intend to consider the performance of bodily difference in theater as a reminder that all bodies are socially constructed. This follows Tobin Siebers's research on disability theory, in that social attitudes and institutions determine, far greater than biological fact, the representation of the body's reality.[3] Thus, bodies that lack our own bodies' predictability disquiet us, and we demand explanations that allow us to regulate those exceptional bodies within our narratives of the world.

Western history shows the fundamental place that difference has occupied in society's understanding of humanity. From the Greeks and Romans up to the medieval era, the different body was clear evidence of a disruption in the natural (i.e., European) order. Therefore, abnormal births were often considered religious omens that required study, as they could be symbols of upcoming fatalities or prophetic signs. They were often included in early cataloging of portentous events. Called *portenta* or *monstra*, these abnormal births were supposed to warn of the gods' unhappiness with the citizens. Aristotle considered such newborns to be monsters (*terata*), and his careful classification of them eventually brought about the science of teratology, the study of abnormalities in physiological development, in the eighteenth and nineteenth centuries. Cicero discussed these births as portents of the will of the gods and considered the newborns useful for divination. These first careful studies of western difference already identified monstrosity with excess, defect, or hybridity. Thus, these studies gave rise to the figure of the monster, and if we focus on the lexicon of the word, we can simplify the term as referring to all things considered unnatural.

> It is difficult to generalize . . . but *monstrum* does seem to have been early identified with unnatural births or composite creatures and to have been seen as a warning. Its closest synonym, "prodigy," is likewise a thing rather than an event, and may be alive, but it may also be something inanimate (a comet, for example) to which we attach a prophetic significance.[4]

The divine significance of the exceptional body continued to exert a fascination beyond the classical era since, as manifestations of the portent of the gods, they allowed humanity to imagine, consider, and revise the natural order of things. For example, in Renaissance England popular "monster ballads" cautioned against immoral behavior, meaning that a child's cleft palate was the result of a mother's lewd talk. Furthermore, abnormal births were considered not only an attribute of the iniquity and immorality of the parents but also of the imminence of God's wrath to be visited on humanity.

The study of nature's monsters was of great importance to Renaissance empiricist science, as it afforded the opportunity to closely examine all aspects of nature, including the hidden mysteries that lurked beyond humanity's gaze. The philosopher Francis Bacon argued for this close study, viewing monstrous births as a necessary point of reference that would allow the scientific mind a further understanding into the regularities of organic life: "He who is acquainted with the paths of nature, will more readily observe her deviations; and vice versa, he who has learnt her deviations, will be able more accurately to describe her paths."[5] Of particular significance here is the implication that arises from this natural curiosity about the abnormal body. As noted by Bacon, it is through the careful understanding of "deviance" that one can hope to understand oneself. Through our modern gaze, the study of the freak throughout history clearly reveals the ambiguity that this figure produces on the "normal" individual's social consciousness. The freak provokes repulsion and fascination. Above all, what becomes clear in this chapter's study of the genealogy of freakery is that this ambiguity stems from our own problematic gaze as we recognize a part of ourselves projected on the freak: our own perceived deformities (real or not, physical or moral), which we constantly attempt to banish or at least hide. Above all, and as many scholars have pointed out, the freak is a subjectivity that serves as a repository of our deepest social fears and anxieties.[6] It should not surprise us, then, that historically we have expended such an effort in the process of dissecting and categorizing such notions of difference.

Of particular importance to western cataloging and categorization of the monster is the work of the French surgeon Ambroise Paré, who in 1573 created a treatise on all sorts of marvels, from conjoined twins to unicorns and sea devils. The importance of Paré's efforts lies beyond any medical relevance since his work is a scientific and literary document that reveals the surgeon's interest in the architecture of nature. Paré believed his catalog of monsters provided a study of deviations from the normal course of nature; they were counternatural phenomena. As was the case with most European medical discourses of the time, Paré's research straddles science and religion, often finding divine explanations and interpretations for cases of anomaly. Paré's study of monsters offered an alternative perspective on the subject, which allowed for the logic of science to cast the foundation for the study of bodies as demanding regularity rather than exceptionality. Therefore, the basis of study moved, as claimed by Garland-Thomson, from wonder to error; the monstrous, by the seventeenth century, was no longer a divine warning but rather a curiosity that delighted man's whimsies concerning the strange.

What is absolutely clear in the depiction and study of bodily difference is the significant ways in which each historical period conditioned the hegemonic gaze on the monstrous in order to convey what constitutes the natural order of things. So as to fully comprehend the political and social significance of those ways in which corporeal difference has been categorized and named, which is similar to what Michael Baxandall has termed "the period eye," we should consider those changes in both representation practices and modes of observation as related to marginal figures. After all, in the study of freakery within theatrical discourses, one of the most important tools for the dismantling of codes of normativity is a careful consideration of the spectator, meaning those who observe and consider what they see as related to categories of normal or abnormal. It is in those moments of question that the theatrical representation of freakery acquires a political overtone. Here Jacques Rancière's notion of the emancipated spectator is imperative. Rancière calls for a type of spectatorship that moves toward an active participation in the action observed so that there is a process of learning as opposed to a seduction by images as forms of entertainment.

> Emancipation begins when we challenge the opposition between viewing and acting; when we understand that the self-evident facts that structure the relations between saying, seeing and doing themselves belong to the structure of domination and subjection. It begins when we understand that viewing is also an action that confirms or transforms this distribution of positions. The spectator also acts, like the pupil or scholar. She observes, selects, compares, interprets. She links what she sees to a host of other things that she has seen on other stages, in other kinds of place. . . . They are thus both distant spectators and active interpreters of the spectacle offered to them.[7]

The performances examined in this chapter, as well as throughout the book, aim to dismantle notions of normativity that have reified a fundamental "Latin American" identity and created a stigmatized otherness; race, class, gender, sexuality, mental condition, political leanings, and so on all constitute elements of an enfreaked body that is easier to marginalize than accept. Since these are theatrical performances creating an instance of dissidence toward the status quo, the artists push for the spectators to act as emancipated viewers who should "actively interpret" the political ramifications of the freak body in performance.

Furthermore, the ways in which we construct meaning behind categories of difference or marginality say a lot about the underlying myths that form our cultural and social foundations, as they reveal shared attributes across a culture in time. When scholars (and spectators) study the freak, the monster, the savage, or any other "abnormal" subjectivity in theater, they are primarily considering the representation of the archetypal outsider. Therefore, these representations are inherently political, as their social construction becomes a significant category of inquiry. In this chapter, my focus of analysis follows the reformulations and reconsiderations of corporeal difference as I move from the perspective of the abject (the monster) to one of deviance (the freak). In this analysis, I consider three theatrical and performance pieces that (1) allow us to trace corporeal difference from a historical perspective, as presented in the play *De monstruos y prodigios: La historia de los castrati* (*Of Monsters and Prodigies: The History of the Castrati*) by the Mexican company Teatro de Ciertos Habitantes; (2) push us to consider the legacy of exhibition practices through the performance piece *Hecho en Perú (vitrinas para un museo de la memoria)* (Made in Peru [Showcases for a Memory Museum]) by the Peruvian collective Yuyachkani; and (3) encourage us to study hegemonic visual discourses as presented in *Fauna*, by the Argentinian writer and director Romina Paula. The purpose of this study is to reveal the practices and cultural logic that construct certain corporeal variations and assign them meaning. For, as Garland-Thomson has intelligently asserted, the freak is a historical figure that is ritually fabricated over and over from what hegemonic society (and in this case different instances of Latin American societies of power) considers bodily and behavioral variations. These differences are then appropriated in the service of shifting social ideologies so that social fears and anxieties collapse within one fixed notion of otherness: the freak. In order to emphasize the importance of historical, social, and cultural perspectives in the naming of cultural difference, I use the terms *monster* and *freak* interchangeably in this chapter, as I develop a genealogy through these plays that reveals the evolution of the terminology as the historical periods changed and scientific knowledge expanded, so that what was the monster of antiquity eventually became the freak of modernity. What should remain a constant in this chapter's understanding of corporeal otherness is that the freak exists for the purpose of exhibiting and performing difference, and so, as a sociocultural construct, the exhibition and understanding of these bodies vary according to the historical and cultural context.

DE MONSTRUOS Y PRODIGIOS: LA HISTORIA DE LOS CASTRATI OR THREE CENTURIES OF MONSTROSITIES FACE THE MODERN SPECTATOR

I want to begin by considering how particular Latin American theatrical discourses have dealt with this genealogy of the freak as they move from discourses of monstrosity to those of modernity. A pertinent example is the piece *De monstruos y prodigios: La historia de los castrati* (*Of Monsters and Prodigies: The History of the Castrati*, 2000), by Teatro de Ciertos Habitantes, a play that recounts three centuries of history on the perception of difference.[8] Founded in 1997, Teatro de Ciertos Habitantes has become one of the most recognized companies in Latin America due to its innovative and avant-garde stagings, which include *Becket o el honor de Dios* (Becket or the Honour of God, 1998), *El automóvil gris* (The Gray Automobile, 2002), *¿Dónde estaré esta noche?* (Where Will I Be Tonight?, 2004), *La piel* (The Skin, 2006), *El Gallo* (2009), *Todavía . . . Siempre* (Still . . . Forever, 2012), *La vida es sueño* (Life Is a Dream, 2013), and *Quijote, vencedor de sí mismo* (Quijote, Victor over Himself, 2016). The company's productions are not numerous after almost twenty years of success, but what matters to the company and the director is that they produce plays of great quality in small quantities. Their reputation has allowed them to thrive in international theatrical circuits and become an obligatory reference for any critic of Latin American contemporary theater. Ciertos Habitantes, performance scholar Katherine Zien writes, is a company that attempts "to forge that which might be called a 'global aesthetic,' which joins avant-garde universalist-interculturalism to contemporary neoliberal cosmopolitan multiculturalism."[9] *De monstruos y prodigios* is a clear attempt to forge this aesthetic. What best characterizes the company is its creative process, which consists of long periods of experimentation dedicated to specific artistic purposes and investigations. The company's poetics require continuous renovation and bring together various registers that require the sensibility of multidisciplinary artists in order to tackle the various expressions of their art; these range from the use of musical instruments, dance, and opera singing to martial arts and Sufi dances. The company's aim has always been to explore the human condition through theatrical work, so the exploration and rehearsal process includes a rigorous scenic, visual, and corporal investigation, which has been at the core of its work.[10]

The company's first play, *Becket, o el honor de Dios,* was a defining moment in the Mexican theater scene, primarily because of its innovative staging. In this adaptation of Jean Anouilh's play, five actors play multiple roles (the original play requires thirty actors) on a stone stairway inside a convent, the only stage. The staging required the actors to make very precise movements set to live music. Originally the company planned on twenty presentations, but the play was such an enormous success that the season extended to fifty-one sold-out performances. Yet it was its second play, *De monstruos y prodigios,* that brought the company international recognition. The play, written by Jorge Kuri, premiered in Spain in 2000 and continued with a long and successful string of performances that lasted until 2011.[11] The story spans several centuries, from the seventeenth to the present, and focuses on the Italian castrati, whose voices were considered a true phenomenon of human nature. The performance itself was created as a didactic concert of sorts, director Claudio Valdés Kuri explains, since the text is written as a scientific treatise. These narrations/treatises are told by a few main characters, who add their own performative subtexts to the play as they alter the dramatic text through their playful gestures and the incorporation of elements unrelated to the main purpose of the play/treatise (music, dance, mime, etc.). The theatrical text lacks any intrigue or action; it is a treatise that seeks to conduct an overview of the central issue: the rise and fall of the virtuous figure of the castrato. Theater scholar Rosalina Perales suggests that the work "inserts the castrati as part of the marvels and monstrosities that history has created and from which no culture is exempt, not Mexico or Europe or Latin America."[12] The lack of specificity in terms of a "national" theme situates the performance within a global context as the director is more interested in showing the effects of hegemonic discourses on culture through a more impersonal perspective.

De monstruos y prodigios focuses on the shifting valuation of the castrati throughout history. The play depicts different events in the lives of these opera singers, from the separation from their parents at an early age through the arduous training process and their triumph in the artistic scene of the time. The text gives an account of the success and decadence of the Italian castrati, culminating with the story of the last castrato, Alessandro Moreschi, who is not physically onstage but whose voice is preserved in a recording. The main narrative is interspersed with musical numbers that appear at different times during the performance and disrupt the structure of the more scientific narrative text. Accompanying the castrato onstage are

Fig. 2. *De monstruos y prodigios. La historia de los castrati*. Actors Luis Fernando Villegas, Kaveh Parmas, Javier Medina, Miguel Ángel López, Gastón Yanes, and Raúl Román. Photo by Eniac Martínez.

a barber-surgeon and an opera critic, who happen to be conjoined twins named Ambroise and Jean Paré (of course, paying homage to the author and book that inspired the play).[13] This two-headed character (who at times is two individuals, at others one entity) represents the two extremes of science/reason and art/intuition,[14] and along with the singing teacher, Professor Galluppi, they are the narrative voices that guide the audience through this scientific conference, which spans three centuries of history. Completing the set of monsters onstage are Quirón, a centaur who is also introduced as the Parés' pupil, and Sulaimán, a "savage" slave from the Orient (as the Paré brothers explain) who appears mostly naked except for an elaborate loincloth. Sulaimán is the first character that we see; he is onstage as the audience enters the theater. Yet he remains silent throughout the play, simply obeying the orders given to him until the final moments of the performance, when he is able to impose his own discourse and becomes, within his own freak discourse, a new protagonist of history.

The premise of the play is quite simple: through the perspectives of art and science (Jean and Ambroise Paré, who are often referred to in the singular as Doctor Paré), the spectator is told about the rise and fall of the castrato. This also becomes a narrative about taste and aesthetic value. In the words of Claudio Valdés Kuri, the director of this play:

> There was a time when beauty was of the highest value. It was a divine gift, and there was no price high enough to prevent one from wanting to reach it. In the eighteenth century, the castrati, those sacred monsters, those children whose voices were surgically molded, represented the height of sublime artistry. *Of Monsters and Prodigies* is a performance that aims to give an account of the development, plenitude, and decadence of the history of the castrati. It is a history that also accounts for three centuries of human action and thought, from the succulent extremes of the baroque to the technological beginnings of the twentieth century.[15]

It is not surprising that most of the play's action begins during the baroque period, the era that witnessed the rise of the castrati, focusing especially on the Italian opera tradition (as opposed to the more reserved French opera) as the great spectacle of passions. After all, baroque opera sought to indulge one's personal urges. It was, in the words of Jean and Ambroise Paré, "a celebration of epidermal pleasures" that focused on a moment of sublime happiness.[16] It is pertinent to use the work of Mikhail Bakhtin on the medieval carnival to understand the play's use of the Italian opera. His approaches regarding carnivalization and the grotesque and hybrid body provide the necessary tools for the study of artistic phenomena that propose a parodic inversion of the status quo. Bakhtin understood the carnivals of medieval Europe as fleeting moments in which the legal, political, and ideological authority of both church and state was suspended (or inverted) during a period of anarchic and liberating celebration. Terry Eagleton has pointed out that this was a "licensed" form of transgression.[17] But Michael Chemers notes that the transgressions of the freakish body in Rabelais "is welcomed by Bakhtin with open arms, as the same transgression present in social revolution, of liberation from oppression, from fear, even from death itself."[18] Thus, the carnival had true liberatory potential because it could allow new ideas to enter public discourse (in other words, it was a moment for even the most ridiculous notions to be present and celebrated). *De monstruos y prodigios* presents us with two operatic possibilities: the French opera, guided by rules of propriety; and the Italian opera, which, as the characters in the play describe, is the "sole distraction for an audience capable of extending an evening of music until the wee hours of the night, in a carnival of multiple pleasures, of social and gastronomic enjoyments."[19] Similar to the Bakhtinian carnival, Italian opera serves to dismantle the normative hierarchy, a space of liberation that celebrates what would otherwise be considered an aberration of nature: the castrato. It represents an explosion into a realm of free thought and action as it eliminates the ideal of the normal in favor of pure pleasure. The Italian opera becomes, then, the primary space in which monstrosities can become prodigies.

The main monster onstage is, of course, the castrato, a male subject who, through a medical procedure, has had his testicles removed before reaching puberty in order to preserve a sweet voice and prevent the arrival of a deeper, mature voice. The choice of an actor for this role was deliberate and an essential part of the performance. Javier Medina, who plays Il Virtuoso, is an opera singer with an unusual vocal range. He suffered from leukemia as a young boy, and due to his radiation treatments his throat never developed, so he became a man with a child's throat. Medina, then, is one of very few male singers with a natural soprano voice. His own suffering during an adolescence filled with rejection and a lack of understanding for his condition inspired the first instances of research into the history of the castrati by the director, who is a close friend of the actor.[20] As the program notes state, the particular interest in the castrati stems from their social construction as a figure filled with internal contradictions and extravagances. If we are to focus on corporeal differences as modes of representation and sites of interpretation, the castrati constitute a constant defiance of the male body. They exist outside the norms of morality and rationality, appreciated because of the inherent beauty of their voices but also because, even when celebrated for their physical beauty, they were considered "safe" physical objects of desire. The castrati, a "fusion of the monster and the angel," with their angelic voices and the roundness of their cherubic bodies, seduced all who listened in a perturbing manner. When considered as a representation of corporeal difference, their freakery arises from both an excess of beauty (in their voices) and a lack of gender normative codes (genitalia and muscular bodies). The disruption they caused to the social order, which eventually led to their being categorized as abominations, stems from this ambiguousness, which, "along with excess and absence, are the threatening organizational principles that constituted freakdom."[21]

After Sulaimán receives the audience, which enters the theater, the play begins with one lonely figure onstage, Quirón, the four-thousand-year-old centaur who appears behind a stable door that covers the lower part of his body, thus keeping his condition as a centaur from the audience.[22] This mythical creature, brilliantly performed by Miguel Ángel López, speaks directly to the spectators as he imparts his academic treatise: a history of monsters that refers back to classical thought, where monsters were considered sacred figures. Quirón points out that, throughout the history of humanity, the word *monster* has been applied to anything that cannot be explained within the order of nature. In the play, he quotes directly from Ambroise Paré's treatise *On Monsters and Prodigies*. This constitutes a direct nod to a European (i.e., hegemonic) view of monstrosities as a form of creating and conditioning a cultural gaze on the abnormal body. As he proceeds to enumerate and describe different monsters in history, such as the "Mollusk Boy" (who was born without bones) or the "Piedmont Devil" (who was born with a series of horns on his head), Quirón finally leads us to our monstrous protagonist—the castrato—who is described as one more in this long list of monstrosities.

> We shall now focus on the most exceptional monster, within the realm of what has been a most frightening seventeenth century. It is a sort of androgynous or hermaphroditic figure that is a man, a woman, and a child at the same time, whose body is inclined toward voluptuousness, with the mouth, waist, arms, and a bosom rounded and chubby like a woman's. Aside from their notorious plumpness, they are characterized by a lack of hair, beard, or moustache; a thoracic deformity; and, on some occasions, a disproportionately small head compared to the rest of their enormous bodies, which, at the same time, stand in contrast to their very high-pitched voices, reminiscent of a prodigious and heavenly bird. . . . The mystery of this phenomenon lies in the ineffable pitch produced by his voice, a sublime and sensuous sound that transports people to states of profound nostalgia: his chant incarnates the mystery of a voice that constantly negotiates the abyss between the monster and the prodigy.[23]

In terms of this first representation of the castrato as a monster, Robert Bogdan's study of the stylized representations of freaks is extremely helpful in understanding the admiration that these opera singers merited. Bogdan explains their "aggrandized status" as a mode of representation in which the superiority of the freak is emphasized. In the historical freak shows, many performers were not physically disabled but were presented in a way that highlighted certain traits as their difference (e.g., the bearded lady). These staging practices led Bogdan to affirm that "freak as a term is not used to mean people who have certain physical conditions. Freak is a frame of mind, a set of practices, a way of thinking about and presenting people. It is not a person but the enactment of a tradition, the performance of a stylized presentation."[24] And, in *De monstruos y prodigios*, the "stylized presentation" of these two freaks (Quirón and the castrato) becomes a skillfully organized game of gazing projected on the spectator.

The fact that Quirón remains partially covered at all times prevents us from ever seeing that which makes him a monster (his lower animal half). The same can be said for the castrato, for even though we may observe the femininity of his body, we are unable to actually see his genitalia or that which renders him an aberration by normative standards of gender. Yet, the ways in which we, as spectators, assume what is hidden from our curious gaze varies greatly in these two characters. Quirón provokes a sense of fascination, as we are aware that he is a mythical creature who belongs to a long line of classical heroes (as clearly described by the brothers Paré) and is aligned with a sacred notion of monstrosity, as he belongs with "everything that cannot be explained" to human beings.[25] On the other hand, the castrato is described through the discourse of science as Jean and Ambroise Paré rationalize the process of castration at the start of the play: "Now, the act itself has to be rapid: it starts with an incision on the groin, through which the barber pulls the string . . . (*Jean finalizes the extraction*) *voilà!*, and the testicles. You proceed then to the complete removal with a knife. . . . Ambroise, *s'il te plaît* (*Jean asks Ambroise to make the cut*)."[26] The precision with which the "creation" of a *castrato* is formulated onstage produces a morbid curiosity about that which we cannot see but are fully aware has happened. At the same time, the procedure is presented with a great deal of absurdity. The actors asphyxiate one another while demonstrating anesthesia techniques. They also almost kill the child they are operating on as they clarify that "the percentage of children's mortality oscillates between a 10 and 85 percent."[27] Furthermore, the two supposed specialists are clearly confused about whether the correct term for the operation is *ornithology* or *orchiectomy*. Thus, the creation of the castrato is clouded by an absurd sense of entertainment in this medical theater presented by the brothers Paré, who try to pass off this practice as the creation of beauty. In contrast, it is very significant that our first encounter with the castrato is through the words of Quirón, who prepares us for what we are about to encounter. In this contrast of monstrosities, we become aware of our own sense of perceptions or the fact that "the trajectory of historical change in the ways the anomalous body is framed within the cultural imagination . . . can be characterized simply as a movement from a narrative of the marvelous to a narrative of the deviant."[28]

This movement, from the marvelous to the deviant, is of particular importance in the Ciertos Habitantes' play, particularly because Quirón is a classical figure of mythical proportions—a monster from the minds of the ancients. These wild beings were, claims anthropologist Roger Bartra, crucial figures in Greek thought as they helped to demarcate the limits of civility. To Bartra they were "important elements for structuring the relations between a wild existence and a civilized life. They formed a myth with twin poles, one as a wild man who was humanoid and the other as a wise and just man who was bestial."[29] As such, Quirón's perspective on beauty and monstrosity derives from the classical division of the Apollonian and Dionysiac types of beauty. Apollonian beauty required order and harmony, a measured notion of beauty. Yet this aesthetic is complicated by the presence of chaos, which disquiets and perturbs the beauty of reason. Dionysiac beauty, then, is a more dangerous and uncontrolled aesthetic, difficult to categorize and contain. In *De monstruos y prodigios* the castrato contains both of these forms. On the one hand, the physical aspect of this singer contains a variety of gender codes, making it difficult to interpret his voluptuous and, as we shall see, seductive body. Yet his voice is sublime harmony, absolute perfection. Quirón describes, then, a body in discordance with the beauty of his voice. The impossibility of categorizing the castrato as either Apollonian or Dionysiac is problematic for the centaur, as he does not know how to interpret the emotions awakened by the voice that the singer emits. During the first operatic performance of Il Virtuoso, the character of the castrato as he sings "Per la Gloria d'adorarvi" by Giovanni Battista Bononcini, the stage notes state that Quirón appears onstage "frightened by the castrato's voice, which he aims at with his bow and arrow."[30] In the performance, the centaur follows the castrato's movements onstage with his weapon, yet he is slowly seduced by his voice, falling into a sort of sexual rapture and exaltation, which leads to uncontrollable applause. At this point, Professor Galuppi demands that the brothers Paré "control their beast," which they do by offering him a carrot. Quirón is utterly offended and leaves the stage.

AMBROISE: Poor thing . . . he doesn't know he is a monster.
JEAN: What happens is that these kinds of mythological figures, such as the centaur, have a conflictive character, changeable, since its personality oscillates between the rational . . .
AMBROISE: . . . and the emotional.[31]

Quirón, in his study of monstrosity (he is the character who "teaches" us the history of monsters), departs from a classical perception of the monster and moves beyond a consideration of beauty. He is one of these figures; as a centaur—half man, half beast—he cannot consider himself a monstrosity but rather a marvelous creature. Therefore, what he exhibits toward the castrato is a fascination with him as prodigy, something with an elevated meaning.[32]

The curiosity and awe that the castrato produces in Quirón is slightly different from the perspectives adopted by Jean and Ambroise Paré. The brothers, figures derived from the historical doctor, continue to maintain a fascination with monsters and marvels; they collect such objects and keep the body of the Mollusk Child "in a small laboratory, inside a bottle with formaldehyde."[33] Yet their fascination straddles natural scientific curiosity and symbolic power (reason and emotion), and they often lean toward a more naturalistic exploration of the castrato's anatomy, as presented in their first scene, where they perform the castration of a child.

> JEAN: Gentlemen, there is no use in skimming books nor chatting nor cackling in a surgery lecture if the hand does not act as reason dictates. This is all: a potion with a high content of opium (*Ambroise hands him the potion*) *merci*, so as to completely neutralize the sensations of the child. Of course, most of the time, the barber is content with oppressing the carotid arteries in this way (*Jean presses Ambroise's carotids as an example*) to momentarily interrupt circulation. The patient then finds himself in a state that is quite close to a coma. He has been previously submerged in a bath of freezing milk to soften the genitals and, of course, to avoid . . . (*Ambroise, who is asphyxiating, asks Jean to release him*) *oh pardon!*, the bleeding.[34]

The first instance of castration by this two-headed scientific monster (Jean and Ambroise Paré) leads us to contemplate the symbolic duality that permeates the entire play as we are to question the transitionality of historical perspectives on the castrato: the monster or the prodigy.

At the height of their success in the opera world, the castrati were highly regarded for their almost impossible to achieve musical feats. They were, culturally and artistically, phenomena very specific to their historical context. The conditions that surrounded their rise are unrepeatable in more modern times since, besides the now illegal surgical intervention necessary to produce a castrato, they had a very strict musical education. For many centuries, these singers gave their lives to art, even when for the most part the decision was not theirs to make, since they were most likely children when they were castrated. In the performance, the rigid structure that allowed for the creation of such a prodigious being comes to life through the figure of Professor Baldessarre Galuppi, a monster in his own right, as he is the one who decides which children should be castrated.[35] Galuppi describes the details of the severe education implemented in the musical development of the castrati as the audience becomes aware of their tragic commodification. The purpose of such unyielding training was their exhibition to a public that could be moved and made to desire these sublime figures.

> JEAN: Later, businessmen avid for opera figures will come,
> AMBROISE:. . . . and they shall have to compete with the courts of Europe in search of young castrati, so as to turn them into the most beautiful ornaments of their chambers or chapels.[36]

As valuable commodities in the opera world, they are often described in the play as adornment, yet it is possible to also infer the freakery innate in their exhibition as an extreme that means to cause awe in the spectator. In other words, the othering gaze of the spectator objectifies the castrato onstage through a process of consumerism. This is similar to what Carlos Jáuregui considers the consumerism of the other: a form of cannibalism that signals the persistence of colonial structures and the appropriation of difference through a process of cultural consumption.[37] In the case of *De monstruos y prodigios*, we are forced to consider the implication of the castrato as a freak as we become privy to the commercial exhibition associated with this figure and the tragedy of his existence. Regarding the artistic (and commercial) exhibition of the castrato, we must consider the problematic issues of choice and consent as presented by David Gerber. By foregrounding the issue of exploitation, Gerber disagrees with Bogdan's narrative of the implications of social construction in the display of the freak in favor of a consideration of the matter of free will on the part of the performer. Gerber bases his claims on a desire to remoralize this form of entertainment as a product of unequal social relations. This becomes a crucial issue in the analysis of the castrato, as his freak subjectivity has been imposed on him through forced surgery as a child, and so he has no other option as an adult than to be a castrato. This also depends, of course, on whether or not he also has the talent to perform as demanded. The castrato is a commodity, and as such he is utterly dehumanized in the eyes of the audiences that go to the opera to enjoy his beautiful voice while also being morbidly intrigued by the ambiguous figure. And so, in terms of their configuration as a freak without a choice, the castrati's singular tragedy stems from the spectator's gaze on them: "Did the audience understand the show as a *performance* and attach value to those who were at the center of it? Or did people come to be fascinated by the unusual, to stare, to be horrified, and to engage in loathing at a *display*?"[38] Thus, the castrato becomes a singularly tragic freak who devotes his life to performing while being considered only a display. As Galuppi states, "How can you not understand, then, the mixture of grudge and sorrow that must be added to the feeling of uselessness of a life based on one single objective: vocal success?"[39]

The baroque period privileged beauty over reason; in this search for sublime beauty the castration of a child was not considered immoral by any means. Thus, the great drama that surrounds the castrati and the underlying theme of the *De monstruos y prodigios* is developed through the tension between the discourse of the unreasonable baroque period and the extreme reason of the Enlightenment, as represented in the antagonistic perspectives of Jean and Ambroise Paré. It is not gratuitous that this scientific "monster" (as conjoined twins) guides the audience as we move from one historical period to the next, as we are meant to grasp the significance of culture and politics in the historical development of taste and our understanding of normativity.

JEAN: Gentlemen, in the middle of the Enlightenment, all of Europe finds itself immersed in a polemic.
AMBROISE: All of Europe? You and I are in a polemic.

(They fight each other managing to tear apart different parts of their [shared] gown)

JEAN: Take off that wig! [. . .] It is the symbol of decadence (*they struggle*). Then I will take it off (*Jean takes it off his own head*)
AMBROISE: [. . .] The French have initiated a violent opposition to the castrati, basing it on their . . .
JEAN-AMBROISE: . . . "scientific" reasoning. (*Jean puts a cap on his head, which Sulaimán gives him*)
AMBROISE: Scientific? With those caps?
JEAN: Gentlemen, we are talking of a combat . . .
AMBROISE: . . . whose origin happens to be political. (*Sulaimán gives Jean a glass of wine and to Ambroise a pipe*). When attacking the art of the Italians, the French do not seek anything but to add a victory to their . . .
JEAN-AMBROISE: . . . Imperialist pride.[40]

The significance of the brothers' dialectics responds to conflicting eighteenth-century aesthetics. Theater scholar Juan Villegas delves into this notion and points out, "Aesthetics becomes the meaning of life and, in relation to artists, they are given special powers and conditions within society. In exchange for this endorsement and pseudofreedom, the artist is used or punished according to his service to the holders of power."[41] Thus, a taste for the castrati was to be found among the upper classes and church officials, who were willing to sacrifice human beings in the name of aesthetic pleasure. As the semiotician Umberto Eco explains, conflicting ideals regarding taste are more understandable if we recognize the evolving perspectives that led into the nineteenth century. After all, in the eighteenth century the rigorous coherence of neoclassicism is met with an aristocratic, rococo preference for giving oneself to the *douceur de vivre*. This is the century of Kant and Rousseau but also of the guillotine—a period of great contradictions: "[A] more attentive eye will have no trouble in descrying a younger and more dynamic entrepreneurial nobility, whose tastes had by that time become effectively bourgeois, modernist, and reformist."[42] Changes in societal power structures bring about a change in aesthetic perspective, and so the prodigies of the past become the monsters of the present. Yet, as the castrato loses his ethereal symbolic value, he is no longer desired or admired, and therefore he cannot be considered a commodity. It is at this historical juncture of the play that Napoleon comes onstage, and, with the explosion of a canon, everything changes. As we move into the nineteenth and twentieth centuries, it is no longer possible to maintain the notion of monstrosity that these characters, such as centaurs and castrati, elicited in previous periods. The advent of modern thought does not allow for their mythical quality. And thus Quirón reappears onstage without legs as a victim of war violence; Ambroise and Jean Paré have been separated and appear as separate beings; and the castrato loses any quality of marvel. After the Age of Reason, their corporeal differences are no longer tolerated, for their ambiguities make them far too removed from acceptable, knowable humanity. They are at the "corporeal limits of subjectivity," in the words of Elizabeth Grosz. As characters who represent bodily difference, they now suffer from social marginalization, especially the castrato, which transforms them into freaks. In other words, "[W]hat makes a freak is not just being unusual or atypical," explains Grosz, for "more than this is necessary to characterize their unique social position. . . . He or she is considered simultaneously and compulsively fascinating and repulsive, enticing and sickening."[43] The castrato has no other value than as a simple curiosity, as explained by Jean. On the demise of the castrati, he notes, "The Vatican believes it has finished off castrati, expelling them definitively from its

Chapel; however, prior to dying, Alessandro Moreschi agreed to have experiments performed directly on his person, in the year 1904."[44]

While the castrato's condition as an ornament is put on full display throughout the play, there is a significant point of comparison between this character's "appreciation" and that of Sulaimán, the Paré brothers' servant. Sulaimán, who is always referred to as "negro" (black), represents absolute otherness in the form of the savage. As a matter of fact, this character could be said to evoke the medieval construction of the monstrous races: examples of barbaric and incredible specimens of nature's most deviant possibilities. The singular body has provoked reverence and dread throughout history, and throughout the Middle Ages the work of the Roman author Pliny gave rise to a profound interest in races of men considered fabulous monsters believed to live in faraway lands. The descriptions of these races, from the Greco-Roman to the Latin Middle Ages, demonstrate a fascination with the strangeness of other peoples and places while also revealing an implicit rejection of the "other." The monstrous races were always in faraway lands (such as India or Ethiopia) that evoked mystery in the medieval mind while also exhibiting a marked ethnocentrism that made the observer's culture, language, and physical appearance the norm by which to evaluate all other people. Therefore, one could assert that the construction of the monstrous "emerges from culture-bound expectations even as it violates them."[45] As western Europeans shifted their interests from India and Africa to the so-called New World, the perspectives on the monstrous races changed. First, the monstrous men of antiquity were reduced to a single figure—the hairy wild man—and, second, this figure became conflated with the aboriginal people found in the New World. Therefore, it is of utter importance that in the play Sulaimán, who is first equated with the Orient (through his name), has an identity that dissolves into the word *negro* as he evolves in the collective imaginary of the play from the monstrous races of the past to the feared cannibals of the "New World" and the savage masses of "the popular."[46]

In his seminal work, *Canibalia*, Jáuregui produces a thorough analysis of the ways in which the inhabitants of the Americas have been perceived throughout history as the eternal instance of monstrous difference and analyzes the figure that best contains this imagery: the cannibal. The cannibal is the eternal other who has always inhabited the exotic lands of the Americas. Cannibals evoked the Cyclops and cynocephali of ancient times, which quickly evolved into the wild indigenous men who had to be enslaved in order for the foreign invaders to gain access to the gold and riches of that new land. "Cannibalism," he writes, "becomes the product of a tau-

Fig. 3. *De monstruos y prodigios. La historia de los castrati.* Actors Gastón Yanes and Raúl Román as Jean and Ambroise Paré, and Kaveh Parmas as Sulaimán. Photo by Christa Cowrie.

tological reading of the savage body: the cannibal is ugly, and those who are ugly are cannibals. . . . Far from finding a moment of semantic appeasement, the *cannibal* constantly slides throughout a nonlinear space: the space of colonial *difference*, a murky mirror in the figuration of the other and the self."[47] And so the colonial gaze has established a semantics of difference in which certain bodies are configured as liminal entities that can only be understood through their association with notions of monstrosity. This is clearly the case with Sulaimán. He is a freak because he is different, a savage who doesn't speak in the language of his masters and therefore a body to be conquered and enslaved.

In the context of *De monstruos y prodigios*, Sulaimán is established from the beginning as an abomination in terms of difference: he is always treated as an outsider whose only purpose is to serve others. Furthermore, he is revealed to be a eunuch, a practice condemned by Jean. In contrast to the castration, Jean says, "you should not confuse this practice with the Orient's barbaric customs."[48] The notion of duality that permeates this work presents us with Sulaimán as the unappreciated double of the castrato. As explained by director Valdés Kuri, "[T]he history of the castrati begins with the eunuchs who sang to the harems in Spain. The practice of castration ended in Spain with the expulsion of the Arabs from the Iberian Peninsula, but those practices were only transferred and further developed in Italy."[49] If the castrato is only appreciated through the exhibition of his voice, Sulaimán has no possibility of appreciation by those around him as he is nothing more than a silent exotic creature with no redeeming qualities. His aboriginal persona incorporates those mythic qualities that have characterized Europeans' vision of the New World's native inhabitants. As a character, he is dressed in an intricate loincloth that evokes the Middle East, yet the Paré brothers constantly comment on his blackness, even though the actor playing this character is not black. It appears as though the terminology used to address him combines and dissolves all forms of otherness into one word that embodies rejection: black.[50] Thus, Sulaimán appears in the eyes of the other characters, as well as the spectators, as a liminal entity empty of any clear identity markers other than his savageness. Even worse, whereas the castrato can become a prodigious monster due to his seductive qualities, Sulaimán can be nothing more than an erotic trope of wild, limitless passion. He is an ethnographic metaphor of the wild man who will rape the women and kill the men and must therefore be contained. The notion of his possibly dangerous nature is promptly destroyed through humor in the play, as Sulaimán must be limited to the role of a controlled and nonthreatening slave.

JEAN: Men and women . . .
AMBROISE: . . . succumb before the pleasure of such disturbing
    beauty. Is it the exceptional power of their singing that clouds
    reason?
JEAN: Or is it the idealization of a supernatural being who partakes
    of both sexes without enduring either's limitations?

(Sulaimán is entangled in a sexual rapture that captures Dr. Paré's attention, as well as Galuppi's and Quiron's. At first they are all shocked, but when Sulaimán reaches his climax, they all burst out laughing)

JEAN: He's in heat.

(Jean-Ambroise and Galuppi surround him)

ALL: (Making comments, mockingly, at the same time) This is a man. A
    macho. A purebred stud.

(Galuppi pulls down Sulaimán's loincloth. It is revealed now that Sulaimán is a eunuch. They all stand paralyzed. Jean picks up from the floor the fake penis of the slave and hands it to him)

AMBROISE: *(Disgusted)* Jean, no, Jean, Jean . . .
JEAN: *Pardon, mon ami.*[51]

In this case, the performance clearly marks the perspectives of "civilization and barbarism" that so colored the colonial vision of otherness. Yet, following on José Martí's conception of *Our* America, this constructed difference disintegrates before our eyes, as the spectator can clearly identify the cruelty with which Sulaimán is disqualified from the category of human and classed as nothing more than a passionate animal.[52] Roberto Fernández Retamar reminds us that for Martí "there is no battle between civilization and barbarism, only between false erudition and nature."[53] Thus, civilization is nothing but a false pretense under which the contemporary European man operates to assert his natural right to colonize foreigners who resist the normalizing category of European or European American. As the slave, Sulaimán functions as a stand-in for the Latin American condition because he represents the barbarism that has been associated with those native to the Americas as a means of colonizing peoples and lands: "The presumed barbarism of our peoples was invented with crude cynicism by those who desired foreign lands . . . those who, with equal effrontery, give the 'popular name' of 'civilization' to the contemporary human being who comes from Europe or European America."[54] If anything, Sulaimán embodies the ethnographic image and cultural metaphor of the savage as seen through the lens of the colonizer, especially because of his wild eroticism, "a trope that involves the fear of dissolution of identity, and conversely, becomes a model of appropriation of difference."[55] Sulaimán is important because he allows for an understanding of otherness as it has permeated the cultural anxieties about difference that began during the colonial period and continue to affect our own definitions of self and civilization in modern Latin America.

I would even venture to compare Sulaimán to the figure of Caliban, the Shakespearean character who has become an allegory for postcolonial Latin American identity. If we are to consider the pervasive rhetoric of colonial thought as a hegemonic global model of power that, as it was articulated within the Conquest, continues to position notions of race and difference as modes of exploitation, then Sulaimán (and even the castrato) emerges as a figure of exploitation that continues to be dominated by a Eurocentric knowledge seeking to maintain practices of domination based on injustices and an established misunderstanding of alterity. Thus, as the world of legitimate knowledge that both Ambroise and Jean Paré have inhabited as the sole space of power begins to disintegrate with the advent of capitalist modern thought, Sulaimán becomes the Caliban that Fernández Retamar described: a figure that attempts to decolonize his culture and resists the invasion of the invader. It is precisely because of this aspect that I consider Sulaimán to be the most critical character in the play, even more so than the castrato. After all, the castrato represents a prodigious monster that can be admired for his vocal prowess; he is the freak that does not produce fear but pity. As Jean explains, the discourse of reason dismisses the castrato as a deformed, asexual being created by a cruel culture. Citing the words of Rousseau, he announces, "After many heated discussions, he has chosen to talk of castrati as true monsters, yes, gentlemen, 'monsters,' whose existence is an offense to reason."[56] The characters quickly dismiss these opinions as frivolous whims of modern thought, but this is contradicted by their actions toward the slave. While this conversation continues, Professor Galuppi "(*Approaches Sulaimán who has stopped handing out the hors d'oeuvres among the public and throws him a glass of wine*) [shouting] Work you beast! Work!"[57] Indeed, the cruelty that these characters are unable to enact toward the castrato is very much present in their relationship with Sulaimán. And here is where Fernández Retamar's thoughts resonate, as Sulaimán becomes the voice of the people, the popular sectors of society that will no longer tolerate the conquering presence.

From the beginning of the play, Sulaimán is treated as the freak before a series of monsters who have found, at one moment or another, a legitimizing discourse for their existence, even as they are visually outside all notions of normalcy. Yet the slave continues to be disposable, not even allowed to have a language with which to talk back. This all changes when Sulaimán takes on his role as a possible Caliban. Sulaimán, who has been denied a language and any access to official knowledge, suddenly appropriates "official" language (in this case French) to interrupt Jean and Ambroise's debate regarding the lack of merit in French reasoning. After a series of what we assume are untranslated insults in his native language, Sulaimán cries, "Je suis un homme, et je suis un homme libre, et je peux pedir tous que je veux. Vous êtes des imbecils, des imbecils. L'egalité, liberté, fraternité!" (I am a man, I am a free man, and I can say what I want. You are imbeciles, imbeciles. Equality, liberty, fraternity!).[58] This is a cry filled with irony since it is the slave who claims the human rights granted by the French Revolution. Yet, as a symbol of Caliban, Sulaimán reappropriates the language denied to him in order to declare himself a man. Fernández Retamar writes, "Prospero invaded the islands, killed our ancestors, enslaved Caliban, and taught him his language to make himself understood. What else can Caliban do but use that same language—today he has no other—to curse him?"[59] And so Sulaimán evolves in his representation of monstrosity from an elaborate, fictional monster to the freak masses of otherness, those marginal sectors of society that continue to be disposed of by the hegemonic sectors of society. Sulaimán becomes the voice of the marginal who attempt to rise and become the protagonists of history even as they are constantly shut down, "the people who, for centuries, have had no voice and at certain moments in history find a voice. . . . Sulaimán represents the masses in the sense of the people. He is the voice of equality; everyone has the same rights, which are rights of humanity."[60] This marginalized figure, the other, is the only character who rises and enunciates the discourse of reason. However, he is immediately shut down by someone in the audience, who yells "I do not come to the theater to be insulted! Do you think I do not understand what you say, black man?"[61] Although this person is a complicit spectator who has been asked in advance to say these lines, in the majority of the stagings the rest of the audience is usually shocked and begins to shush and silence the "screamer."[62] This interruption in the action, along with the reaction of the spectators, has a clear purpose, as it makes clear the artificial nature of all discourses. This should resonate with Rancière's words about the emancipated spectator, as the dramaturgical purpose of this action points to the "opposition between viewing and acting." The audience member who silences Sulaimán (as the other) seems to force the rest of the audience to actively react against his marginalization while challenging "the structures of domination and subjection" that often prevent opposition (even in something as simple as the fact that one should be quiet in the theater). [63] At the same time, the interruption of Sulaimán's assertion of self reminds us of our own compliance in the marginalization of the freak, as we dismiss his agency with insults that remove any trace of his humanity and only privilege what makes him "less than."

Everything changes in the play with the triumphant entrance of Napoleon on his horse and the beginning of a war, which leads to the complete decadence of all characters onstage. With the changes brought on by the historical moment, the legitimizing discourse also must change, which leads to the castrato becoming "an object of pleasure and shame." Valdés Kuri explains:

The entrance of Napoleon onstage is intended to signify the triumph of reason, nothing more. His moment in history (and in the play) arrives. He is the one to light the cannon onstage and make everything explode, because in the history of the castrati the most famous episode is Napoleon's war against them. Napoleonic culture is what truly brought the demise of the castrati.

Along with Napoleon's entrance, the characters become individualized since the cannon that explodes onstage separates the conjoined twins and eliminates Quirón's animal half. History and the official discourse have definitely changed. This brings absolute chaos onstage, and, after much confusion (during which the characters sing the history of western music, culminating with the "three tenors" and leading to the most banal moment of pop music) and violence, most of the characters face death onstage.[64] Their monstrosities obliterated, they are unable to function within a modern, rational discourse that condemns their concepts of beauty and order as nothing more than freakish aberrations of the past.

In the end, we find only Sulaimán and the *castrato* alone onstage, and all that is left of the latter's voice is a recording of Alessandro Moreschi, the last *castrato*. They both sit sadly on the stage listening to this. Sulaimán, the character who, as the voice of the people, had always been relegated to the margins of all discourses, is now in charge of narrating the end result of an era. It is no longer possible to incorporate the *castrato* within the official language, since the legitimizing gaze that once proclaimed him a sublime prodigy has now become obsolete. History has changed its official discourse, which leads to new conceptions of beauty and order. Thus, the final monologue becomes a powerful reminder of the prickliness of humanity, which will quickly dispose of those who don't fit neatly into the composition of its quickly changing conceptions of normalcy.

> If we could recapitulate musical history, the phenomenon of the castrati would claim our attention as a prodigious event that arose in the splendour of baroque art, only to definitively disappear and occupy a place in the gallery of mythical beings. If it was true that this phenomenon existed since medieval times, the lights of the "Century of Reason" ended this myth by calling it frightening and finishing off a prodigy that sacrificed all its being to the service of art. That was how the pitch of an indescribable voice that transported people to celestial sensations was completely lost from the stages.

(*He takes a banana from the pocket of his pants and peels it*)

The most important thing: the discovery of one of the most touching and spellbinding myths of musical history since Orpheus.
The adventure lasted three centuries, defying all laws of morality and reason, to conclude the impossible union between the
monster and the angel.

(*Sulaimán gives the banana to Il Castrato, kisses him, and exits. Il Castrato cries completely alone, center stage, while the historic recording* **Ave
Maria** *by* **Bach-Gounod** *sung by* **Alessandro Moreschi** *is heard*)[65]

Like an animal to be exhibited, a remnant of the past to be viewed and to
astound those who will be surprised by the primitive violence of his origin,
the castrato has no place in modernity. It is the end of an era, however, not
the end of a discourse, as the spectator should be aware that we, too, are the
product of that mode of thinking. Hopefully we are made aware that history does not present a "truth" but a perspective that legitimizes certain
monstrosities over others in order to declare them prodigies.

A LATIN AMERICAN FREAK SHOW: IDENTITY POLITICS
IN YUYACHKANI'S *HECHO EN PERÚ*

As we have seen thus far, the movement from the monster to the freak in
Latin American theater cannot escape the construction of colonial otherness that developed from the relationship between "conqueror" and
"conquered." Within the Latin American construction of identity, the categories of otherness continue to expand through the specter of a long
history of colonial power founded on violence perpetrated on and fear of
difference. Aníbal Quijano explains the ghostly presence of colonialism as
follows.

[I]n spite of the fact that political colonialism has been eliminated,
the relationship between the European—also called "Western"—
culture, and the others, continues to be one of colonial domination.
It is not only a matter of the subordination of the other cultures to
the European, in an external relation; we have also to do with a colonization of the other cultures, albeit in differing intensities and
depths. This relationship consists, in the first place, of a colonization

of the imagination of the dominated; that is, it acts in the interior of that imagination, [and] in a sense, it is a part of it.[66]

Quijano offers a clear analysis of the structures of power and domination that have "seduced" with an image of European superiority while also exploiting those deemed inferior. These actions are continuously legitimated through racial configurations: "Coloniality of power was conceived together with America and Western Europe, and with the social category of 'race' as the key element of the social classification of colonized and colonizers. Unlike in any other previous experience of colonialism, the old ideas of superiority of the dominant, and the inferiority of the dominated under European colonialism were mutated in a relationship of biologically and structurally superior and inferior."[67] Quijano's phrase, "coloniality of power," can be extended to the construction of freakery in the Latin American racialized other as the remnants of the violent conquest of those monsters that inhabited the "New World" are transformed into the exploitation and exhibition of racial difference as a systematic rendition of freak identity imposed on the marginalized racial sectors. The imposition of a racialized freak revitalizes the implied danger of those sectors of society that do not "benefit" the nation's path toward modernity and power. The traditional order of violence in Latin American society, then, insisted on the continuation of a colonial order that excluded the masses and the racialized other as it restricted classes through a powerful system of elites. This cycle of control reached its zenith in the nineteenth century and continued to the present through an oligarchic order that continues to repress the majority: "[I]n so far as the mass of the population was socially and culturally excluded from the national projects of the criollo elites, the latter were unable to perceive the collective expression of the popular masses in any other way than as putting the oligarchic states in great peril."[68] The tensions produced by this continual fear of the rise of the other have led to a history of violence that is especially marked in a country like Peru, where racial and class tensions remain an unresolved issue.

From 1980 to 2000, Peru was marked by the emergence of terrorist violence that brought, in turn, the emergence of state terrorism and the high cost of thousands of lives of Peruvian citizens, especially indigenous peasants in the highlands. This period of violence began in 1970, when Abimael Guzmán, a professor of philosophy, formed the group Shining Path in the mostly indigenous region of Ayacucho. Guzmán based the group on Maoist ideals and quickly garnered a student following that aimed to launch a revolution against the principles of imperialism and domination. During the 1980s the group's tactics became more violent, and in 1984 a second militaristic group appeared: the Tupac Amaru Revolutionary Movement (MRTA).[69] This was a process of violence that at first was concentrated in the provinces but eventually also brutally shook the capital of Lima (though not until the 1990s) as the government used military and paramilitary forces to combat the group. Every Peruvian was affected by the escalation of violence in those years as the state's military campaign victimized all those accused of protecting the terrorist organizations.[70] In addition, the Shining Path and MRTA often violently recruited individuals into their ranks and the people who lived in the crosshairs became unwilling victims of this war. As theater scholar Hugo Salazar states, in those decades the "culture of violence imposed its statute upon Peruvian society, and with this it reformulated and redefined our own scene and that of our criticism." [71] This meant that the theater of the eighties was profoundly influenced by these violent events, also known as the Dirty War, which translated into specific themes in theatrical production, such as metaphors of the political situation, a deep focus on the effects of violence, an act of denunciating the loss of the disappeared, and a nationalization of classical texts to express violent experiences. In the 1990s there was a decline in terrorist violence, especially after the capture of Abimael Guzmán. The government of Alberto Fujimori imposed neoliberal policies that sought to introduce a new era of globalization. In those years, Lima was transformed. First the margins of the city were expanded to accommodate the migration of people in search of new opportunities, and then the northern and southern parts of the city were further developed so that certain areas of the city were filled with casinos, supermarkets, and shopping centers. At the same time, this economic policy increased levels of unemployment and underemployment. This, in turn, increased the overseas migrations initiated by the previous government, as much of the population residing in Peru wanted to leave the country because they saw no future there. Unlike the revolutionary values of previous decades, the neoliberal ideals the government established in the 1990s implemented and promoted values like individualism and extreme market competition. Terrorist violence may have disappeared, but it was replaced with an increase in economic and ideological violence as a result of Fujimori's neoliberal policies, a violence that continues under the government of Alejandro Toledo. Such drastic changes call for a transformation in theatrical themes and forms, as artists consider the role of memory, religious syncretism, and the relation of identity and isolation in a country that is barely able to confront its recent past.[72]

It is within this context that the Peruvian activist performance collective

Yuyachkani celebrated its thirtieth anniversary in 2001. This was a difficult period for the country, as its citizens came to terms with the overt corruption of the previous government of Fujimori and began to demand an official acknowledgment of what had transpired.[73] The corrupt governments of the past had created a society where fear was the institutional, cultural, and psychological repercussion of violence, and this "culture of fear" was embedded in a generalized climate marked by the trivialization, or even ignorance, of the horrors that had occurred in the past thirty years. And so Yuyachkani decided to create the performance piece *Hecho en Perú (Vitrinas para un museo de la memoria)*(Made in Peru [Showcases for a Museum of Memory]) as a possible way of asserting and establishing a memory of the past.[74] As company director Miguel Rubio explains in the program notes:

> A present without memory condemns us to a depleted future, therefore a belief that the present doesn't owe anything to history leads us to believe that we have no obligation to the future. On the contrary, it must be repeated that the faculties of memory and imagination are complementary because they allow us to represent what is no longer and what is not yet. Yuyachkani's work is presented with the conviction that the present is the site where, with turbulence, the waters of past and future converge.

The efforts of past governments to create a homogeneous national identity that could stand against enemy forces, as well as the Shining Path's Maoist-inspired ideology, which called for the erasure of individual difference in favor of a standardized mass of "the people," had led to an impossible present where difference continued to be a negative marker. With *Hecho en Perú* the company sought to create a memory of those fraudulent identity categories as constructions that only benefit those who are in power or seek power. The importance of this performance is precisely the study of those representations of identity through a decontextualizing stylistic form, an aesthetic conviction that is also a crucial element of the company's performance practices.

Francine A'ness explains that the members of Yuyachkani often draw on "nonnaturalistic performance modes for their political potential. Their aim was to not only denounce but, moreover, to defamiliarize the violence they were living. By defamiliarizing it—donning masks, setting the action in the distant past, translating the contemporary world through allegory and myth, and using song and dance—they were able to expose the absurd and dehumanizing effects of the violence in a way that rendered it coherent and viewable."[75] Their aesthetics of defamiliarization are primarily created through a strong reference to traditional indigenous images and folklore. Andean music, masks that reference an Andean cosmology, accents from all parts of the country, and folk dances and dresses are all resources that can be understood as actions for identity empowerment. But, as Luis Ramos-García clarifies, the use of traditional Peruvian aesthetics has more to do with the company's desire to produce theater as ritual: "Rubio's theatrical discourse intends that the ritual of theater affects or provokes a dynamic utopian return to something lost: a real or imaginary state in which its members remain connected with nature, and with their Quechua or Aymara gods. . . . It is a set of practices that serves to define a cultural identity as opposed to nonculture, codifying an existing social structure and strengthening its forms and values."[76] This is especially significant in a country that often negates its autochthonous culture and relegates it to the margins, where the white elites consider indigeneity a marker for alterity and poverty.[77] After all, the rejection of these identities has formed a part of the national discourse that can be considered "fantasies of power" (following Slavoj Žižek's idea that "what precedes fantasy is not reality but a *hole* in reality, its *point of impossibility* filled in with fantasy") and constitute the ways in which hegemonic discourses continue to produce constructed images of the nation, culture, and ethnicity in contemporary Peru.[78] The identities we find in *Hecho en Perú* tell us more about the delusions of the "conqueror" than the "conquered."

Grupo Cultural Yuyachkani (which means "I'm thinking" or "I'm remembering" in Quechua) was founded in 1971 in Lima as a collective that understands theater as political action and a way to promote the investigation of cultures in Peru. For these purposes, in their forty-six years together the members have conducted workshops in marginalized communities, where they investigate and absorb the valuable corporeal and scenic diversity that exists within Peruvian popular culture.[79] As Miguel Rubio, artistic director of the company, explains in his program notes, Yuyachkani "tries to build a theatricality that is fully conscious of our culture and memory; we want to create Peruvian theater with all the complexities that this entails. In order to accomplish this we have to bring into the theater Peruvian diversity; here is where we will find the basis of our identity." The collective has always maintained this as the foundation of its work, and as such it has never ceased to be directly involved in the sociopolitical problems of the country, even during the difficult decade of the 1980s.

With *Hecho en Perú* the company puts on display the personification of the effects of the violence and trauma that affected the country. The piece consists of a "gallery" of identities that presents the viewer with six different showcases in which actors illustrate scenes and icons from contemporary Peruvian culture. Even though the piece is subtitled "A Museum of Memory," the physical structure of the space, as Miguel Rubio asserts, was inspired by the circus sideshows (or freak shows) that would visit his hometown when he was a child.[80] Considering the social and political significance of the traditional freak show in the cultural imaginary, it is particularly telling that the company chose these aesthetics to stage the piece. Rachel Adams reminds us that "With its heterogeneous assemblage of bodies, the sideshow platform is both a source of entertainment and a stage for playing out many of the century's most charged social and political controversies, such as debates about race and empire, immigration, relations among the sexes, taste, and community standards of decency."[81] Thus, the freak show becomes a sort of political and historical heterotopia, following Foucault's notion, where the anxieties and fears of a nation can be translated and performed. The physical space of the installation was created following these same aesthetic practices. There is a man in the street (similar to a freak show announcer) who calls out to the passersby, inviting them to come in and "see culture! Be a part of the history of our country! For the memory of our past!" The performance took place inside a shopping mall in downtown Lima, with a multitude of people walking by and coming in. The spectator or visitor entered the building, which was in the style of a rectangular exhibition room: on both sides of the space there were three showcases, or *vitrinas*, leaving empty space throughout the area for a sort of large corridor where spectators could walk or stop by any of the showcases. There was almost a claustrophobic feeling as one entered the space, with a multitude of people gathering around the different *vitrinas*, unable to determine where to look next. The spectators could not passively observe the different actions; instead they had to actively wander around the space, and, as Beatriz Marcos suggests, "This is a suggestive approach in that it promotes what is dynamic and participatory in the construction of collective memory (against traditional musealization)."[82] The hall had low lighting, with strings of colored lights hanging from the ceiling and loud music playing (mostly cumbias and other types of popular music). Each individual in the *vitrina* was an exaggeration of a particular sociocultural identity in Peru. And their exaggerations were concentrated on the body as action.

There were six figures represented in the *vitrinas*: the Andean indigenous identity (El Dorado, performed by Amiel Cayo) from the historical figure to modern conflicts; the immigrant who has decided to leave his country with whatever means he has been able to accumulate (Desembarque-Landing, performed by Augusto Casafranca); womanhood (Pieles de mujer–Woman Skins, performed by Ana Correa) and the different roles in society to which women must conform or break in order to become leaders of the nation; the Motherland (Madre Patria, performed by Teresa Ralli) with all of its possible disguises and allegorical meanings; faith and popular religion (La Mano Poderosa–The Powerful Hand, performed by Debora Correa) along with several icons that signal our need to believe in something; and, finally, corruption at its best in the figure of Vladimiro Montesinos (El Asesor–The Assessor, performed by Julián Vargas) and his sinister practices.[83] Following in the tradition of a Barnum and Bailey collection of human oddities, the performance offered a panoramic view of some of the most sensational forms of alterity at that given moment, and from multiple perspectives for understanding forms of deviance. Each performance in the *vitrina* lasted about seven minutes, all occurring at the same time and repeating the action. This hybrid cast constituted a series of varied curiosities indiscriminately categorized as freaks by a social system that fails to separate difference from deviance and where the marginalized members of society face systematic alienation in a political system that allows figures such as Montesinos and Fujimori to create a system of persecution and destruction.

I find this to be a particularly interesting example of a visual movement away from the idea of the exhibition of the monster and toward the exaltation of freakery that appeared in the sideshows of the nineteenth and early twentieth centuries. The nineteenth-century conception of the modern body led to the exclusion of those who did not conform—the ill, the insane, and the sexually dissonant—to the political and economic pressures of modernization.

With the union of commercial and scientific interests, mass culture gave rise to the freak show, among other forms of mass entertainment that continued to rise with the development of the entertainment industry. With the advent of the technological reproducibility of the lithograph and photography, the nineteenth century was a period when our connection to the experience of materiality was astoundingly altered. The notion of visual culture expanded the historical narrative as societies experienced a paradigm shift that accounts for the centrality of images in the belief systems of contemporary society. The images that would capture a nation also revealed the shared attributes across a culture in time. Literary critic Leslie Fiedler explains that with the advent of modernity and the heightened attention devoted to visual appearance, the term *monster* was stripped of its previous connotations and became a term more closely aligned with artistic fantasy (e.g., characters such as Dracula and Frankenstein) akin to the horror film genre.[84] As the monster acquired a more mythical dimension and developed into a figure that is "not real," the Victorian freak show became an institution in itself where observers could see "real" anomalies that would assure them of their normalcy: "[T]he true freak stirs both supernatural terror and natural sympathy, since, unlike the fabulous monster, he is one of us."[85] The freak show exposes our own primordial fears regarding our individuality and ability to comply with the conditions of normalcy.

Similarly, *Hecho en Perú* exhibits the idea of national identity as a series of problematic figures that force the observer to move beyond traditional binaries and stereotypes as it decenters and "enfreaks" the major tropes that constitute the Peruvian national consciousness. The nation, for example, appeared through the figure of the woman (Teresa Ralli as the Motherland) dressed in white robes crossed with a red cloth (the red and white of the Peruvian flag). Her head was covered with olive branches, her face a mask of white makeup that evoked the image of a Japanese geisha. After waving the national flag, she sang "Baion japonés" (a popular rock and roll song from 1957 by the Argentinian group Los cinco latinos), an obvious reference to Fujimori's quick departure. Ralli cries onto the red cloth and finally sits down to read the "Motherland News, the ones that always tell the truth." She reads about all sorts of political scandals in the current media. This performative action throws out the question of what constitutes national identity in a nation that has so carefully cultivated ignorance and forgetfulness of the violence that has been perpetrated on so much of its population. The pain brought on by so much violence has to move beyond empathy and solidarity with the victims and instead be directed toward each individual citizen who stood by while all this happened. Who belongs to this Motherland and who was allowed to be exterminated? The period of violence in Peru succeeded in dividing the nation through a false conviction of national identity, or, as Victor Vich clarifies, one must question "the production of the main metaphors that became the ideological sustenance for the hegemony through the development of the 'dirty war' in Peru. . . . How diverse types of utterances constructed altered images to represent the country and an 'Other' supposedly external and different."[86] In this performance, Yuyachkani finds a way to put into play not only the memory of cultural and social violence but also the notion of national identity itself. The "freaks" that are put on display are caricatures of foundational myths, archetypes, cultural icons, and even national foes.

With the end of an era comes the creation of new subjectivities, and, as Josefina Ludmer clarifies, in the context of Latin America the cycles of fin de siècle have led to historical processes filled with symbolic value that in turn constitute entrances into modernity that transform the cultural discourses.[87] In the nineteenth century there was a direct correlation between the nation and Latin American modernity that focused on the construction of national identities. Yet in the twentieth century we were faced with a blurring of the national referent in favor of global capital influxes that sought to erase borders. As Ludmer points out, this favoring of capital over national identity led to the exclusion of several components in the creation of modern citizenship: "[T]he excluded from Latin American modernity at the end of the nineteenth and twentieth century were women, blacks, homosexuals. It is from their existence that one can critique nation and modernity: from their territories, representations, and bodies."[88] In the midst of the Fujimorian spectacle that had overtaken the nation during the last two decades of the twentieth century, Yuyachkani put on display the freak show that the nation had become.

By then it was common practice for the bodies that represented dissidence to lose all sense of value in the eyes of those in power. Rubio writes that "the bodies of us, Peruvian citizens, were degraded to such a point that it became an everyday occurrence to see them massacred, mutilated, and exposed to the weather, buried in clandestine mass graves, or, even worse, disappeared."[89] At a time when the country made a freak show of victims of violence by exhibiting the punished bodies of individuals considered to be outside the norm for reasons of ethnicity or morality, Yuyachkani replied by exhibiting national images that had precipitated the violence itself as the country's true freaks. This is obvious in the *vitrina* that featured Montesinos (El asesor). Here Julian Vargas sat on a bed in what appeared to be a small bunker (by now Montesinos had fled the country), his face covered with a very lifelike mask of the man. He looked at the audience, provoking them with body language that aggressively seemed to ask "What are you looking at?" The room was cluttered with papers, boxes, and bottles. More important, a television showed a constant loop of the vladi-videos, emphasizing the role that the media had in manipulating the images of difference as deviance. "The assessor" goes through his daily routines, defecating into a bedpan, playing with the torso of a naked mannequin, and sleeping in his underwear and a girdle. He is put on display for all his abnormal behavior and his institutionalization of fear, which trivialized the horrors committed around the nation. Montesinos was a clear manipulator of the mass media, creating a state of fear for the "subversive element," which the state trans-

Fig. 4. *Hecho en Perú. Vitrinas para un Museo de la Memoria.* Actor Julián Vargas as El Asesor. Photo by Elsa Estremadoyro/Archivo de Yuyachkani.

lated as the indigenous populations. Miguel Rubio himself recalls a time when, while teaching a workshop in mountainous Ayacucho, a young actress lamented the imagery that accompanied those living in the most vulnerable areas of the country: "[W]e don't want to continually be seen as savages that kill each other. Ayacucho is not only death, we live here."[90] The *vitrinas* would serve as living exhibitions where the national spectacle could be made into a carnival of oddities that presented events from high politics to the appropriation of national myths and popular culture. I find it particularly useful to reflect on this work through the lens of the historical freak show as it leads us to consider the inflexibility of a national consciousness that, with the passage of time, becomes more dogmatic, especially as the company converts national icons into freaks as a reflection on the cracked mirror that is national identity politics.

Garland-Thomson has identified the freak show as a particularly important trope for its "counternarrative of peculiarity as eminence" with an explicitly political and democratic agenda.

Straddling the ideologies of the traditional and the modern, the freak show manifested a tension between the older mode that read particularity as a mark of empowering distinction and a newer mode that flattened differences to achieve equality. In such a liminal space, the domesticated freak simultaneously embodied exceptionality as a marvel and exceptionality as anomaly, thus posing to the spectator the implicit political question of how to interpret differences within an egalitarian social order.[91]

Thus, as a trope of difference, the freak show does not attempt to deny or normalize the stigma associated with it (since the "freaks" themselves would not have the power to do so) but instead embraces it and discovers within it an intense subversive power to revise oppressive disability narratives in favor of transgressive and liberating ones. In the case of this performance, the aesthetics of freakery allow for a very interesting game that involves the gaze of the spectator and the experience of a shared space as it comments not only on a memory of past atrocities but also the "idea" of a national identity (something so intrinsically tied to past violence). It is important to remember the special significance of this, since the characters onstage are aberrations of foundational myths, national archetypes, cultural icons, and despised figures. What connects the showcases in which actors and actresses illustrate visions and scenes of contemporary Peru is not a cohesive narrative but instead the gaze of the visitors as they decide where to look and how to interpret notions of difference.

In each *vitrina* there is a rectangular platform with its own lightning and sound. Each actor or actress inhabits an object's installation within the performance space. Some showcases project video effects over the performer's body. The bodies onstage are unpredictable, as spectators are aware of the anomalies within each representation, from the exaggerated and erotic appearance of an indigenous man to the use of masks and face paint and the grotesque movements performed by the body. Interestingly, though, most of these figures deal with societal issues corresponding to a lack of tolerance that has led to increased violence, such as religious beliefs, indigeneity, and gender violence. Ana Correa explored this last issue in the *vitrina* Pieles de mujer. With her face painted in red and white, like the national flag, Correa knelt before a set of candles, preparing a bundle of items that she later carried to a side within her stage space. Her head was covered in a black shawl, and behind her a video constantly projected images of different instances of violence against indigenous populations. She eventually took off most of her clothes until she was left in a short black slip of a dress, her long hair loose. Her movements, which had started off slow and fluid, became agitated and incoherent as she moved around the set of candles.

After taking them and balancing them on her chest to calm her movements, Correa blew out the candles. There were many actions occurring in this space, but the principal issue was the innate violence imposed on fixed social identities (women and indigenous communities) to legitimate a model of repression that, as Quijano asserted, has been in operation since the colonial period. These are society's freaks, and the performance forces us as spectators to face the fact that when, traditionally, there is a cultural and social dictate that promotes intolerance, facing (in a closed space) those we marginalize becomes exceedingly difficult. For as much as we have progressed as a society, and our relationship with difference has evolved as we reframe our perspectives within a variety of registers over time, the uneasy human impulse to textualize, contain, and explain our most unexpected corporeal manifestations to ourselves has remained constant. Culturally, we associate difference with our anxieties, questions, and needs. When society uses singular bodies as images from which to coax anxiety and fear, these bodies can also become politicized as they reflect distorted national values and identities. Yuyachkani sought to build on the political implications of difference, creating an experience that could only occur outside the theater. Ileana Diéguez explains, "[O]utside of the safe spaces, the actors did not represent, they actuated like 'liminal entities' generating individual performances that formed a sort of scenic collage, through a parody exploration of the devices and effects of the media."[92] In other words, *Hecho en Peru* carnivalizes a series of social problems to denounce the manner in which the mass media had exploited the identities contained in each *vitrina*. This could be best achieved though a process of enfreakment, exploring how each body on display mediates the social anxieties of a system founded on fear and violence.

Yuyachkani very much plays with the exhibition of bodies within a space and reimagines it as a site for staring (as Garland-Thomson reminds us, "[W]e stare when ordinary seeing fails, when we want to know more").[93] It becomes an interesting revision of Foucault's panopticon and a powerful commentary on modern society. As the panopticon made the individual always visible to the eye of power, the free movement of the spectator through the *vitrinas* and the bodies on display calls for an undifferentiated public in a space that is organized around the crowd as viewers. As such, the spectator becomes a witness to the messages of the bodies on display and thus a vehicle for inscribing and broadcasting the messages that discourses of power continue to hide within society. Diana Taylor furthers this notion: "Yuyachkani attempts to make their urban audiences culturally competent to recognize the multiple ways of being 'Peruvian' at the same time that they denounce the multiple ways in which the body of a nation has been corrupted."[94]

Let's expand on one example—the *vitrina* for El Dorado. Peru has had a very conflictive societal view of ethnicity, especially during periods of extreme violence, as the indigenous populations were not only the victims but also the protagonists of conflict. During the Dirty War much of society was indifferent toward the acts of terrorism that destroyed the indigenous peasant populations. In the capital city, the presence of those fleeing terror could only be understood as an inconvenience. Yet Peru continues to be a country that benefits from its indigenous past (and present) for capitalist gains such as tourism. Thus, Yuyachkani plays with the notion of El Dorado, that mythical place that promises riches from the Inca Empire. In this *vitrina*, the actor portrays the "*indio*" through the assigned condition, meaning the stereotypes of exoticism and sexual tourism. This creates a contrast between the rejection of the indigenous self as a marginal element of society and the use of a "sanitized" indigeneity through a marketplace that wishes to attract capital, as well as creating a national identity. This allows for an understanding of the figure onstage as narrating a process of enfreakment for indigenous identity. Therefore, as with freak shows, the marketplace has demanded that indigenous Peru be institutionalized as a site where one can "admire" nature's other.

Bogdan reminds us that the historical freak shows exhibited not only the "physically disabled" but also the "exotic ethnic," framing them in a way that heightened their differences from viewers, who were in turn rendered comfortably common and safely standard by means of this exchange.[95] Theirs were bodies that transgressed rigid social categories such as race, gender, and personhood. External objects associated with wildness or otherness exaggerated their forms. In the case of El Dorado, the actor Amiel Cayo fluctuates between different perceptions of modern Peruvian society. The space has a cross in the background, where golden hands and a golden mask hang. A series of masks surround the actor, who changes into different personas during his performance cycle. He first appears as the *indio*, with the corresponding accessories, including the coca leaf that he chews on. Yet these "typical" artifacts are contrasted with his sunglasses and, as we soon see, his revealing Speedos. Through the modern artifacts, the actor becomes a sexualized other, spilling oil on his skin, sensually rubbing it over his body, and eventually hanging a number (69) on his bathing suit as he flexes his muscles for the audience. One can perceive that a history of freakness is imposed on the racialized body of the indigenous performer. In other words, ethnic freaks are not physically anomalous within

Fig. 5. *Hecho en Perú. Vitrinas para un Museo de la Memoria*. Actor Amiel Cayo as El Dorado. Photo by Elsa Estremadoyro/Archivo de Yuyachkani.

the context of their own cultures; instead, it is their presence among those who live differently that serves as the basis for their display. And, so the actions of El Dorado allow us to understand the colonial gaze that has been cast on the indigenous other. As Bogdan explains, "[W]hat made them 'freaks' was the racist representation of them and their culture by promoters. . . . The exotic mode emphasized how different and, in most cases, how inferior the persons on exhibit were."[96] Within the context of Peruvian society, the complex manipulations placed on indigenous identity by those in power are exposed on this stage, as El Dorado becomes not only an eroticized figure of consumption but also a martyred Christ figure through which governmental policies are able to claim a so-called progressive economic and cultural doctrine.

The showcases that compose *Hecho en Peru* question and expose the fear injected in society that characterized Fujimori's dictatorship so that citizens would continue to accept his authoritarian rule in a space of mediatized manipulation. All aspects of modern Peruvian society are staged in this gallery, as spectators are invited in through the premise "la cultura es para todos." Yes, culture is available to all, but how do we consume it and those represented by it? As Fiedler has stated, "The freak is a historical figure ritually fabricated from the raw material of bodily variations and appropriated in the service of shifting social ideologies. In short, we show the freak of nature to be a freak of culture."[97] As Yuyachkani carnivalizes the media spectacle of the dominant society that was Fujimori's Peru, it is necessary also to reflect on the possibility of developing strategies and rituals from the citizen that can parody those same media through which the establishment is legitimized. Yuyachkani pushes the spectator to question the ways in which identity in Peru is conformed and consumed, for whenever we discuss issues of deviance we have to look at those in charge of telling us who the deviants are and what they are like. As spectators we act in a collective moment of looking at these "abnormal" identities, the freaks of society, a society based on a state violence that is just starting a process of healing and remembering. *Hecho en Peru* acts as a carnivalization of social problems that should not be forgotten.

CAMERA OBSCURA: MEDIATIZING THE FREAK, FINDING OURSELVES IN ROMINA PAULA'S *FAUNA*

If the nineteenth century brought forth the advent of the freak show as a place where the everyday citizen could gaze on and confront his or her uttermost fears through the terrifying forms of otherness (the exotic dark-skinned savage, the deformed body, the ambiguously sexed body, the exaggerated body, etc.), the twentieth century evicted this form of amusement from the realm of popular culture as a consciousness of human rights and social ethics prevented the live exhibition of those bodies for profit. This does not mean that freaks disappeared from the collective consciousness; their exhibition was simply displaced to other forms of visual consumption. Rachel Adams explains that the freak show is integral to developing political and social consciousness and an unavoidable part of societies' negotiations of meaning: "[W]ith its heterogeneous assemblage of bodies, the sideshow platform is both a source of entertainment and a stage for playing out many of the century's most charged social and political controversies, such as debates about race and empire, immigration, relations among the sexes, taste, and community standards of decency."[98] Modern notions of human rights and the medicalization of disabilities removed this platform, and new forms of mass entertainment brought the figure of the freak to television and film, where we could once again gaze on our greatest fears from a safe distance. Leonard Cassuto observes that

> freak shows have not so much disappeared as dispersed. Just as freak show spectators could once wander from booth to booth in a sideshow tent, viewers may now flip from channel to channel. . . . The freak show remains alive and well, then, a still viable prism for collective anxiety—but with a change. Mass culture would have us believe that freaks now write their own script from their own lives.[99]

Thus, freaks were moved from the monsters of mythology and cabinets of curiosities to sideshow tents and popular forms of media where the same issues could be explored through different genres from the horror film to today's reality television.

The twentieth century brought us the implementation of new forms of visual culture and consumption: mass media, film, and television. If photography fundamentally transformed the ways in which we imagined and experienced the world in the nineteenth century, cinematic culture transcended notions of nineteenth-century modernity as a realm of both experience and representation. As Walter Benjamin theorized, forms of media and technology become social facts, as there is a direct correlation between a period's visual technologies and its structures of understanding. In the words of Guy Debord, "As the indispensable decoration of the objects produced today, as the general exposé of the rationality of the system, as the advanced economic sector which directly shapes a growing multitude of image-objects, the spectacle is the *main production* of present-day society."[100] In this present-day mediatized society, with the heightened importance of visuality, film and other forms of visual media have reappropiated the freak show in order to produce spectacles based on the fears and insecurities of modern society. The film industry allows for the creation of all sorts of made freaks that can accurately respond as allegories of our deepest insecurities and anxieties. One of the best-known examples would be Tod Browning's cult masterpiece *Freaks* (1932), a film that subverts the notion of normative standards in order to denounce class antagonisms. When the film premiered, in the midst of the Depression era, it was a failure. As Adams explains, the main reason for its failure was that the US public was more concerned with film as entertainment through the magnificent musicals Hollywood was producing. *Freaks* put on display that which it wished to ignore, an identification with the other that lacked any form of disguise.

> Not only did [*Freaks*] reanimate the conventions of a mode of live entertainment that many Americans were eager to erase from cultural memory, it also explored the way that cinema could intensify and prolong the experience of a live sideshow by bringing the freak off of the display platform and onto the screen.[101]

Freaks were meant to stay in the marginal tents of the circuses and not be displayed on the "silver screen" as stars. Yet the revival of the film in the 1960s and its devoted fandom raise the questions: What happens to the freak as it is removed from its traditional confines of the sideshow and moved to other locations, such as film and television? Is this yet another form of exploitation? Or does the screen become the main space through which, as a society, we can understand and explore the fears and issues that plague us? And, although both are forms of popular culture, film had different aspirations as it became associated with artistic forms, aesthetic value, and glamour.

Romina Paula's play *Fauna* (2013), directed by her and staged by her company, El silencio (The Silence), explores the ways in which film has a way of altering our perception of that which is around us, even before it appears onscreen.[102] Born in 1979, Paula is considered one of Argentina's new generation of prolific playwrights in Buenos Aires' independent theater scene who are finding new ways of interacting with the economic and political upheavals of the past few decades. She has worked as an actress in films and theater in addition to being a director and playwright. For this play, Paula was inspired by Dorothea Lange's quote "The camera is an instrument that teaches people how to see without a camera,"[103] as she approached the play itself as a film without a camera or screen and an exploration of our understanding of the world through technological means. The central plot in *Fauna* follows a film director, José Luis (portrayed by Rafael Ferro), and an actress, Julia (portrayed by Pilar Gamboa), who is also his muse and the impulse behind his new film endeavor. They go to the countryside to research the myth of Fauna, a sort of Amazonian woman known for being both extremely cultured and savage who dressed as a man for years in order to participate in intellectual circles at the university. They want to make a film about her life, and with the help of Fauna's adult offspring, the intelligent María Luisa (portrayed by the veteran actress Susana Pampín) and the wild man Santos (portrayed by Esteban Bigliardi), they will attempt to piece her life together. In the midst of the reenactment of Fauna's life, the four characters become involved in a tragic story of unrequited love, as Julia decides to no longer continue her affair with the married José Luis and falls for María Luisa, while Santos declares his attraction for José Luis. The four characters rehearse scenes from the movie as they discuss which elements of Fauna's life should be represented and how much veracity can be found in the stories about her. The constant question that plagues the characters is whether or not telling the truth about her life is important. After all, how does one represent theatrically the life of a woman, who never appears onstage, in a film about her life outside the confines of normalcy? Or, as the theater critic Denise Mora explains, "What is not there can be magnified with words. The fact that Fauna does not appear, is not visualized, makes her sublime and mysterious."[104] The fact that she never appears onstage only fuels the myth that surrounds her, as that which is absent can easily be aggrandized through language, in this case the language of representation (film and theater).

The main character, Fauna, has died, but she is constantly remembered as "a sort of Amazonian, a cultured and savage woman" (program notes) who lives in the midst of the Argentinian *litoral*, the northeastern part of the country, surrounded by great rivers and jungles. She was an insatiable reader who recited poems by Rilke, a woman who combined great force and vulnerability and whom the characters onstage attempt to re-create. The performance questions the artistic process of representation itself, but it does so through the process of creation since the play itself is about the process of recounting a life for a film. And in doing so, we, as the audience watching this process unfold, are left to question how the enormity of a freak identity (Fauna) can be represented through the retelling of stories

Fig. 6. *Fauna*. Actors (left to right) Esteban Bigliardi as Santos, Rafael Ferro as José Luis, Pilar Gamboa as Julia, and Susana Pampín as María Luisa. Photo by Sebastián Arpesella.

when she is no longer able to represent herself. How much will her character be distorted? Similar to Benjamin's view, it is not simply that the age of mechanical reproduction ushered in the culture of the copy but that these copies influenced our definitions of authenticity and originality in unsettling and unexpected ways (Benjamin's notion of the aura produced by confrontation with the actual presence): "[T]he desire of contemporary masses to bring things 'closer' spatially and humanly . . . is just as ardent as their bent toward overcoming the uniqueness of every reality by accepting its reproduction."[105] We are more convinced by the illusion of the copy as reality as we are overcome by a desire for encompassing all truth. In the case of this play, Fauna is the desired object, which none of the characters can fully apprehend.

To understand Fauna as a freak, one must first understand her constant straddling of a feminine and masculine identity that is associated with her savage nature. Fauna may not be a freak in the traditional sense of physical anomaly; she is a freak due to a series of behaviors and practices that situate her on the margins of what is culturally or socially acceptable. She first adopts a masculine identity in order to attend the reading circles at the university, which were conducted by only men. Fauna decided to dress as a man and participate. "She read everything that she could get her hands on. She read in German, in English, in French. At one point she began to study Russian to read all the classics, but I'm not sure if she ever really learned well enough to read,"[106] explains María Luisa, her daughter. Fauna's curiosity about life and literature, along with her thirst for knowledge, is partly what makes her a freak in the eyes of traditional society. She is a woman who chooses to dress as a man in order to access this knowledge. Her curiosity is reflected in Paula's own understanding of the role of theater in life: "[T]heater is a vital practice, it has to do with a concern about who is that person you represent, it is never a certainty. In my case it does not arise from a theoretical or intellectual place, but from anxiety and curiosity." [107] The term *curiosity* is at the center of the action in this play: Julia, the actress, first encounters Fauna from afar and is driven with curiosity about the identity of this woman, which steers her to convince José Luis, the director, to film a movie about her life. Fauna's entire life is guided by curiosity and a thirst for knowledge, which leads her to dress as a man and to spend her life in isolation exploring books and nature. This curiosity has removed Fauna from the realm of socially acceptable behavior, as it is an act of defiance.

> Curiosity is a vice that has been stigmatized in turn by Christianity, by philosophy, and even by a certain conception of science. Curiosity, futility. The word, however, pleases me. To me it suggests something altogether different: it evokes "concern": it evokes the care one takes for what exists and could exist; a readiness to find strange and singular what surrounds us; a certain relentlessness to break up our familiarities and to regard otherwise the same things; a fervor to grasp what is happening and what passes; a casualness in regard to the traditional hierarchies of the important and the essential.[108]

Instead of following Foucault's admiration for such a state of being, which coincides with Fauna's own attitude toward learning, those around her would have considered her curiosity to be an unnatural condition for a woman such as herself. For example, the play begins with Julia reading some lines from a poem by Rilke that Fauna translated from German into Spanish. José Luis immediately replies that the poem is "too pretentious" for the film and the character of Fauna: "It isn't important. I don't mean to say that it's not important, but it isn't relevant, that's what I meant. When you say it like that it sounds pretentious and, besides, books do not fit her."[109] Based on the image of Fauna that the director will forge for the film, her condition as an intellectual cannot be adapted to the freak subjectivity he wishes to exhibit: Fauna as a savage woman/man who never allowed herself to be integrated into society. José Luis's perspective on the star of his film is very much in line with the structure of the freak show (and today's mediatized narratives of alterity), as he wishes to create a particular persona for his film. As Nadja Durbach reminds us:

> The showman's narrative and the promotional materials that surrounded these shows reinforced these themes of primitiveness, savagery, and thus the necessity of imperial rule. Freak shows were highly structured experiences that were invariably framed by a story about the anomalous body on display. The presenter's patter, important at most freak show performances, was particularly essential to the success of these shows, as it transformed otherwise unremarkable individuals into bloodthirsty savages.[110]

For his film to succeed, José Luis must create a consumable image of Fauna as spectacle, and any trace of her intellectual identity has the possibility of removing the freak specter from her character, thus rendering her incompatible for consumption. He is more comfortable with the idea of Fauna's behavior as out of bounds (dressing as a man) than Fauna as an intelligent woman. Even as María Luisa explains that her mother loved Rilke, José Luis's reply is a simple "[T]he truth doesn't necessarily matter."[111]

All the characters onstage straddle the line between feminine and masculine identity. Julia, the actress, decides to dress as a man to get into character; María Luisa, Fauna's daughter, begins the play dressed in a pair of man's overalls but later (after Julia has declared her love for her) changes into a "more feminine" blouse; and at one point the actors question whether the director José Luis's version of Fauna is more feminine than Julia's. The constant question onstage is the possibility of finding both, the feminine and masculine, in one person. This gender ambiguity, which slowly creeps into all the characters onstage, is what creates such discomfort in both Julia and, especially, José Luis. They have come to the *litoral* to film the life of Fauna, a freak they assume they have nothing in common with but who will be an interesting character for a film. Instead, the study of Fauna's life leads them to question their own identities as "normal" citizens. In the words of Elizabeth Grosz, Fauna embodies an "intolerable ambiguity" that is assumed to be external to their own conditions.

> The freak is an object of simultaneous horror and fascination because, in addition to whatever infirmities or abilities he or she exhib-

> its, the freak is an *ambiguous* being whose existence imperils catego-
> ries and oppositions dominant in social life. Freaks are those human
> beings who exist outside and in defiance of the structure of binary
> oppositions that govern our basic concepts and modes of self-
> definition. . . . Freaks cross the borders that divide the subject from
> all ambiguities, interconnections, and reciprocal classifications, out-
> side of or beyond the human. They imperil the very definitions we
> rely on to classify humans, identities, and sexes—our most funda-
> mental categories of self-definition and boundaries dividing self
> from otherness.[112]

In addition, Fauna's gender ambiguity embodies the savage freak, a being
that was in essence a cultural artifact for a utopian vision—a way of imagining a euphoric state of being associated with complete, uncivilized freedom. This vision of Fauna is closely related to Bartra's notion of the wild
man/woman in western civilization. As he points out, the wild man is a
European invention that "conditioned the emergence of the notion (and
praxis) of civilization."[113] This idea, as previously discussed, was later
transposed on the indigenous cultures of the Americas along with the notion of barbarism. In other words, the savage man was already a part of
European iconoclastic history, and within the colonial context it was easily
applied to the "savage" populations that the conquerors encountered as
this was the only way in which these others could be understood. Therefore, Fauna, as a wild woman of the Americas, conforms to this notion of
savagery as "the wild man reflected a condition of a degenerate individual,
far from the city, and fallen from grace."[114] This savage nature is transferred onstage to her daughter, who makes José Luis very uncomfortable
with her vast knowledge of literature, and her son, who constantly questions the representation of their mother by these outsiders.

In the case of María Luisa, her presence brings about a contradictory
reaction: she is both the savage woman and the cultured intellectual. For
Julia she becomes a proxy for Fauna and therefore intimidates her. For José
Luis she is nothing more than an object of study to help him create his own
configuration of the Amazonian Fauna. At one point, after María Luisa
questions Julia and José Luis about their romantic nature, José Luis quickly
dismisses her question by replying, "Looks are deceiving, María Luisa, you
should know that better than anyone else."[115] When María Luisa questions
this statement, the director's answer is to point out her constant use of literary quotes, and he asks her to recite one for this situation. In his mind, it is
impossible that a woman who lives "as a savage" could also have such in-

Fig. 7. *Fauna*. Actors Pilar Gamboa and Susana Pampín. Photo by Sebastián Arpesella.

tellectual capacity unless her use of literary quotes is a form of mimicry, which would bring her closer to a circus freak, an exhibition staged for his amusement. Santos, on the other hand, is a complete wild man. He first appears onstage in a furry coat, reminiscent of primitive man. His own sister describes him as "particular" and "a little bit of a savage." This invites a discussion between Julia and José Luis about whether or not Santos should appear in the movie, for why would such a wild man want to be in a film? Here we have a more complex discussion of aesthetic judgment in the arts and the relationship between freaks and bad taste. Within the hierarchy of taste, the freak appears as a grotesque figure, an object of curiosity, and as some visual media (such as film and photography) move into the realm of high art, the appearance of freaks in these media causes controversy. There is a desire for a marked distinction between genres, and the freak show is a reminder of past "misconduct" in bad taste. In the case of this play, Santos allows José Luis to bring authenticity to his film about a marginal figure. And, as María Luisa points out (most likely ironically), "That's the point of the cinema, right? To make things beautiful?"[116]

The relationship between María Luisa and José Luis (notice the parallels in their names) in relation to Fauna brings about an interesting comparison regarding the creation and telling of her story. Both characters, the director and the daughter, wrestle for control over the story that should be told, and both act as the directors of Fauna's life onscreen: José Luis as the creator of her fictional story and María Luisa as the one who attempts to present the facts. María Luisa represents the ambiguity between savagery and civilization; she has great intellectual capacity, yet she wishes to remain separate from society. In the performance, Susana Pampín represented this character as a larger than life persona, with very exaggerated movements and a sort of arrogance in her tone of voice. After all, she is fully aware of the distortions that occur regarding her mother's life story on film. José Luis, on the other hand, is only interested in creating a particular image of Fauna based on a fictional life of abnormality. This particular image of Fauna as freak is based on Julia's first encounter with Fauna years before. Her description of that moment is plagued with images of terror and desire before the unknown character she can see from afar.

> One day I saw her, it was like an apparition. . . . [S]uddenly from the intense green comes a horse, with a woman mounting it, bah, a person, I didn't know what I was seeing, first I see this imposing horse. . . . And on top of the horse, like an effigy, this being, this person, with a hat, stout, beautiful, a gorgeous being, imposing, hieratic. . . . [S]he looked at me for a second, I don't know how to explain what I felt, a commotion, I couldn't understand if the terror that I felt was because I was in danger because of this presence, but at the same time it wasn't just terror, it was something else, it had to do with pleasure, perhaps idolatry?[117]

Julia continues by stating that she tried to visit Fauna but was discouraged by the townspeople, who told her that Fauna lived in the jungle, was unsociable, and lived surrounded by "crazy people." Julia's disparate feelings toward Fauna are a common theme in the theorization of the freak. She finds herself observing a figure that stares back, someone she cannot understand but who forces her to feel her own anxieties about her identity as a fragile woman.

As a matter of fact, the uneasiness that Fauna brings forth in Julia and José Luis is part of a long tradition: the myth of the Amazon. The Amazon is a liminal being who enables us to define the limits of civilized space. According to Bartra, she breaks with boundaries between culture and nature through her gender ambiguity, the domesticity of the female and the violence of the male: "For the Greeks, civilized space was associated with men, whereas women were, to some extent, comparable to wildness. Amazons combined wild features with notoriously masculine traits such as a love of war and great horse-riding skills as they brandished the typical double-edged axes."[118] This image is what José Luis wishes to portray in his film through Julia, who is by no means an Amazon. In the performance, her first appearance almost ridicules this notion, as she recites Rilke's poem from a makeshift horse onstage (a saddle on top of a wooden structure). Julia is dressed in denim shorts and a feminine blouse, giving the appearance of a young girl, an image that is exaggerated by Pilar Gamboa's naturally child-like voice. There is no force to her presence; it is mostly fragility, which is countered by María Luisa's character. In fact, when Julia narrates her first encounter with Fauna, it is María Luisa who sits atop the "horse," a re-minder of her mother's power. Julia understands this force, which she wishes to emulate, but in the end, as Santos reminds her, she is nothing more than an impostor.

> SANTOS: Listen well, phony Fauna.
> JULIA: I don't understand, why do you speak to me like this?
> SANTOS: I said listen, don't talk. Listen. . . . We already had a Fauna, we don't need any other, there will never be another like her and it is a perverse gesture to try to emulate her for something as frivolous as a film.[119]

There is recognition, at least by Santos, that these "outsiders" are drawn to Fauna as a freak because she will be exhibited as if she was the only one of her kind (which was also what drew crowds to the freak shows). Fauna is the lost (and last) Amazonian, an anachronistic relic of the past. Through her gender and social behavior, as well as her ethnicity (considering that she is not a city dweller but an other from the jungle), she will be trans-formed into a freak on film.

From his first appearance onstage, Santos has questioned the ability of film to tell the truth, at least as it relates to the presence of the natural self (his own savage nature). He denounces Julia as someone who is attempting to appropriate his mother's identity without any understanding of her es-sence. This, in turn, becomes a further insult to Fauna, as the actress and the director are attempting to capture an aspect of Fauna as freak that is inex-pressible, much less through film as fiction. The fictitious nature of any representation of Fauna is prevalent in the performance, where the specta-tor is always outside (the fourth wall is never broken), while the actors themselves act as spectators during the rehearsals of the scenes. There is a continuous observation of the act of representation, which in turn is interrupted by questions about the authenticity of the "Fauna" onstage from the actors themselves. What has modernity done to the freak? The media age attempts to deconstruct the freak persona for mass consumption, and, as we observe in this play, the one who is left without a voice is the freak herself. Mass media, as an integral part of the market economy, become another form of coloniality, which excludes those on the margins from establishing their own identities through their own voices. Through their paternalistic "good intentions," both Julia and José Luis deny the possibility of Fauna's existence on her own terms, an idea that is defied by Santos, who exclaims when José Luis wonders where they came from, "We didn't come from anywhere, we have always been here. You two were the ones who came looking for us."[120] Indeed, the two of them attempt to "discover" their existence through a fictional retelling of their stories that doesn't include their own perceptions of their lives. Their presence in the *litoral* becomes a sort of perverse voyeurism that leads to the horror of identification as the characters project their own fears and fantasies on the freaks before them (present and absent) and are shocked by what answers them back.

ENFREAKMENT AND THE COLONIAL GAZE

This last instance of the freak onscreen allows us to consider the move from monster to the banalization of difference for mass consumption. In all we are left to consider the ambivalent categories of fiction and reality in relation to freak identity, as history has established a clear desire for the creation of a figure that can encompass our social anxieties regarding civilized normalcy. The need to satisfy this desire has clearly led us to the categorization of certain bodies and behaviors as the safe harbors of freakery. In the case of Latin America, it is clear that the colonial gaze continues to exert its power through the process of enfreakment and has determined our identities as the Calibans of modern society. This is further problematized, as is the case in the pieces by Yuyachkani and Romina Paula, by an internal, national "othering" in which Peruvians and Argentines are implicated as the ongoing colonizers of the indigenous, women, nonconformists, and the economically disenfranchised. Through an understanding of the move from monster to freak, it is possible to understand the particular space that Latin America occupies within the global order, which continues to exert the coloniality of power that Quijano so aptly describes.

If the different body has historically fascinated and frightened the western cultural imaginary, the period of colonial imperialism (beginning in the fifteenth century and extending to the present time) easily transferred the stigma of difference to the native bodies of the Americas, an idea that is clearly apparent in *De monstruos y prodigios*. The neoliberal Latin American state and its pursuit of modernity at the cost of those individuals that continue to embody those notions of dangerous difference established by the colonial mind further problematize this. Instead of promoting the economic boom and social equality promised by capitalist administrations, neoliberal policies in Latin America, as we will continue to see throughout the chapters of this book, produced a dirtying of society. The search for order, production, and control, for the semblance of cultural modernity that led to the implementation of a neoliberal system, is a false divider. Zygmunt Bauman asserts that "the world is neither orderly nor chaotic, neither clean nor dirty. It is human design that conjures up disorder *together with* the vision of order, dirt together with the project of purity."[121] The only way to create the idea of order and control is by disposing of those bodies that cannot fit neatly into the social system, by finding and categorizing them as dirt: "It is by being assigned to waste by human designs that material objects, whether human or inhuman, acquire all the mysterious, awe-inspiring, fearsome and repulsive qualities."[122] As these three performances demonstrate, the internalization of the colonial gaze continues to present all forms of otherness as threats to the order and safety of the nation. The continuous fear of difference, in the terms established by US-dominated capitalism, will require a constant revision of what constitutes a freak identity in order to continue staging nonconforming replies to such categories.

TWO | ## Danger Unleashed

The Pathology of Difference as Deviance in the
Latin American Neoliberal State

In her seminal book *Extraordinary Bodies: Figuring Physical Disability in American Culture and Literature*, Rosemarie Garland-Thomson refers to the story of Julia Pastrana, a woman who was exhibited across the United States and several parts of Europe in the nineteenth century under the name "The Ugliest Woman in the World." Pastrana's tragic story is an example of the ways in which freaks have been pathologized by modern science to illustrate what constitutes identities, behaviors, and physicalities outside the norm. Pastrana was a Mexican woman, born near Sinaloa. She suffered from hirsuteness (excessive body hair) and gingival hyperplasia (which thickened her lips and gums), for which she was described as resembling a bear or "the link between mankind and the ourang-outang" by several of the medical pamphlets that accompanied her exhibition. A short woman of four feet, six inches, Pastrana was often exhibited in ornate costumes to perform songs and dances, and when she died during childbirth in 1860 (while on tour in Russia), her body was preserved, along with the body of her child (who inherited her condition), for continued exhibition. Her husband and manager, Theodor Lent (also the father of the child), sold their embalmed bodies to the University of Moscow for its anatomy museum. Very little is known about Pastrana's life, as the pamphlets that accompanied her exhibitions told stereotypical stories of her as a member of an indigenous tribe in Mexico or a missing link. Many doctors examined Pastrana in life and death, including Dr. J. Z. Laurence, who published about her in the well-known British medical journal *Lancet* in 1857. Roger Bartra points out that even Darwin himself was interested in this savage woman (though he never did see her), briefly discussing her in his *Variations of Animals and Plants under Domestication*.[1]

The tragic story of Julia Pastrana provides an interesting point of departure for this chapter, as one can observe the interest in her as a *specimen*, a medical anomaly that illustrates how modern medicine transformed the discourse of monstrosity into the scientific study of freaks through a pathology of difference. In the previous chapter, I discussed the multiple ways in which monstrous bodies had been at the center of myth and religious and philosophical thought, expanding in the early modern period into the study of medicine. Yet in the nineteenth century there is a clear movement from the classification of the divine monsters of the past to the biological explanation of the freak. This also meant, in the case of Pastrana, as well as many other examples, that her body had equal value alive or dead, as it was nothing more than a specimen suited for "medical advancement." Garland-Thomson explains, "[A]s the nineteenth century progressed, the ever-worrisome freak was cast less in the language of the marvelous and explained more and more in the ascending scientific discourse of pathology."[2] What can be observed is a movement toward scientific reasoning with regard to what constitutes normalcy and a growing fear of the unknown that led to the categorizing and containing notions of abnormality as deviance. Society moves to legitimize its own impulses for a "normal" identity, preserving a status quo that will keep a perceived balance of power between "sensible" normalcy and feared abnormality (a category that moves the mythical monster of the past toward notions of mutation and freakery as the century progresses in medical advancements). In order to do so, modern society depends on the "truths" provided by science, law, and medicine—discourses that create a cultural imperative for classification. Thus, that which defies classification can be excluded or regulated through the institutions created to enclose those society considers to be an affront to the privileged category of normalcy.

This chapter deals with the discourses of science and medicine as a hegemonic political gaze that categorizes certain modes of behavior and corporality as dangerous difference. It is through this lens (science and medicine) that I look at three recent plays: *De un suave color blanco* (Of a Soft White Color, Teatro Malayerba, Ecuador), *Vacío* (Emptiness, Teatro Abya Yala, Costa Rica), and *NK 603: Acción para performer & E-Maíz* (NK 603: Action for a Performer & E-Corn, Violeta Luna, Mexico/United States). These performances allow me to trace the way culture-bound categories of difference are constructed as deviant, requiring institutions of power to step in and restrain or contain such individuals, or freaks, in order to maintain order and keep society safe. I trace these ideas through the three performances to establish (1) the formation of a pathologized body through the institutionalization of women in *Vacío* (I focus on womanhood because it is the central theme of the play and because it complicates categories of identity as the freak is placed within a rigid, biological hierarchy of normalcy);

(2) the further deformation of the pathologized body through the reinforcement of scientific discourse in a neoliberal world order that seeks to exploit that which it deems different, as exemplified in *De un suave color blanco*; and (3) how the category of normalcy is further muddled in the modern globalized world of genetic experimentation so that the idea of freakery as an identity category expands and doubles through the mutation of the natural environment, the central critique of *E-Maiz*.

Hence the performances produce a defamiliarization of these identity categories (normal/different) to show how the concepts of abnormality and deviance are produced through legal, medical, political, cultural, and literary narratives that embrace an exclusionary discourse in order to maintain control of the social body. In particular, these three performances illuminate the particularities of Latin America as related to the power struggles concerning discourses of science and medicine. This is in line with Gareth Williams's claim regarding the implementation of strict biopolitics through institutionalized forms of control in a quest for economic and political domination. In other words, a biopolitical ideology leads to a new economy of the modern concept of personhood. In a geographic area that continues to be impacted by issues of machismo, sexism, and homophobia, the Latin American history of violence perpetrated on the different body or behavior is particularly dire, from forced sterilizations of indigenous women to the continued femicides across the nations and the disappearances of student and political activists, all in the name of preserving the status quo. In addition, Latin America has historically been a laboratory in which transnational corporations conduct experiments, as well as exploiting the natural resources of the area, which has often led to violent abuse of the native inhabitants, especially women.[3] The three plays examined in this chapter delve into the violence associated with the exploitation that an unrestrained discourse of science and medicine imposes on the individual who does not fit within the parameters of normalcy established by such powerful agents.

We must first establish what constitutes the category of normal. Traditional scholarship refers back to the importance of Aristotle in establishing a norm with which to measure all other forms of physical variation. He develops a taxonomic system in his *Generation of Animals* for the purpose of discovering the "norm" in biology through a hierarchy of binary opposites. Thus, the normal and abnormal are defined against each other and invested with their own set of desirable and undesirable characteristics. Aristotle establishes the "type" to be able-bodied males, and so the "first beginning of this deviation is when a female is formed instead of a male."[4] This means

that "we should look upon the female state as being as it were a deformity."[5] Besides the relative value he assigns to femaleness by equating it
with aberrations (a point that is taken up in a later chapter), Aristotle establishes (for western thought) a norm by which we will measure all variations. Garland-Thomson notes:

> [B]y defining femaleness as deviant and maleness as essential, Aris-
> totle initiates the discursive practice of marking what is deemed
> aberrant while concealing what is privileged behind an assertion of
> normalcy. This is perhaps the original operation of the logic that
> has become so familiar in discussions of gender, race, or disability:
> male, white, or able-bodied superiority appears natural, undis-
> puted and unremarked, seemingly eclipsed by female, black, or dis-
> abled difference.[6]

The Aristotelian tradition continued and even exploded in the sixteenth
and seventeenth centuries, as scholars studied and collected "monsters" in
the scientific spirit of determining their possible origins, leaving the medieval wonderment and religious connotations behind. The pathology of difference brought forth a desire to collect all sorts of specimens in order to
determine, through various forms of experimentation and dissection, the
causes of difference—an idea that continues to this day as we marvel at the
wonders of genetic mutation and the indecipherable language of genes.[7]

This emergence of deviant subjects from a medical perspective is closely
related to the coining of the word *norm* in its modern sense as "constituting,
conforming to, not deviating or different from, the common type or standard, regular, usual" as the pioneer in disability studies Lennard Davis has
explained.[8] He dates the appearance of the word in the English language to
around 1840. Before this, when the concept of normalcy didn't even exist,
the word *ideal* was used in the seventeeth century to capture the image of
the divine body. But with the emergence of a number of phenomena, such
as industrialization and urbanization, which led to the emergence and consolidation of the middle classes in Europe, there came the concept of "the
average man," understood as "both a physically average and a morally
average construct."[9] Everything outside this norm became abnormal. And,
of course, a society operating with the concept of the norm is crowded with
freaks that resist the "tyranny of the normal" and affirm their deviant subjectivities from the margins of society because there can be no norm without the existence of the abnormal.

If we are to understand the category of "normality," we must first establish that it is a genetic impossibility that depends solely on taste. Biologist Armand Marie Leroi explains that genetics is a highly complex area that we have yet to completely understand and the category of "mutation" is simply an individual distinction, a "deviation from some ideal of perfection," as humans differ from each other in many ways at the genome level and there is not one standard (or perfect) genome by which we shall all be measured.[10] For Leroi, the idea of perfection is a problematic concept dependent on culture and history.

> The only reason to say that one genetic variant is "better" than another is if it confers greater reproductive success on those who bear it; that is, if it has a higher Darwinian fitness than other variants. It is likely that the most common variant is the best under most circumstances, but this cannot be proved, for the frequencies of gene variants are shaped by history, and what was best then need not be best either now or in the future. To prefer one polymorphism over another—or rather to prefer the way it surfaces in our looks—is merely to express a taste.[11]

Each of us carries a great deal of mutation in our genes, but as a society and culture we determine the type of mutation that is deemed acceptable in order to create a type of normalcy that has little to do with scientific truth.

This chapter, as opposed to the previous one, focuses on a theoretical framework from the West, where these restrictions and confines have been established. It is necessary to understand the categories of inquiry from this perspective because it was western thought that created the theories and relations of power in terms of which the different body is often read. At the same time, these discourses of power come from a premise that functions more like a myth—the idea that western thought originated with the classical Greeks. It is necessary to dismantle the notion that western ideas are "pure" forms of classical thought; instead, one must recognize the "unsullied" nature of a discourse that has been intersected by Semitic, African, and Asian identities, as well as a history of colonization. In order to dismantle these ideas, it is from the West that I interrogate the identity politics that are associated with normalcy and abnormalcy. Although I trace this type back to a western paradigm, I acknowledge that in modern Latin American society it is this same assumption of normalcy that contains so much cultural variation in a hierarchy of oppression against indigeneity, womanhood, sexual diversity, and many other forms of difference. As mentioned in the previous chapter, the colonial gaze that continues to persevere across the hemisphere maintains a discourse of power in which the different body (according to gender, race, or physical ability) constitutes a cultural text, which must be inscribed with centuries-old meanings required to assert social relations of power and stigmatize difference.

The same can be said for the concept of the abnormal as deviant, as its terminology and associations are quite porous and have more to do with an individual's expected function in society. Michel Foucault examined this idea in many of his works, but it is especially in *Discipline and Punish: The Birth of the Prison* and *Abnormal: Lectures at the College de France (1974– 1975)* that he delves into the notion of the abnormal as a historical construction formed through "a regular network of power and knowledge."[12] He analyzes the body as deviant in terms of history: "a political history of the body."[13] He traces this history in the first lectures of *Abnormal*, where, through the analysis of specific criminal cases, he considers the ways in which medico-legal practice produces a morality or psychology through a language necessary to produce the idea of a dangerous individual. The purpose of such a practice is to impose the power of normalization. These institutions constitute themselves as the authorities responsible for determining and controlling "dangerous individuals" through techniques of power and knowledge: "[A]long with other processes, expert psychiatric opinion brought about this transformation in which the legally responsible individual is replaced by an element that is the correlate of a technique of normalization."[14] Foucault's notion of power is linked to what he deems to be a model of exclusion that is not necessarily a system of unleashed violence but rather a physical and calculated exercise of power on the body, a notion that he explored in *Discipline and Punish*.[15] The conception of power that concerns Foucault is based on a model of rejection and negative practices.

> I think we still describe the way in which power is exercised over the mad, the ill, criminals, deviants, children, and the poor in these terms. Generally, we describe the effects and mechanisms of the power exercised over these categories as mechanisms and effects of exclusion, disqualification, exile, rejection, deprivation, refusal, and incomprehension; that is to say, an entire arsenal of negative concepts or mechanisms of exclusion.[16]

According to Foucault, exclusion was the prevalent model until the late seventeenth century. He emphasizes how this model evolved into the approach of constant surveillance, which he exemplifies through the treatment of plague victims in the eighteenth century: "I think the replacement of the exclusion of lepers by the inclusion of plague victims as the model of control was a major phenomenon of the eighteenth century."[17] The constant observation and control over those deemed unacceptable has a final goal of "normalization" through constant intervention on the subject. Therefore, this is a model based on "discipline-normalization," unlike the previous models of absolute repression: "Repression is only a lateral and secondary effect of this positive power, a power put into place, in its modern form, by apparatuses of discipline-normalization."[18]

The question remains, How were individuals determined to be "dangerous" enough to fall into these models of control? Here Foucault turns to the field of knowledge, a concept he examined in *Discipline and Punish*, as the issue at hand in the examination of the individual. He relates knowledge to the notion of panopticism as the examination embodied "a mechanism that links a certain type of formation of knowledge to a certain form of exercise of power."[19] As he explains in *Abnormal*, these examinations were meant to determine the capacity of an individual to act dangerously, a determination based on a previously established norm. In other words, what matters is the individual's *potential* for being dangerous and therefore representing a sort of abnormality.

Following Foucault's set of ideas, deviancy is clearly demarcated as a theatrical representation of danger contrasted with institutional conceptions of normalcy. Garland-Thomson points out:

> The meaning attributed to extraordinary bodies resides not in inherent physical flaws, but in social relationships in which one group is legitimated by possessing valued physical characteristics and maintains its ascendancy and its self-identity by systematically imposing the role of cultural or corporeal inferiority on others. *Representation* thus simultaneously buttresses an embodied version of normative identity and shapes a narrative of corporeal difference that excludes those whose bodies or behaviors do not conform.[20]

Within the context of this chapter, these ideas lead to an analysis of performances that aim to consider issues of control and dominance on bodies that are deemed different. This allows me to consider ways in which modern institutions of power (mainly science, medicine, and law) construct our social understanding of the freak through a long-standing tradition of the examination of abnormal qualities that often have little to do with the individual and more to do with his or her ability to conform to the established norms. In other words, the performances provide a lens through which to understand cultural constructions of freakery as they stem from discourses of power that develop from cultural expectations.

A very useful concept for understanding the intersection of the body and culture is that of stigma, which encompasses a multiplicity of social processes through which society marks unpredictable bodies and modes of behavior. The pioneer in the study of stigma theory was the sociologist Erving Goffman, whose methodology allows us to better understand the ways in which stigma is necessary for society's characterization of certain traits as deviant, a form of social behavior that he believes extends across all cultures and histories. Goffman's theories have been crucial to several scholars who study freakery and disability studies, including Robert Bogdan, Rosemarie Garland-Thomson, and Michael Chemers. His work focuses on how characteristics that are stigmatized also determine what constitutes the normal individual and, in addition, how these "deviant" characteristics are determined themselves by dominant social groups in power that seek to legitimate the status quo. Goffman's oft-cited work, *Stigma: Notes on the Management of a Spoiled Identity*, offers a model of human interactions with regard to behavioral and physical characteristics out of which stigma is usually constructed. They include various physical deformities; unpredictable individual behaviors and blemishes of individual character; and race, religion, ethnicity, and gender.[21] Goffman's primary interest revolves around human interactions, in particular the way individuals present themselves to others as actors in different situations, something he found akin to the theatrical stage.

The central idea for Goffman is that people who are stigmatized are expected to continue to perform their inferiority so as not to continue to elicit resentment from "normal" people by performing in ways that do not correspond to their capacities.[22] Nevertheless, he emphasizes that any human trait can be characterized as a stigma, which brings forth his most important idea: stigma is a social process that fully depends on the social context. Similarly, Garland-Thomson explains, "Stigma theory reminds us that the problems we confront are not disability, ethnicity, race, class, homosexuality, or gender; they are instead the inequalities, negative attitudes, misrepresentations and institutional practices that result from the process of stigmatization."[23] Thus, stigma has less to do with the body or behavior itself and is more related to the social framing of such "spoiled identities" within a cultural milieu.

This leads me to this chapter's underlying question: Why can't we perceive difference without assigning a value? A value oftentimes is associated with deviance and requires it to become pathologized and thus contained in some way, as it is deemed out of place and inappropriate for the traditional order of society. I am particularly interested in the way Garland-Thomson deals with this issue, as she turns to the work of Mary Douglas and her concept of dirt, which she relates to Julia Kristeva's notion of abjection. Says Garland-Thomson, "Hygiene and pathogenicity, Douglas points out, are relatively recent legitimations for the concept of dirt as a cultural contaminant. Dirt is an anomaly, a discordant element rejected from the schema that individuals and societies use in order to construct a stable, recognizable, and predictable world."[24] Thus, social stigma becomes social dirt. And in the context of this chapter, performance practices bring to the stage certain instances of social dirt as a form of *contamination* and project them onto certain individuals who have been characterized as different in order to denounce the way the freak has been swept up in a complex matrix of political, historical, and scientific phenomena. In the specific context of Latin American theatrical practices, one must take notice of how these discourses aim to categorize individuals along racial and sexual lines and how the performances I analyze denounce these instances unapologetically through the representation of the freak on the stage in order to disrupt the social acceptance of normalcy as a category of humanness.

In her work, Douglas deals with notions of pollution as taboo, especially as these relate to systematic classifications of human value that present an absolute intolerance for all forms of anomaly. Most societies function through a normative ordering system through which categories outside the ordinary are displaced into classifications such as "aberrant" or "anomalous," which in turn constitute elements of pollution, an affront to order, and are not to be tolerated.[25] In order to deal with elements of difference, society establishes certain strategies through which it frames and responds to the extraordinary. Douglas perceives these strategies in five specific patterns.

The first strategy is reducing the ambiguity of that which we do not understand into one assigned, absolute category, what Douglas terms a "master status." This implies that an individual will be reduced to one totalizing aspect of his or her identity (black, gay, woman, "rape victim, etc.) in relation to which all other traits will disappear.[26] Besides the absolute categorization of individuals, Douglas considers elimination as a second strategy, meaning the complete eradication of "drastic" forms of abnormality (which we find in the eugenics movement and all forms of reproductive control). A third strategy is avoidance, which relates to Foucault's notions of exclusion and regulation. Forms of segregation are established for the control of anomalous individuals in institutions such as asylums and prisons. A fourth strategy labels individuals as dangerous (which also relates to Foucault's premise that individuals are considered abnormal at the level of their potential for dangerous behavior rather than their actions). This action is defended through the institutionalized assumption that one is protecting society from a threat to the social order and is extended to different bodies that are often deemed to be out of control. In addition, the act of labeling individuals allows for a pathologized categorization of difference that relies on relationships of control (often patronizing relationships that establish a division of power between the one who diagnoses the individual and the individual who must be controlled). The fifth strategy (which Douglas finds to be the least common as it is the most positive of the five) is the incorporation of the anomalous individual into ritual in order "to enrich meaning or to call attention to other levels of existence."[27]

Douglas's strategies are very obviously at play in the social criticism that the performances analyzed in this chapter aim to produce. The different characters in these performances have been categorized through a scientific framework that seeks to establish a biological order. Oftentimes, these attempts at categorization focus on physiological and behavioral features that only confuse an understanding of sex and humanness. I chose to read the characters in these plays as freaks and not as simple stand-ins for categories such as "the disabled" or "the other," because their differences exist in a sphere ruled by public exhibition, performance, and consumer culture. Their enfreakment may be physical at times (of course, as a theatrical representation) and at other times behavioral or moral, but either way the characters in these performances embody a pathology of difference that keeps them on the margins of the social order. At the same time, these performances produce a critical distance from any projection of a passive freak. In the plays the freaks that the western imagination creates for its narratives can be monstrous avatars of the other that at any moment may destroy the very society that imagines them.

VISIBILITY IN THE ASYLUM: THE THEATER OF MENTAL ILLNESS AND FEMININITY IN *VACÍO*

Founded in 1991, the theater troupe Abya Yala has created over twenty pieces in which its members explore the political realities of Costa Rica, from the corrupt political system that has landed two past presidents in prison to an ever-increasing level of poverty and the social formation of gender identity.[28] Their transdisciplinary performances are vastly different from one to the next, but what remains clear is their complex relationship with the spectator, who must be maintained on the edge of discomfort. In addition, music is an important element in their performances, and *Vacío* (Emptiness, 2010) is no exception.[29] It remains one of their most successful productions and continues to this day as part of their repertoire. Inspired by Mercedes Flores Gonzalez's 2013 book *Locura y género en Costa Rica (1910–1950)* [Insanity and Gender in Costa Rica (1910–1950)], *Vacío* seeks to explore the relationship between maternity and mental illness. Director Roxana Ávila and dramaturg Anabelle Contreras continued their research by exploring the archives of the San José Asylum (which included letters from the female patients that were later incorporated into the performance).

Twelve women are onstage; some are musicians, others dancers and singers. The spectators are seated at small tables distributed throughout the theatrical space, with no central stage except for scattered platforms where the musicians sit and the singers sometimes perform. The tables rock back and forth like cradles and have five holes in which to place the glasses that will eventually be passed out to each audience member. As the public enters, ten women walk around the space and continue to rock the tables, making sure they are never still. These women wear high heels, which amplify the sound of their feet obsessively moving as they rock the tables. As Ávila explains, "This already suggests, to the audience, something outside of reality, establishing an obsessive action, even as it is logical, functional, and necessary (one must not let children cry, even when there are no children)."[30] Hanging from the middle of the space is a contraption that holds an aerial dancer and a hanging microphone next to her, the end of which the actresses can reach.

The performance is composed primarily of songs interrupted at times by one androgynously dressed actress, Andrea, who is costumed in a breastplate made of resin, with long pants and short hair. She does not do what the rest do, nor does she interact with the public. She circles the stage, solemnly stating the clinical cases (directly taken from the archives of the asylum). In addition, there are intimate, short monologues whispered into the hanging microphone by some of the actresses, as well as into the ears of some of the spectators. There are also moments when the actresses pass letters to some of the audience members; they are fragments of actual letters written by the women in the asylum.

As previously discussed, within the realm of the normal and abnormal, womanhood has often been portrayed as that which marks a different body—Aristotle's first instance of a "deformed" body. *Vacío* allows for an

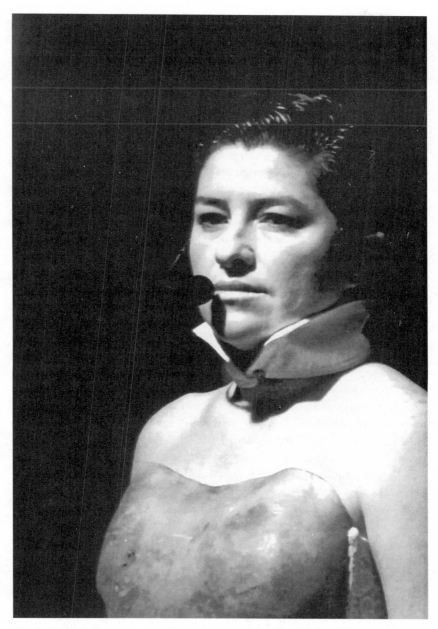

Fig. 8. *Vacío*. Actress Andrea Gómez as the voice of medicine. Photo provided by Roxana Ávila.

interesting case study of a (re)reading of this inherited history, as it builds on the complex characterization of femininity as a contradictory symbol of life (motherhood) and nation (*madre patria*, literally "mother/fatherland," the "homeland" in Spanish) and also abnormal behavior or an unstable mind (the "feeble" mind of the woman), consequently challenging the definitions of motherhood and maternal frustration. Even though the focus of my analysis, then, is based on feminine characters, I want to link the female category to a pathologized body through the assertion that throughout history womanhood has been a stand-in for the universal and eternal other: the freak of nature. Thus, through the unique case of women in an asylum I also form a general case for the unique body under clinical surveillance and the ways in which this performance undermines and critiques this condemnation of the female body.

Womanhood has a tendency to be equated (predominantly in western history) with instances of contamination and otherness. Femininity is closely related to notions of illness and contagion, starting with the coming of menstruation, which not only signaled a woman's fertility but also her condition as easily prey to passion and other contaminants that can pollute a rational mind. Often a woman's capacity for violating the laws of nature (and man) was associated with her womb. As Barbara Creed explains, "[W]hen woman is represented as monstrous it is almost always in relation to her mothering and reproductive functions."[31] As a matter of fact, "from classical to Renaissance times, the uterus was frequently drawn with horns to demonstrate its supposed association with the devil."[32] This association between the feminine reproductive organs and evil points to a historical perception of the capacity for unnatural behavior and abnormality that is housed within the female body itself. From the beginning of *Vacío* menstruation appears as an unstable moment for womanhood: "With the first appearance of their menses, organic intellectual disorders can be noticed." This statement, which is one of the performance's first lines, suggests the perceived inability of women to behave or even think rationally, as their bodies have betrayed them. The intention is to reveal a historical demonization of femininity that encompasses the body itself as the site for abnormality.

As Carlos Jáuregui and Paola Uparela Reyes explain in their study of feminine sexual organs, until the eighteenth century the vagina was not to be seen or studied, even in medical treatises, as it was deemed a humiliation for the medic (thus births were left to be dealt with by midwives).[33] Gynecology and obstetrics were among the last medical practices to be recognized and appropriated by the scientific establishment since it was not until the eighteenth century that studies on anatomy "looked down" on the female sexual organs. And even then, gynecology was not concerned with the female body but rather a specific fragment of it: the reproductive organs. Jáuregui and Uparela compare this fetishized gaze to the freak body: "[W]e are before a knowledge that is properly a fetishist, founded upon a tropological arrangement through which the genitals, specifically the vagina, become a synecdoche."[34] Thus, there is no female subjectivity in the sciences; instead there is a fragment of the body that becomes a visible icon, which stands in for, in this case, all female conditions within a sociopolitical context.

This problematic medical gaze is at the center of the performance of *Vacío*. The medical representation of the female sexual organs as an abject monstrosity that must conform to the aesthetic parameters of the masculine gaze is conducive, in the play, to the freak subjectivity through which the female body is constantly exhibited. This gaze is problematized in the play as the audience is invited to read against it. For example, one of the actresses sings the bolero "Como fue" (As It Was), a very romantic song about the particular aspects of a woman that made a man fall madly in love with her.[35] With a deep, sensual voice the singer moves seductively on a small platform where she performs, her silky green dress clinging to her body. Very light percussion accompanies the song, so it is almost an a cappella version of the original. This emphasis on the singing allows the audience to focus on the words, as the singer stands alone on her small stage. At the same time, some of the other actresses lie on the floor, while others mimic the performance of everyday "female" housework (cleaning floors, sewing, sweeping). Andrea speaks over the song with a detailed description of a clitoris by a medical doctor: "After separating the large labia one can see on the top of the vulva two fleshy excrescences. In some women they extend so monstrously that it is necessary to mutilate them . . . in order to prevent a repugnant imperfection not conducive to the caresses of the other gender." At this time, the women lying on the floor make disjointed movements with their arms and legs, extending and contracting their bodies as if they were in the midst of a convulsion.

The clear relation between feminine beauty and masculine desire that the song states, along with the acceptable roles for women mimed by the actresses, exemplify a characterization of "normal" femininity according to social standards: the classic housewife and mother. However, this mold of perfect beauty in the play is only so in the eyes of a masculine aesthetics that will go so far as to "mutilate" the body of a woman for the pleasure of the man. Hence a patriarchal system of medical knowledge does not offer shelter to women placed on the margins of their classification structure, starting with the "imperfections" of their vulvas. On the contrary, a traditionally masculine scientific discourse has relegated women to the private sphere of the household where their primary purpose is to take care of others. This notion of normalcy extends to the stigmatization of women who do not "perform" womanhood as expected by the institutions of control and will label her "mad" in an effort to control her behavior (as presented in the play). And even though, as director Ávila explains, Vacío is a play that narrates the cruelty encountered "by our grandmothers and their mothers," it is an inherited history for Latin American women who continue to contest traditional notions of femininity in a historically patriarchal society. [36] In this way, the performance deconstructs romanticized and idealized notions of motherhood.

This model of maternity was the pillar on which the division between public and private was sustained in the first half of the twentieth century in Latin America. The importance of maternity for the construction of the gender/sexual system (as developed by Gayle Rubin) required the joining of a multiplicity of discourses and praxis from several apparatuses of knowledge: medical, legal, political, educational, philosophical, and religious, and adding even the emerging technologies of mass culture.[37] Vacío calls attention to this rigorous model of classification, which has mapped the social attitudes toward womanhood and places special emphasis on the confluence of these various discourses within mass culture. At two moments in the performance, some of the actresses stand on an elevated stage and present versions of commercials and public service announcements created for the purpose of "helping" women to better play their assigned roles. These range from commercials for medical syrups that will "put an end to the turmoil and agitation your wife suffers" to radio programs geared toward women that tell them "you are ignorant. The doctor is going to recommend. Do not invent anything for yourself, only the doctor knows" and newsreels about the beauty of Marilyn Monroe (who, interestingly, is played by the darker skinned of the actresses, which I find to be a clear commentary on standards of beauty). These momentary interruptions effectively demonstrate the impact of the medical discourse on societal perceptions about behavior as it seeps through the realm of mass culture.

Through these standards, individuals (in this case, women) who did not conform to the medicalized hierarchy of normalcy were deemed imperfect and thus became pathologized individuals that had to be contained (at the very least until "cured"). At the same time, body and mind remained intertwined as the so-called violent behaviors of the body (in the case of Vacío,

overt sexuality, the refusal to take care of the household, the general unhappiness with the role of motherhood, etc.) revealed a disabled mind. The
freak constructed through medical discourses was made popular because
of a public fascination with the unstable body and mind, as disability
scholar and artist Petra Kuppers asserts: "[D]isabled people are often asked
to describe their experiences, and to open up their personal histories to
both the medical gaze and public curiosity."[38] The display of mental illness
was astonishingly obvious with the medical theaters of the past and our
continued fascination with it can be appreciated through the success of
contemporary talk shows in the current age.[39]

Foucault's mapping of social attitudes toward madness in western culture centralized the function of "reason," language, and institutions to
regulate and control medically defined mental illness. For this reason, one
must track the powerful institutions, principally the media, schools, and
hospitals, that act as markers of social stability against the instability of, for
example, the symbolic power of mothers, which is reconfigured in service
to patriarchy (i.e., the nation). My particular interest in *Vacío* is not only
because it produces an analysis of woman as freak in terms of a pathologized mode of behavior, but in addition because it expands and emphasizes female sexuality and maternity as markers of feminine abnormality
through the lens of scientific discourse. This performance seeks to connect
mental illness to the repression of women and their sexual freedom. In
other words, following the historical framework of medical discourse, the
female body carries with it a series of markers that construct it as
"different"—a stigmatized body. In addition, feminine behavior must be
conducive to placating the abnormalities to which it is predisposed (passion, immorality, evil). Thus, woman is confined to prescriptive models of
behavior (mother, caretaker, wife, daughter) that if not followed will only
lead to her isolation and containment under the watchful eye of the medical institution, which will make her comply or remain isolated in the space
of the asylum.

As the director of the play explains, the women that inspired this performance were often placed in insane asylums and "locked in by another's
voice, not their own. They were there because their husbands, fathers, etc.
decided that they should be there, without any sort of confirmation or acceptance. They were doubly silenced: by a voice of powers that placed
them in the asylum and once they were there, the letters that they wrote to
their families were never sent."That is why in *Vacío* there is a special interest in presenting the silenced words and thoughts of those interned in the
controlled space of the asylum. The letters that the actresses pass to certain

members of the audience have inside them the secret thoughts of those women (they contain actual transcripts of letters found in the asylum in Costa Rica) that were never able to reach their addressees. The audience, then, becomes the intermediary through which their voices are finally heard. Even if only some of the audience members are privy to the letters, it is, as Ávila states, a sacred moment in which the women in the asylum are finally able to have their voices heard. The same can be said for the microphone that hangs on one side of the space. Whenever an actress stands below it to speak, a soft red light illuminates the area. This is an intimate space, the one moment in silence where all the attention is focused on the woman that speaks and tells her secrets, such as "In what corner of life will happiness await me?" or "I hope the baby falls to sleep and my husband does not return for dinner," all the intimate thoughts that, if said aloud, would categorize a woman at the time as insane.

The "fairer sex," then, has often been portrayed as a body in need of care, as it is prone to diseases of body and mind that can render it unstable. In the nineteenth century, advances in psychiatry attempted to delve into what were considered the mysteries of womanhood. This only led to the notion of woman as having a "feeble" mind prone to passions and a lack of control. Argentine playwright and theater scholar Marcos Rosenzvaig asserts that "insanity is the result of a 'moral weakness' for the field of nineteenth-century psychiatry," which meant that "such a misrule of the senses needs an order, and nothing works better to reestablish order than repression. Repression led to 'reflection,' and this was considered fundamental to keeping away from contamination and sin."[40] It should not be surprising, then, that women who did not behave according to the established notions of femininity should be categorized as hysterical and relegated to the controlled spaces of the asylum.

Often the ruling category for "normal" female behavior is related to a woman's ability to meet the demands of motherhood. Women are expected to aspire to norms of femininity that include ideal motherhood, where mothers are positioned as ever-available, ever-nurturing providers of involved and expert mothering. In the case of Latin America, this is a crippling performance of womanhood that has often led to problematic binary definitions of normalcy (the classic mother/whore division) founded on a patriarchal system that seeks to infantilize and control feminine behavior.[41] Building on this history, and seeking to dismantle the categories themselves, Abya Yala created *Vacío*. It is an instance of what Kuppers reflects on: "By structuring the visibility machine of performance, we intervene in the violations of the 'medical stare' at different bodies."[42]

Fig. 9. *Vacío*. Aereal dancer Liubov Otto with several of the actresses and dancers. Photo provided by Roxana Ávila.

In the play, maternity becomes a pathologized condition, for which the
women onstage must be removed from society. As the audience, we inhabit a space that does not belong to any notion of reality. It is as if we are
inside the minds of the women who are now able to have some sort of
agency outside the real world, although, at the same time, this private
space of the mind continues to be observed and controlled by a discourse
of power that circles around them (as Andrea moves around the stage in a
clockwise circle reciting the medical records in a monotonous voice). Because of this, even within the private enclosure of the female mind there is
a disparate ambiguity regarding the space the woman inhabits—from the
private confines of the home to the public exclusions in society and finally
the isolation of the asylum for constant observation. The crossing between
maternity and the binary public/private was of great relevance, especially
at the beginning of the twentieth century. The social discourses of the beginning of the century condensed and established the ethical value that
determined the space of maternity as destined for womanhood in Latin
American culture. One could say that it was during this time period that
the sexual/gender feminine identity was crystalized through the construction of maternity.[43]

The image of the benevolent mother, then, becomes a constraint on the female identity, and in the play this is dealt with in a particular manner. During the song "Versos a mi madre" (Verses for My Mother), a very nostalgic homage to the compassionate and generous mother, the notion of an ideal motherhood is dismantled through the physical performance of the actresses. While one of them sings the verses "My mother is a poem of white hair, who always has on her lips a gesture of forgiveness," another stands on a corner and takes off the top of her dress (the only instance of nudity in the play). She proceeds to use the ribbons of her dress to bind her breasts in a mechanical manner. Through her actions, motherhood becomes a source of pain and confinement, a predicament that was imposed on the women in this space, isolating them from society when they were unable to fulfill their duties. This symbolic space of maternity was well formed through the discourses of medicine, religion, law, politics, and education. Medical discourses, in particular, were foundational in their consecration of the maternal function of women. From the symbolic discourse of medicine, produced primarily by males, a series of public policies were designed that situated women in a specific and unique function: the sacred mission of an educated and pure maternity. To access this space and adequately fulfill their preassigned social function, women should become that which can be equated with the progress of the nation: they should be the caregiver who is always protected.[44]

The challenge of undoing the discursive and hegemonic practices that license men as truth-bearing bringers of rational solutions to the "unbound" behavior of women must be addressed, in the play, through a questioning of language itself. This is in line with what Luce Irigaray has already said regarding the instabilities of language and the efficacy of scientific discourse.[45] The lack of subjectivity in scientific writing (as the basis of western medicine), its rejection of the "I" of the speaker in favor of an apparently objective "one," is nothing more than a disguise for a manipulative order that harms the individual. In the play there is a pursuit of a more truthful discursive space in which the "I" of identity is known, exposed, and shared. For starters, there is no continuity or formal narrative of any sort in the performance. The same can be said for the use of formal language, as ideas are expressed through incomplete sentences interrupted by medical language and songs. For example, the use of popular songs is often contradicted by the performer's movements, as can be appreciated in one particular moment of the performance. Andrea (the voice of medical discourse) explains in a monotone, "When the husbands slap the wives, or hit them with sticks or threaten them to kill them with knives, or stones, or

machetes, or guns, according to the Penal Code, the penalty will be delin-
eated according to whether the wounds or blows prevent her from working temporarily or for life. San José, 1841." The rest of the actresses have
stopped moving and stand in place while stomping their feet in unison on
the floor. This moment is interrupted by another performer whispering
into the microphone, "This body hurts so much . . . it must be this bed
squeezing me from underneath," and she is immediately interrupted by
another medical statement discussing the rape of a woman by her father
and uncles. In the midst of the story, the singers begin to sing "Mama Said"
by the Shirelles.[46] At that moment, the other performers thrash about on the
floor, requiring the attention of the audience to be focused on their bodies
as they recoil and contract on the floor.

The movements of the actresses on the floor remind us, of course, of
hysterical seizures as described in the nineteenth century, especially
through Jean Charcot's photographs of asylum inmates. This idea is reinforced in the next scene, when Andrea narrates the symptoms of a hysterical woman. The aesthetics of hysteria that Charcot created through his
medical research and visual testimonies greatly contributed to the struggle and stigma of those diagnosed with the condition, as they became the
stages for the visible evidence of difference. As Kuppers explains, if one
studies the performative aspects of Charcot's photographs, it is possible
to discern the issues of power and gender that are at play in the staging of
the pictures.

> The supposedly "neutral" medical gaze onto the patient is refig-
> ured, shows its own technology of knowledge, when performance
> enters the field. The medical stare with its attendant effects on
> power relations becomes visible in our historical reading of Char-
> cot's work, and attunes us to the performative and rhetorical func-
> tion of contemporary representations of "madness," or other invis-
> ible impairments.[47]

Vacío aims to raise suspicion about these technologies of knowledge that
claim to make visible that which is not clear to the rest of society by exploiting our fears of the unknown and manipulating our limited popular knowledge about mental illness. The performance "widen[s] the gap between
seeing and knowing" as it attempts "to make visible the technologies of
meaning that impart authority on medical knowledge."[48] In order to do so,
the performance relies on scenes like the one described above. The obvious
implication there is that womanhood often falls prey to the violence exe-

cuted by masculine power, leaving her helpless in a society that emphasizes the need to "put up" with such trauma as this is just part of being a
woman. What the audience sees onstage are women resisting trauma, expressing a violent force against a system that refuses to let them exist as
they are. The message, though, is not explicitly stated; instead, bodily
movements and the performers' active inhabiting of the space replace language. The play shows a discontinuity of language within the space of the
performance itself in a manner similar to what Hélène Cixous explains: "[S]
o few women have as yet won back their body. Women must write through
their bodies, they must invent the impregnable language that will wreck
partitions, classes and rhetorics."[49] This is crucial for the purposes of dismantling the categories of femininity that are at play. Cixous's call to
arms—"write yourself. Your body must be heard"—becomes a mode of
communication that departs from our usual understanding of language.[50]
Instead, the play depends on a form of bodily communication intercalated
with text and music to produce an affective message that can only be perceived through the emotions provoked through all these signs.

It is useful to turn to Homi K. Bhabha to further understand the effect of
this structure in the play. Borrowing from Roland Barthes, who narrates an
episode in Tangiers that he describes as a "stereophony of language" that
became an instance of a "non-sentence" or existence "outside the sentence,"
Bhabha considers the possibility of exalting affect over the authority of language in order to understand the multiple possibilities offered by cultural
difference.

> At the point at which the hierarchy and the subordination of the
> sentence are replaced by the definitive discontinuity of the text, at
> that point, the subject of discourse spatializes and moves beyond the
> sententious. It turns "outside" the sentence to inscribe the boundar-
> ies of meaning (not its depths) but in the affective language of cul-
> tural difference.[51]

It is possible to enact a sort of affective understanding that speaks to the
unconscious of cultural difference ("social and sentient," as Bhabha explains) if one operates outside the sentence. In this sense, affect becomes
the universal that binds us all together regardless of language. This can
mean "writing aloud" (as Barthes proposes) a sort of hybrid language
"lined with flesh, the metonymic art of the articulation of the body not as
pure presence of Voice, but as a kind of affective writing, after the sumptu-
ousness or suffering of the signifier."[52] This is an important notion, as it

breaks with the hierarchy of language through an affective relationship with space. For the purposes of *Vacío* it is a vital element for the understanding of the piece, as the meaning is found in a sort of in-between space that is experienced in the midst of the dissonance (to the senses) produced by the music, language, and movement that occurs throughout the piece. The multiple personal encounters that occur between the actresses and the spectators (the whispers, the letters, the short monologues) rely on an affective understanding that moves beyond the formality of language toward "the affects of life," as Barthes explains.

The questioning of the formal hierarchy of language is best exemplified in the performance through the clinical language of medical cases, which constitutes a predictable language of subjection and control from an institution created for the control of those deemed abnormal. Foucault's well-known warnings about institutional politics of cultural control in the areas of both "madness" and institutional incarceration are embodied in the way this play enacts the power of normative discourses around knowledge, history, genealogy, and medical science to shape experience and understanding. The first words of the play, stated by Andrea, the androgynous figure of the law, claim, "Today, the fourth of May, in the center of the capital an expensive building shall be inaugurated with the assigned mission of restoring the health of those most wretched in society: the mentally ill. This building, which could be called a TEMPLE, will be devoted to the worship of the most sublime virtue: charity. San José 1890." The space of order and control is challenged by the performance space, one of absolute disorder that is ruled by passions. If, as I have previously asserted, the language of institutions determines what constitutes normalcy, the space inhabited in this performance allows for the complete disarray of such a construction by removing the formal elements of language in favor of a communication focused on the senses (music, touch, movement).

Vacío's ending reinforces the affective communication displayed onstage as a way of dismantling and questioning the dominance of a patriarchal scientific discourse. The last "confession" on the microphone tells the story of a woman who lived in a small town with twelve other women. No one took any notice of her existence, yet "she continued living in this town without any resentment of what they did to her." The music has stopped and the women's voices explode in a cacophony of overlapping texts: "My mother lied to me and her mother lied to her," "insolent mother, admirable mother," "Where were you, mother, when the fathers signed the masculine contract behind your back and the back of all of your descendants?" And of particular importance is one statement that stands out amid the other voices: "You have been reduced to silence. They shut your mouth with a penis or a child. Then they made you speak a language that is not your own to convince you to send your children to school, church, the military, the asylum, jail, to their death." The voices in discordance go on and on until the final statement: "The emptiness . . . woman does not exist. This is the lack that we carry with us." The damage that is produced by the false idol of motherhood has been passed on for generations, from mother to daughter. This specter has been sustained by the medicalization of nonnormative behaviors that aim to liberate women from such constraints, and even as it extends to all individuals who do not conform to the parameters of normativity, women have been, historically, the primary sufferers of the stigma of mental illness. Deviant behavior is a category of inquiry as it is applied to those who defy established categories of identity and, in the case of *Vacío*, women who do not follow in the footsteps established for them by a patriarchal society.

With the last words from the chorus of voices, the aerial dancer (who has remained on the metal structure throughout the play, performing movements and at times dancing to the music) falls to the floor and the lights abruptly go down. This is not the end, though. After a few moments, a voice begins to sing "El silencio es sexy" (Silence Is Sexy), the song by Blixa Bargeld. This phrase parallels the well-known saying in many Latin American countries aimed mostly at women: "Calladita te ves más bonita" (You look prettier when silent).[53] When the lights finally come back on, it is Andrea who stands at the hanging microphone repeating the phrase while the rest of the actresses move from side to side or convulse on the floor. What becomes clear throughout this play is that silence is not sexy; it is death. Women have been condemned to silence, and when they dared to speak against those norms that marginalized them they were condemned as freaks—hysterical women that were exhibited in medical theaters or photographed to be studied and contained until they learned to behave. Garland-Thomson explains that "women with disabilities, even more intensely than women in general, have been cast in the collective cultural imagination as inferior, lacking, excessive, incapable, unfit, and useless."[54]

The larger political dimension of the issue involves challenging prejudice such that mental disability can be understood as "human variation, rather than essential inferiority."[55] *Vacío* undermines the visible discourses of mental difference by undoing those fixities and categorical differences through an affective discourse that transforms the medical freak into an individual with a clear voice. From the removed space of the asylum, the "crazy" women offer a criticism of what has been considered legitimate order, progress, and rationality in a capitalist system for its lack of morality. The women in the asylum provide a clear humanist rationale in contrast to the inhumanity of a political doctrine that has no ethical consideration for life. Locked in a separate space from society, the women in this play are the other—the freaks whose existence is not recognized by a capitalist logic that is intolerant of difference. Yet it is only in this removed space (separate from the ontology of capitalist reason) that the "insane" can exist as a form of resistance and denounce the insanity of this system, which categorizes difference as deviance and provides an empty appearance of what constitutes reason and normalcy. The female body in *Vacío*, through which modern political discourses have enacted great restrictions in the name of social order and control, becomes the space through which subversive ideals are performed to disband discourses of power.

MEDICINE AND LAW: FRAGMENTED IDENTITY IN A NEOLIBERAL WORLD ORDER, THE FREAK IN THE THEATER OF MALAYERBA

The categorization of human difference in terms of abnormal/normal has had a continued impact on the globalized discourses that have brought along the establishment of a neoliberal order in a vast part of Latin America. Neoliberalism, as an economic discourse, is related to market fundamentalism, which proclaims that when the market is left alone to do its functioning without state interference it will be sufficient to generate wealth and distribute it evenly in any given society. The expectation is that long-term economic dynamics generate the necessary measures to overcome any conditions of poverty. As discussed in the introduction to this book, in Latin America neoliberal economic policies were imposed through the "Washington Consensus," a term derived from the conference that the Institute for International Economics convened in 1989. This meeting was called to consider the various aspects that should be taken into account for the structural reforms that Latin American countries should implement in order to overcome the chronic "underdevelopment" and indebtedness of their current conditions.[56]

Nevertheless, neoliberal policies have promoted major social changes that contribute to ever-increasing poverty and unemployment across the continent, the growth of a precarious life in an unsafe environment, and the consequent militarization of many countries. As theater scholar Beatriz Rizk explains, "[T]he neoliberal model, which was supposed to finally push Latin America into 'modernization' . . . has failed to settle the, everyday more profound, gaps between the ruling classes and the rest of the population. It has characterized itself by a high level of corruption that has reached, in many countries, the most visible spheres of power."[57] There are various ways to discuss and approach the term *globalization*.[58] In the analysis proposed here, we should understand it as the multinational integration and extension of markets. For many this phenomenon is the epitome of capitalism. Its defining characteristics include an increase in both physical and virtual communication (transportation and technology), an easing of state control, and a growing porousness of the borders of nation-states. Much of Latin America took this "neoliberal" turn in the 1990s. Neoliberal policy changes included the opening of markets for goods and capital, the privatization of state enterprises, and the removal of tariffs. Above all, the role of the individual in society has continued to be affected as we function through the lens of interchangeability: in the global market, what is valued is the constant production of goods and commodities for the well-being of those who have the means of acquisition. Thus, the rest of those individuals become nothing more than components in the machinery of productivity as interchangeable laborers.

In terms of normality/abnormality, the individual as commodity faces an even greater pressure to fit into the approved category for belonging in the modern nation, as those who do not fit will not be able to enjoy the riches of the nation and are deemed noncitizens of the state and thus erased. The neoliberal order has brought on contributing factors that establish a particular understanding of the role of the body in the national discourse as part of a political economy: what matters is the utility and docility of the individual, and this, in turn, allows for the erosion of the notion of citizenship through the expulsion of the body from the system. The notion of the freak, then, acquires a larger dimension in a globalized community that exhibits a mounting neurosis regarding the case of being a "normal" and useful person, as the "abnormal" is not part of the system. In the twenty-first century we all struggle with the notion of what it means to be a human being within the chaos of a globalized world order. As we saw in the previous chapter, what made one a monster by past standards was linked to religious beliefs that found in the different body a lack of soul. In today's neoliberal world order the freak is the one who is unable or unwilling to follow the economic and cultural norms of the institutions in power.

In the play *De un suave color blanco* (Of a Soft, White Color, 2009), by the Ecuadorian group Malayerba, the aesthetic exercise onstage aims to rethink the experience of violence brought on by an unfettered capitalist imaginary that privileges some individuals over others and has made us question our own humanity as we fail to fit into the mold of normalcy (i.e., economic success) expected in this neoliberal world order.[59] Within a neoliberal economy, this translates into a politics of prevention (which impels individuals, taken over by fear, to isolate themselves in the private sphere of their homes) founded on discourses of fear and insecurity toward that which is not part of the normative standard. In other words, one must fear anything that does not form a part of the known (and safe) worldview. From this stems a generalized distrust of anything on the margins of society, bringing to the forefront issues of generalized insecurity as the primary concern for the "citizen" (and by this I mean those deemed to be so by the social and political order) instead of a global concern with specific issues such as poverty, health, and education. One must question the discourses that emphasize the insecurity of the few over the exclusion and pain of others. As theater critic Beatriz Marcos asserts, maybe it is possible to exorcise the historical experience of collective pain and violence if we are able to create an exercise in critical and narrative distancing in order to reactivate the ethical and political dimension of citizenship.[60] Through theater, Malayerba focuses on the emotional repercussions of violence in a society of fear (fear of difference, the self, those in power, etc.) and reclaims the pain of others from a place of tremendous respect—a moment of "denuncia" (denunciation) against impunity. Thus, the play breaks with the dynamic of fear (of those confined by it) and pleasure (of those in power) present in today's neoliberal system of oppression.

Malayerba was founded in 1979 in Quito, Ecuador, by María del Rosario "Charo" Francés, Susana Pautasso, and Arístides Vargas. The three actors had come to Ecuador exiled from their countries, as Arístides and Susana fled the Argentinian dictatorship and Charo left a post-Francoist Spain. From the start, the company included actors with various backgrounds and nationalities who approached theater making as an artistic, ethical, and technical realm where they could engage in meaningful, creative experiences through which to understand, assume, and confront current sociopolitical processes. The company came into being when Ecuador was in the midst of a redemocratization process after a second military dictatorship (1972–79). The work of Arístides Vargas, one of the most admired playwrights in Latin America, deals primarily with notions of memory, displacement, and marginalization. In the theater of Vargas, as critic Lola Proaño-Gómez explains, "The spectator lives the mystery and experiences the inexplicable of our futile attempt to find answers to the eternal questions, questions about the ultimate meaning of existence in a world where injustice and death reign. In this sense, his productions correspond to the end-of-century climate in the world, and especially in Latin America, regarding the impossibility of seeing a clear future once the great utopias have become impossible to fulfill in the short term."[61] Vargas's artistic oeuvre, then, constitutes a poetics that is not devoid of humor but is also grounded in bitterness and a sense of poetry, which allows for the belief in a world that can be changed.

Here I focus on how *De un suave color blanco* presents the impossibility of forming a coherent reality due to the fragmented identity that is a product of a globalized Latin American culture. Identity today is, according to anthropologist Néstor García Canclini, "ever less shaped by local and national loyalties and more and more by participation in transnational or deterritorialized communities of consumers" created by mass culture.[62] In the case of Ecuador, this is further problematized by a lack of a "national identity" based on something other than the symbols imposed by a hegemonic class at a specific moment.

> The Ecuadorian was laboriously defined throughout the nineteenth century with certain referents to a patriotic history in construction with its heroes and symbols, the national hymn, the progressive institutionalization of Spanish (keeping in mind that it is one among at least, thirty languages spoken in the country) and the creation of imaginary territorial borders.[63]

The lack of a defined national identity that encompasses those outside the spheres of power allows for a continued search that becomes evident in the performance. This search is particularly problematic when referenced through the crossing of law and science in a neoliberal economy that produces an unequivocal category of self in terms of a productive environment. The fundamental questions in *De un suave color blanco* deal with how to differentiate among the multiple and simultaneous realities that are imposed by a world order that varies in perspectives according to the lens through which it is focused. The characters that appear in this play find themselves isolated, doubled, fragmented, or removed completely from a social order that does not privilege the individual but the free market.

The play makes visibility a central issue by leading the audience to question what one is allowed to see given the power of institutions and the need to understand visibility as socially constructed (as opposed to what we can see biologically). In addition, the ability to see is at the crux of social violence on the body since individuals that are deemed to be outside the norm can be easily erased through the discourse of the law (placed in prisons or asylums or even disappeared). Ultimately, those on the marginas are not allowed to predominate in the social order. Rather it is those equipped to perform most forcefully inside the dialectic of law and disorder. This returns us to Derrida, Agamben, and Benjamin, to the notion that the law originates in violence and lives by violent means, the notion, in other words, that the legal and the lethal animate and inhabit one another. This means that certain bodies will be exhibited as infractions on the social order, and society will often turn away as those outside the norm are looked on in order to be punished for their "violations." This form of visibility is the opposite of witnessing: it is an active *refusal* (out of apathy or fear) to bear witness. It is what Diana Taylor terms "percepticide," a form of willful blindness that promotes power for those who control the means of violence: "People had to deny what they saw . . . seeing without the possibility of admitting that one is seeing further turns the violence on oneself. Percepticide blinds, maims, kills through the senses."[64] In this way, "The triumph of the atrocity was that it forced people to look away."[65] Within a region with a history of profound social inequality, the discourses of science and law have depended on visuality to control individuals on the margins (this includes the indigenous, the mentally ill, queer bodies, and the poor) by denying their basic human right to existence. They have become nothing more than entities to be exploited because they, within the visual order of this history, are deemed "less than": the freaks of culture.

In *De un suave color blanco* there is an intrinsic reflection on our own perception of what constitutes humanity in a state of fear. Even those who exist on the margins of the neoliberal order can experience visuality on their own terms. After all, as Jürgen Habermas reminds us, the inclusion of the other implies expanding the limits of community even for those who want to continue to be outside it. The characters in this play inhabit spaces of repression and try to find a means of controlling their realities, and this only becomes possible through the transformation of their physical bodies or bodily functions. The intention of my analysis, then, is to examine how the practices and cultural logic of a neoliberal system that is dependent on the values of modern science for economic gain are able to construct certain corporeal and behavioral variations as deviant and thus are able to maintain the generally assumed opposition between the normal and abnormal body as a matter of moral values that persist because of the fear of a violent system of repression.

De un suave color blanco appeared thirty years after the theater company's founding in 1979. The play is a collective creation that responds to the work of Pablo Palacio (1906–47), the controversial Ecuadorian writer of the early twentieth century and precursor of Latin American surrealism. Palacio was considered a subversive author during his time; the literary world found his work transgressive and accordingly shunned him. His novels and short stories explored the notions of simulacrum and doubling— Palacio found that doubling (in its simulation, disguise, false appearance, or imitation) generated the simulacrum. This is the quality that the author traced through his characters as he displayed an image that responded to the deformed reality that he perceived around him. Inspired by Palacio, Malayerba chose to work with seven specific texts by the author: the short novel *Débora* (1927) and the short stories "Vida del ahorcado" (Life of the Hanged Man) (1932), "La doble y única mujer" (The Double and Only Woman) (1927), "El huerfanito" (The Little Orphan) (1921), "El antropófago" (The Cannibal) (1926), "Un hombre muerto a puntapiés" (A Man Kicked to Death) (1927), and "Luz Lateral" (Lateral Light) (1926). Through an improvisatory process of laboratory exploration of the stories and the issues raised within them, the actors delved into the obsessive universes of the author and presented marginal characters (such as the cannibal, the child abuser, the insane, and the deformed) that exposed the fragility of human behavior and re-created the emotions found in the work of Palacio. Arístides Vargas completed the dramaturgy and took as a thematic unity the universe of doubles so often explored by this Ecuadorian writer. Doubling is tied to issues of memory, as neoliberal practices have contributed to the dismantling and erasure of diverse cultural practices in favor of a monological economy of power. In other words, "One can no longer speak in the name of the collective; human beings . . . are tragically alone and must position themselves in the midst of the uncertainty and skepticism in which they find themselves."[66] Accordingly, the double becomes a complicated character, as each individual works with confronting the other (double) that has been erased.

In the play, Palacio becomes a character that almost never speaks. He is isolated and unable to organize a coherent world because of the constant siege by characters that are doubled in a universe that is in turn doubled. The play is structured in several (apparently) disconnected scenes as follows.

1. The Writer struggles between reality and fiction.
2. The Detective presents the case of a man kicked to death. His hypothesis is that vice killed that man, and he reasons on the subject.
3. An operation separates the Double Woman. In the space of a

medical theater, the Doctor, before the gaze of his students (the audience), and the Mother prepare for the surgery that will separate The Double and Only Woman and thus save her.

4. The Double Woman reflects on her/their everyday reality and the difficulties around this as one woman who is two.
5. The Detective stands before the jury as the defense attorney and justifies the vices of his client in the case of the man kicked to death.
6. The Lieutenant has a double that is completely incompetent when it comes to love and life. He grows tired of his double and decides to kill him and himself.
7. The Double Woman discusses the difficulties of falling in love as a double and reflects on the onset of her death.
8. The Detective finishes his defense as he becomes a transvestite.
9. The Writer-Cannibal introduces his son to the audience, and his paternal happiness turns to cannibal pleasure when he finishes the scene by eating him.
10. The Detective reveals his double and commits suicide by hanging.
11. Three couples (which include the Writer, the Doctor, and the Lieutenant) comment on their incompatibility.
12. A disagreement between the Writer and his Mother leads to his death.
13. The Double and Only Woman dies of autocorrosion.
14. All the men and women wander around the stage amid mousetraps.

The fundamental question is which of these fragments is reality itself, or could it be that reality is made up of several simultaneous realities? The world onstage exists as a labyrinth meant to inscribe in the smallest spaces the largest number of possible roads, in this case to the self. In the performance, this is represented by a series of gauzy curtains that hang one after another across the entire stage, creating various paths through which the characters wander constantly. This physical labyrinth, then, establishes connections and juxtapositions among the different scenes as the characters repeatedly travel through it. In this way, before the amazed gaze of the writer onstage, several marginal characters deemed corrupt by societal standards parade. These so-called freaks can take on very different and controversial appearances, from the transvestite to the cannibal to the deformed, yet each one embraces his or her abject nature. A useful term, and aesthetic practice, to further understand these characters can be the *esperpento*, as defined by the Spanish playwright Ramón del Valle Inclán (1866–1936) in his play *Bohemian Lights* (1920). The main character, Max Estrella, states, "Classical heroes reflected in concave mirrors yield the *esperpento*. The tragic sense of Spanish life can be rendered only through an aesthetic that is systematically deformed."[67] The word *esperpento,* which cannot be translated, implies a grotesque aesthetic and reduces a character (through actions, words, or gesticulations) to nothing more than an absurd puppet.[68] Within the Latin American context, the migration of the *esperpento* to this particular stage brings along "a deformed image of reality or a faithful image of this deformed reality" for the purposes of providing an implicitly critical view of society.[69] As Valle-Inclán reminded us in his play, one must deform the expression itself in order to get to the real tragedy through the path of the grotesque. Therefore, what can be more coherent than the aesthetics of the *esperpento* to discuss characters perceived as freaks in a continent filled with such contrasts and imbalances?

The *esperpentic* world that appears onstage connects the experiences of the characters through the constant fear that characterizes their relationships with their doubles. This fear translates as inaction: characters are unable to come to terms with the "authentic" selves they are (their freak nature before the eyes of the law and science) and the "normal" selves they must pretend to be in order to be accepted by society. This occurs, for example, in the case of the Detective (portrayed by Joselino Suntaxi), who becomes fascinated with the case of the man kicked to death and questions the perception of his vices as they are understood by society.

> To have difficulties in our interpersonal relationships, to not be able to control our nature, to fall prey to misery and despair, to not be able to find a way in life, to have the feeling of being useless, to be filled with fear, to be unhappy, to apparently be of no use to anyone. . . . That's the place to which compulsiveness and addiction, character defects, anxiety, abstinence, and the desire to fill a bottomless void can throw us, like a used shoe! How brutal can we be, to reach the void without return.

The laws of society, which require us to fit into specific categories of normalcy, place an unending series of fears on the individual, who is constantly trying to appease the desire to fit into these imposed yet unattainable norms. The universalizing tendency of the national narratives of development and progress that at once legitimates the state's coercion in

the name of modernity also relegates those subjects that are incommensu-
rable with neoliberal economic politics to the margins through methods of
violence and fear. The abjected social groups, those that do not conform to
the state's biopolitics or those who do not adapt to the economic model of
productivity, are thus denied any orientation to the future other than one
dictated by a colonial neoliberal state. Such are the affinities between the
literary world of Palacio and the dramaturgical experiences of Vargas. Both
are constantly slapping away any reason or logic based on the bourgeois
order, and it becomes the butt of their jokes as they attempt to discredit any
reality based on this logic. In this performance one can find the organic
links between both artists, especially as the play attempts to question the
prototypical cultural "centers" found in law and medicine. The Detective
cannot help but question the humanity of such a process of marginalization
as "we pretend to be one and not the other, the one I would want to be." In
the Detective's imagination, the man who was kicked to death met his demise because he was a homosexual who was read by those around him as
a degenerate, and he died the moment he decided to walk down the street
as his true self. The double, then, is a part of all humanity, and it becomes a
superficial protection against our feared freak identity that we all carry
within ourselves: the fear of being different.

Ultimately, *De un suave color blanco* is a study on the act of representation, questioning whether humanity posits itself as the stage from which to
present its subjectivity, becoming a permanent image. The play begins with
a man writing with chalk on the stage floor "a double person walks through
a double road." It is in those terms that Malayerba's rereading of Palacio
becomes a study of the represented image of the other as the double of the
self. In other words, these characters cannot escape their normal/abnormal
duality and continue to question their authentic selves in order to view,
from the outside, the mechanisms that create or negate their identities. Palacio becomes a character himself, a carefully unfolded copy that remains
hidden behind curtains throughout the performance to remind us that
words, like experiences, are only imitations of realities. This world of shadows leads to the paradox of the normal/freak double as an image that dominates the performance. As a matter of fact, the Detective explains that the
freak is nothing more than a "vice" in this game of doubles, but he can't
conceive of humanity without this vice: "Can one conceive life without
vice? The day will come when they will not be able to conceive life without
this or with this." He repeats these lines as he considers the double nature
of our selves: "We know that experience has shown us that the moment in
which it activates there will be nothing or no one that can stop it; and we

know that it is inside of us, but why activate it? Why do we have this need to make present in our thoughts this labyrinthic and indecipherable structure? Is it in the blood, the flesh, the genes, the semen?" The double as freak, then, becomes that which we do not dare to reveal or be. It is a vice because society has deemed it so, even as it is a part of our selves. The Doctor later condemns it further, as he accuses his double of allowing this "contamination" to take over and prevent him from functioning "properly" socially: "Look at yourself, you have allowed yourself to be contaminated to the point that you are nothing, no one." Yet the fear of the contamination emanates from the fear of the abnormal, from departing too far from the norms of the state. In the words of Arístides Vargas:

> We simulate being in a role in reality, but within us there are others that work differently. This causes our discovery of the world to occur through a paradox: between the ones that function in the world with their social roles stipulated and their integration into a moral universe that is also stipulated and, another self that exists outside of that universe and is often immoral, is corrupt, but lives within the same personality.[70]

After all, as Garland-Thomson reminds us, "whether generating awe, delight, terror, or knowledge," the representation of the freak "emerges from culture-bound expectations even as it violates them."[71]

The freak in the literary work of Palacio is always a privileged character. The characters that appear in his literature are not mysterious creatures; rather their origins are always recognizable in a direct relationship with the world that they inhabit. This takes us back to the *esperpento*. In a social order that deforms reality the characters can only express their identities through the grotesque mirror that reflects their inner struggles to fit into a system that marginalizes them for simply being different. They are a direct product of the society that engenders them. The visually different body has always provoked the imagination, since such "freaks" resist the ordinary and confront the predictable, eliciting both anxiety and speculation in the spectator. What should be clear, though, is that different bodies are fundamental to our understanding of the world around us and the myths through which we make sense of our society. This means that in the performance the freak double becomes an attempt to reverse the state's use of the body for the establishment of a biopolitical social order. Like Palacio, the artists approach the different body as a tool of resistance to the status quo, repelling the notions of progress and ideologies used to create the idea of a nation. Therefore, the freak in this performance becomes a privileged figure as well, with more humanity than the other characters as it emanates from inside our inescapable fears of belonging. At the same time, they are often victims of society because of the differences in their physicality or their behavior.

As I previously stated, this very rich performance is inhabited by a long list of freaks, but the central focus falls on a specific character that clearly structures the performance: the Double and Only Woman. Cristina Marchan and Daisy Sánchez perform this double character, a set of conjoined twins; they always stand together and move in unison. The Double Woman is/are dressed in long white dresses (reminiscent of hospital gowns), and their torsos and arms are painted white. The character of the conjoined twins belongs to Palacio's short story *La doble y única mujer*, a story in which the protagonist "ponders the conundrum of corporeality through her ambiguously double and individual body that defies categorization and makes her the victim of social ostracism."[72] With this story line, then, the play enters the realm of disability as well, as the protagonist understands her torment to be a product of the discriminatory society she is made to live in. Yet her disability is not her identity, as she focuses instead on her way of living, an idea similar to what Carrie Sandahl and Philip Auslander write: "To think of disability not as a physical condition but as a way of interacting with a world that is frequently inhospitable is to think of disability in performative terms—as something one *does* rather than something one *is*."[73] The Double Woman is in search of love, yet each self disagrees on how to approach this search, and thus each is unable to accept the other.

> TWIN 1: I would like to live alone in my own desert, with my own mirages.
> TWIN 2: You assault me when you say that, I shake when you say that. Your desire to be outside me is disgusting.
> TWIN 1: Why must we be so dialectical?
> TWIN 2: Madness is always an option.

The desire of one sister to perform as her "authentic" separate self is questioned by the other, who finds this quest to be a sickness (vice, contamination, dirt) that will spread through them and finally destroy them. The main conflict with this character is the impossibility of producing any action as an individual and viewing death as her/their only escape. The Double Woman, then, interpellates the audience as she/them questions her/their "abnormality" before society's own cruelty and morbidity toward all individuals considered to be different.

Fig. 10. *De un suave color blanco*. Actors Charo Francés as the Mother and Cristina Marchan and Daisy Sánchez as the Double Woman. Photo by Analola Santana.

TWIN 2: I would have liked to be happy without offending anyone.
TWIN 1: I would have liked to talk about trees without this meaning
    having to be silent about so many injustices.
TWIN 2: The leprosy stain progresses with a soft, white color.

The characters' words reveal their freak nature to be socially constructed rather than a fixed, material condition, and their inability to form an expected unity is an adamant refusal to adhere to a static and central point of view as they expose the limits and contradictions of the self.

In the performance, the women/woman's voice is complemented by the presence of the Mother, performed by Charo Francés, who questions her role in the creation of her daughters' enfreaked bodies.

Everything began on a warm August afternoon, after watching all five versions of *Friday the Thirteenth* . . . You may scratch your head and look at each other with knowing glances of disbelief; regardless, I am a mother punished by the excesses of television; for example, in three days I watched all fifty-four episodes of the *X Files*, and in two afternoons I saw the entire series of *I Was Abducted by Aliens*. Never did I imagine that these shows would have such a disastrous influence on my pregnancy and on the most sacred thing that a mother has: her daughter. Well, that is just a way of saying it, since they are really two and one, I mean one and two . . . it is a monstrosity that one must take on.

This monologue is particularly poignant because of Francés's nervous demeanor and her anxious, rapid voice, which conveys her frustration and guilt about her daughter's condition. Everything begins with the Mother, who is made to ponder her own responsibility in the creation of a different body. Even the Writer, in his first monologue, considers this as he searches for his own mother in order to begin the play. The Mother's words situate the origin of the Double Woman's condition within the discourse of the once-popular theory of "maternal impressions." According to this belief, a pregnant woman can influence the development of the fetus she carries by looking at strange animals, images of monsters, or people with disabilities. In the case of the performance, the mother shares the guilt with images of popular culture that mold our understanding of the other. This becomes an interesting alliance, since the Mother's reference to kitschy horror films and TV shows seems to represent the generalized metaphorical freakery of US mass culture. However, the freaks in these films and shows are singular outsiders who refuse integration into the supposed homogeneity of urban life. She has been corrupted or infected by mass culture, which is passed on to her offspring. The Mother's emotions toward her daughters (the guilt she feels for their suffering) and the lack of empathy from the Doctor produce a moment of resistance to the expected meaning of freaks as the spectator comes to understand the influence of mass culture in the condemnation and creation of otherness. Freakery is a material condition imposed on unexpected or deviant bodies that do not conform to social dictates, which, in turn, places restrictions on those bodies. The narrative emphasis on mass culture, as the discourse from which the freak emerges because of his or her corporeal difference, challenges the ancient and invalid notion of maternal impressions by rendering "media" impressions as those which constitute difference. Thus, the Mother's guilt must be rephrased (at least emotionally) by comparing it to an institutional discourse of power and authority that determines the nature of bodies and their respective inclusion or exclusion from society (and feels no guilt about the removal of certain bodies from the social order).

As a matter of fact, the guilt of the Mother stands against the lack of empathy from the Doctor, played by Javier Arcentales, who introduces the audience to the Double Woman as he transforms the space into a medical theater, which, in turn, turns the audience into a group of fellow scientists with a common interest in the phenomenon before them: "Good afternoon . . . As you can observe, this is a singular case. That is a pretty word, singular, because when we use the word singular what we really want to say is . . . Well, you know what I mean (*winks at the audience*)." The Doctor, then, becomes a figure in which the abnormality of the Double Woman is radicalized; his discourse is responsible (at least in large part) for their pathologized identity.[74] The inclusion of the audience in the medical discourse serves as an interpellation that also places responsibility for her/their condition on them (as a stand-in for society), as the audience determines and judges what is normal or abnormal through the absorption and acceptance of institutionalized discourses of knowledge.

The characters' body language is essential to understanding this web of power and emotion. The Doctor is in the center of the space, while the Mother follows him around the stage, pleading for empathy: "Doctor, why do you talk about my daughters as if you were talking about my kitchen blender?" The Doctor's knowledge makes her invisible; he constantly reminds her that she can have no opinion because she lacks the language of medicine and science. After all, while her daughter(s) are dying and blaming each other for their lives, they are also before the cold and calculating gaze of scientists (the Doctor and the audience), who are eagerly awaiting her/their death in order to study her/their body. The Mother challenges this scientific lack of compassion: "Doctor, stop talking, stop saying so many theories, stop cleaning so much metal. Metal, many metals to alter our bodies, to enter our bodies. Why can't they be cotton?" Consequently, the Mother creates a space of affect that cannot be shared by the cold, materialistic world of the Doctor. Her desire to separate her daughters stems from affective guilt and the wish to provide them with an instance of "normalcy" as it is valued by society, whereas the Doctor can only understand the Double Woman through her/their pathology.

The Double Woman sits on the floor in the background (at times both actresses remove the tops of their dresses and expose their breasts as the Doctor examines this double character) while the Doctor and the Mother discuss her fate. The two actresses simultaneously perform a series of choreographed movements, their bodies always close together. These movements are by no means in perfect synchronicity, which is an interesting component of the character as it reveals glimmers of individuality and humanity: an external force against the discourses of power that manages to survive despite the imposed structures that contain them. She/they have had to submit to the Doctor throughout their lives.

TWIN 2: When I was a child and we were children, that degenerate that tried to separate us put his singular hand in my plural sex and this side screamed, but that side was blue like a glacier, frightfully silent and blue like a glacier.

TWIN 1: Then father arrived and said: shut up!, this man broke his back in the university in order to be able to do these things.

The fact that the Double Woman gestures toward the depathologizing of herself and would rather die than continue to fall prey to the Doctor indicates that within their perilous condition there lies a sort of agency that can be understood as political. By simply existing, she/they are a threat to the established discourse of power that the Doctor so clearly depends on, similarly to what Susan Antebi explains: "[U]nlike the classic figure of the *doppelganger*, which may appear and disappear, the double, or twin body, threatens the symbolic order of the paternal, since its unwavering, self-reflectively affirming presence seems to do away with the need for an absent referent."[75]

One could look at these affinities as a comment on the processes of modernization, as it has affected the standardization of everyday life that saturated the entire social fabric, producing and reinforcing the concept of an unmarked, normative, leveled body as the dominant subject of democracy. With its dependence on predictability, the images of mass culture push toward sameness and conformity and reimagine the body, depreciating particularity while valorizing uniformity. As stated by Garland Thompson, during the age of modernization, "[T]he iconography of social status transformed as the polity concerned itself with the subtleties of decoding bodies pressed toward the homogenous, even while the ideology of individualism called for distinction. . . . During a confusing era, the freak body represented at once boundless liberty and appalling disorder, the former the promise and the latter the threat of democracy."[76] Considering that the state forces these bodies to the periphery where they must fend for themselves, when these so-called deviant bodies are intervened on by discourses of power (such as the Doctor's exhibition of the Double Woman in the medical theater) and relegated to institutions (jail, the asylum, etc.) for being illegible to the controlling systems, one must consider the ability to exist and refuse change as a form of resistance to the state's cure. More succinctly, the representation of the sick, grotesque, or disabled as a body that refuses to comply with the norms becomes a form of resistance with its mere existence in the public sphere. These bodies stand as the necessary abjected subjects capable of denouncing the idea of nation and preventing it to hold.

The Double Woman clearly establishes this dynamic on the body, as they explain in one voice: "It has become necessary that I adapt to a series of difficult expressions that only I can use in my particular case . . . Which one of us is the monster? She is the monster, because whoever does not accept themselves as they are can become a terrible monster." This statement functions as a biting commentary on the bourgeois Ecuadorian (and by extension Latin American) society, on those who might absorb and unquestioningly accept the most trivialized and condensed visions of a destructive neoliberal system and then recirculate such ideas. The Double Woman claims this in unison: "They are all me. The street is filled with me, stuck in their tailored suits, their me stuck in their American-style breakfasts, their me stuck in their modern crisis . . . Their little me filled with little dramas that have nothing to do with their huge me, the spine-chilling guilty me that cannot accept their duplicity, their triple, their quadruple human being." There is a criticism, in both the play and Palacio's work, of the generalized fascination with everything foreign at the expense of an understanding of, or interest in, the nation's political and economic problems. As in many other Latin American countries, at the beginning of the new millennium the social, economic, and political panorama of Ecuador was not very positive. According to Michael Handelsman, among the internal and external forces that affected the country were:

> Neoliberal policies, the dollarization of the economy, the Plan Colombia, a general political chaos that has left many Ecuadorians skeptical and disenchanted, and the emigration of approximately a million Ecuadorians in search of better opportunities, which highlights the enormous unrest that has shaped these last years of national history.[77]

In addition to globalization, the country opened its doors to neoliberal policies that emphasized consumerism, coinciding with an economic crisis that almost destroyed the country in 1999. The inefficacy with which society has faced this chaos is expressed in the play through the inability to accept who we are in favor of a transnational economic value into which institutions of power have inscribed the individual without much resistance.

This inability to accept our own selves marks a return to what René Girard terms the monstrous double—the process by which, in response to a society's desire for differentiation from collectively experienced evils, the reciprocal violence of that society is displaced on a sacrificial victim, who becomes a guilty scapegoat: "In the collective experience of the *mon-*

strous double the differences are not eliminated, but muddied and confused. All the doubles are interchangeable, although their basic similarity is never formally acknowledged. They thus occupy the equivocal middle ground between difference and unity that is indispensable to the process of sacrificial substitution to the polarization of violence onto a single victim who substitutes for all the others."[78] Since lived reality can only be perceived through the representation of the double, in *De un suave color blanco* duplicity is necessary for the characters because they are unable to function directly in reality. Vargas has explained that before this impossibility the characters have to invent a double to face their own realities, "but the double, who is meant to function as what they cannot be, also fails; in other words, they are not perfect."[79] As imperfect as it is, the copy appears to be our only access to the established model because of a deep fear of rejection by the established order, an order that relegates power to technological advancements in the hands of a few in order to determine the constitution of functional identity. Queer theorist Paul B. Preciado (Beatriz Preciado) explains:

> If science has reached the hegemonic place that it occupies as a discourse and as a practice in our culture, it is because . . . it works as a material-discursive apparatus of bodily production. Technoscience has established its material authority by transforming the concepts of the psyche, libido, consciousness, femininity and masculinity, heterosexuality and homosexuality, intersexuality and transsexuality into tangible realities. They are manifest in commercial chemical substances and molecules, biotype bodies, and fungible technological goods managed by multinationals.[80]

We have come to depend on the definitions provided by scientific discourse to determine what constitutes our identity, and thus we are unable to understand our actions or ailments without the necessary "substance" to correct them (as prescribed by the "technoscience" to which Preciado refers). Individuals become serial repetitions of consumer identity. And, in this era of mass culture and neoliberalism, the fact remains that the repetition, its duplication in copies, is not a simple accident but the essence of "truth" as it is conceived by economic exploitation.

As previously stated, the double is a constant in the work of Palacio, and in Malayerba's performance the double functions as a means of creating an "other" center, around which individuals constitute themselves. The double becomes eccentric; it situates itself on the margins of the canonical since the body of the woman, or the cannibal or the transvestite, requires a readjustment of grammatical, moral, physical, and social codes—to name just a few of the structures that its presence throws into disarray. By existing as they are within the public space, even as they are removed from society, doubles have created a moment of insurgency as they claim their existence. It is similar to what Ed Cohen argues: the modern body is born/ constructed by the medical and legal discourses of the late nineteenth century, which pushed the state to legally defend the human body. Defending the modern body can also be interpreted as allowing it to attain political valorization; it assuages the individual's weakness by permitting it to accrue value, and with legal possession of the citizen/subject comes access to political and economic rights. If the citizen/subject grows, it becomes an asset to the state. Further, the bodies represented in this performance are exercising forms of resistance by continuing to be infirm and vulnerable when they do not fit into the frameworks of social economic progress. They cannot be reintegrated because they resist the ideas of the modern notions of progress and in fact challenge the state as a patriarchal entity by insisting that the state itself is contaminated.

The Double Woman and the Doctor are not the only characters that explore the ways in which control is imposed from above and outside in order to subdue individual agency, to retain and shape the individual into a specific "way of being," of thinking, which will only empower the capitalist/neoliberal project. The Detective, who becomes his transvestite double, performs the individual's agency to refuse the state's biopolitical agenda. The shifting identity politics of this character poses a particular problem within the context of the law, as it is supposed to operate as an instrument designed to impart order and stability. As the Detective inhabits his own fiction about the man dead from kicks (deemed to be a vicious man by society because of his homosexuality), whom he is defending in a courtroom, he engages in his own repressed desires. He explains the man's actions as follows.

It is as if in a social body, perfectly organized and oiled in order to be happy, a gap opened and an unrestrained desire to be someone else came out, a second I that can play freely, with a certain candor as it is in any game, to do something that is not allowed and that he is not in any condition to do for himself, that's why he needs this other, creating another gender, a third gender, a subgender, a gender that some will no doubt call degenerate . . . My own gaze is tragic, in other words a gaze filled with compassion, because everyone should have the prerogative of making a circus of their own asses.

The Detective's aim is to make visible what remains hidden because of social fears. Revealing his other half, the Detective makes his (perceived) difference visible. As he becomes Ramona and speaks to the jury, he proceeds to place a noose over his head. Like the Double Woman, killing himself (or in their case, allowing themselves to die) will allow the most agency, "and before another group of maladjusted misfits kicks me to death in a dark alley, allow me to commit suicide on this stage . . . If anyone asks about Ramírez, tell them he was an intelligent person to madness, sane to the definite silence." His declaration is a stunned admission predicated on the use of the different body as a spectacular terrain of liminal and nightmarish possibilities. The Detective exposes society's obsession with visually policing corporeal liminality.

The same can be said for the short scene concerning the cannibal. In the original short story, *El antropófago*, Palacio exposes society's double morality through which it punishes the same acts that it desires. The narrator of the short story acts as a sideshow announcer, calling the audience (or the reader) through his pitch and narrative to wonder in awe at the freak on display. He describes his anatomy and tells tales of his actions, ending the narrative with an ironic twist when he asks, "Consider this, through this figure, what would you do if the cannibal had your nose for dinner?" The reader moves from the observer of difference to the observed object of aesthetic difference. In *De un suave color blanco*, this character is fused to the Writer. A group of butchers stand behind the first curtain, hitting wooden tables with their knives. The Writer-Cannibal (played by Gerson Guerra) emerges from among them with a newborn child in his arms (a bundle of blankets). He joyfully plays with him until he is consumed by this happiness and devours him, blood spilling on the stage floor. He then writes with chalk on the floor "Each one is free to eat what they create." The Writer-Cannibal, then, is free to eat his own creations, returning over and over again to the blank page (that soft, white color) to continue for eternity. And so humans, faced with their own inconsistencies and a lack of correspondence between themselves and the world they inhabit, are doomed to repeat and restart their lives in an obsessive circle. As audience members, we watch the characters' inability to move through this labyrinth, always falling prey to their own traps. The characters in the play expose the fragility of our social behavior, and in the tediousness of our social formulas and routine conducts they exhibit our own obsessions with belonging to a sys-

Fig. 11. *De un suave color blanco*. Actor Gerson Guerra as the Writer-Cannibal.
Photo by Analola Santana.

tem that refuses to incorporate forms and behaviors outside the norm. The Writer-Cannibal has the right to consume his own creations and begin again on the blank page. The play ends with the collection of characters wandering through a stage filled with mousetraps, which are activated by their steps.

The fears evoked by the characters of *De un suave color blanco* function as connectors among a fractured societal structure that wants to prevent individual alliances. Yet the characters in Malayerba's play exist on the margins (some in a mental institution, others as freaks to be studied), and through their marginal conditions they find a structure of affective relations that allows them to question the reality of their situations. They are ambulatory characters that lack a definite or defined space. Their existence is an exercise in memory and forgetting since their identity is a consciousness that accompanies the act of thinking itself. In other words, they conform to a genealogy of affect in which their thoughts and acts retain the emotions of remembering and forgetting in a society of mass consumption that has transformed what is valued and thrives on the fugacity of memory. Neoliberalism has established a system that has little to do with Latin American reality, and thus it constitutes a form of amnesia so as to impose a set of doctrines that have failed the majority. It is through a mapping of the characters' emotions that the play constitutes a commentary on the destabilizing societal structures of a Latin America that has turned to a neoliberal world order as an impossible answer.

THE BIOPOWER COMPLEX: THE FREAK IN VIOLETA LUNA'S *NK 603: ACCIÓN PARA PERFORMER & E-MAÍZ*

In this chapter I have traced how institutions of power have, historically, controlled bodies by foregrounding certain bodily or behavioral characteristics as the pattern for normalcy in order to determine who belongs in the modern, neoliberal system (an economic model that thrives on inequality) and who needs to be relegated to the margins and placed in spaces of control (the asylum, the prison). What can be observed is that institutions of power, through the advances of science and technology, create a discourse that stigmatizes certain aspects of the physical body and its behavior as abnormal and thus not conducive to the equal advancement of individuals in society. There is a cost to progress, especially as western medicine aims to legitimate its models against (or in place of) traditional, indigenous knowledge. What has become obvious is that progress does not always improve one's life, especially as modern scientific knowledge attempts to confound rather than inform: the "developed" world prescribes knowledge and science for the "developing" world with utter disregard for the outcomes and context.

Modernity has established a biopolitical relationship between the political body and the individual that regulates and intervenes in the construction of citizenship and social belonging. Foucault, in *"Society Must Be Defended": Lectures at the Collège de France, 1975–1976,* explains biopower and biopolitics as the management of the population's growth through the control of the rate of reproduction in the second half of the eighteenth century. The nineteenth century, Foucault observes, was the time of industrialization, and biopower was diffused through the population with an economic rationale. We are currently living the effects of this displacement of control. Sociologist José Joaquín Brunner notes that modern culture in Latin America emerged from changes stemming from the 1950s (urbanization, the advent of new technologies, and greater education and literacy among others). This led to new forms of production that intrinsically changed our understanding of culture.

> Culture then finally becomes a mass social formation tending to the international, with a progressively industrial highly differentiated base that cannot be controlled from any center. It is a decentered and deterritorialized culture which no longer reflects the people's soul, but the desires, sensibility, and work of a new class—that of the symbolic producers and mediators—and, at the same time, the generative work of millions of receivers-consumers who process, interpret, appropriate, and live this mass of produced and transmitted signs in their own way, individually or, at times, collectively.[81]

For this reason, the role of the state continues to retreat to its basic functions, for "it can no longer mobilize nor imprint order upon the cultural sphere."[82] Power has switched from the state to the producers of technology, which becomes the only clear discourse of evolution and progress. Accordingly, the only "legitimate" knowledge and scientific advancement stem from these spaces. My questions in this section, then, are What happens to local knowledge and technology? If legitimate knowledge comes from a globalized industry that is (de)centered throughout corporations that hold the power of dissemination and advancement, is the ancestral knowledge of indigenous cultures (which constitute the largest percentage of Latin American inhabitants) displaced as folklore? Are those bodies nothing more than visions of a romantic past, meant to be exhibited as remnants of a primitive knowledge?

These are the issues that performance artist Violeta Luna tackles in her piece as she addresses the major changes that have taken place since the implementation of the North American Free Trade Agreement (NAFTA) and its impact on marginalized sectors of society, particularly in Mexico. *NK 603: Acción para performer & E-Maíz* (NK 603: Action for a Performer & E-Corn) focuses on the use of genetically modified organisms (GMOs) and their devastating effect on native culture, the economy, and science. In other words, the performance takes on scientific hubris.[83] It is a reflection on genetically modified corn and its disastrous consequences for life—for the original natural species, as well as for the communities that have cultivated corn since ancient times, which developed entire cultures around it. As the artist explains, "For Mexicans and many other Latin Americans, *maíz* nurtures the body, and also the soul, as native sacred texts tell the story of how our first people were made out of maize. As such, it plays a symbolic role in rituals, and it is also one of our key traditional food sources, from the American Southwest, to Patagonia."[84] Interestingly, Luna approaches the subject by constructing a variant on the freak body. In this performance, we move from the notion of the freak that has been previously discussed—as individuals who assume that their difference is a possible instance of dissidence in the face of a homogenizing neoliberal system of oppression—to a freak produced through technology and science, a body that wants to be invaded by technology and, thus, lose its humanity.[85]

The performance is divided into two spaces within the same stage or enclosed space (depending on where it takes place but always indoors). In the center a long white cloth hangs, onto which various projections appear during the performance. This space is illuminated by a soft, yellow/orange light. The second space is closer to the audience, which usually sits around the space in a semicircle, to the side of the stage. There is a table with various metal surgical tools on it. The light in this space is blue, indicating a colder, less intimate area. The performance begins with calm, acoustic music and the projection of cornfields onto the cloth. Soon the voice of a US farmer can be heard, talking about the impact of genetically modified seeds in farming. Eventually the voice becomes distorted, and only certain phrases can be heard repeatedly, such as "it only affects the corn," "we don't have to work so much," or "it's not fair." The audience begins to hear a sound behind it, as Luna appears wearing a skirt made of dried cornhusks, with a Mexican rebozo covering her torso (which is painted purple with a large ear of corn drawn on her back and corn kernels adhered to her

Fig. 12. *NK 603: Acción para performer & E-Maíz*. Violeta Luna performing indigeneity. Photo by Julio Pantoja.

chest); she has two long braids and a hat, and in one hand she holds a machete while in the other there is a small cloth bundle. Eventually the performance will be divided between a reflection on the ritual aspects of corn farming and the technological modifications and effects of the same as Luna moves from one space to the other. Corn becomes something more than a simple plant, as it is also a symbol of life in the continuation of an indigenous cosmovision of Mexico. In terms of a context for the performance, as performance scholar Paola Marín explains, "Let's recall that the anthropologist Guillermo Bonfil Batalla spoke of corn as the basis of a Mesoamerican civilization process that is still alive in today's Mexico. Consequently, the destruction of native corn implies negative and irreversible alterations, both economically (by the dependence it creates upon the multinationals that produce it) and in relation to a violent split in the ways of living and understanding culture."[86] Technology and science, then, appear as a threat to cultural identity itself.

As was discussed earlier, populations, as a set of living beings, are subject to mechanisms of registration and power that seek the normalization of individuals and encodes them under the sign of capital and productivity.[87] Institutions of power need to control the bodies of the population (biopolitics), and, unlike previous eras, the twentieth and twenty-first centuries have made this possible through a direct collaboration with technology. *NK603* approaches this new relationship between bodies and technology to denounce all those other aspects sacrificed (cultural practices, ancient knowledge, biological diversity, etc.) in the name of evolution and economic productivity. In a society preoccupied with survival—a discourse that has become more and more protrusive as we face overpopulation, scarcity of resources, a widening class gap, and so on—this notion is directly related to biopolitics as explained through Giorgio Agamben's notion of "bare life." For Agamben, the specter of power and violence is a being whose life can be reduced merely to living. Since the emergence of collective power stems from the perception that life itself is in danger and the priority for survival rests on economic advancements and a conducive leadership based on the neoliberal model of success. In the words of Gabriel Giorgi:

> To govern life implies tracing on the continuous body of the population a series of thresholds and roadblocks around which the humanity or nonhumanity of the individual and groups can be decided, and in turn their relation to the law and derogation, their level of exposure to sovereign violence, their place within the webs—every time more limited, more dilapidated in this neoliberal era—of social protection.[88]

This lack of protection for the marginal social body extends, in the performance, to nature itself, as it becomes the embodiment of the people who have been most affected by a negative construct of "science as culture" (borrowing from Donna Haraway, who asserts that "global technology appears to *denature* everything, to make everything a malleable matter of strategic decisions and mobile production and reproduction processes.")[89]

This is clearly obvious in the stage space itself, as the center—dominated by the soft light and white cloth—becomes the space of ritual practices. At the beginning of the performance, Luna stands before this cloth and performs the cultivation of corn, using her machete to plow imaginary fields while behind her images from Mexico's political history appear. These images (from past presidents to farm workers in their fields and the signing of NAFTA) interact with the music, which becomes more aggressive as the sound mingles with voices of protest and culminates with the image of Subcomandante Marcos.[90] At this point, Luna stands with her fist raised and the machete held high, a clear symbol of rebellion. The ritual element slowly appears from this first stance, which denounces specific moments that have affected the marginal communities in Mexico.

After other actions that reference the *campesino* movements and economic issues of the country, Luna uses the corn kernels that were inside the cloth bundle to make an offering. "I wanted to contextualize the piece from two moments that marked the joining of the institutional and the political," explained Luna in an interview. "These were the signing of NAFTA, which put Mexico at a great disadvantage from the United States and Canada, and the rising of the Zapatista movement in Chiapas. The importance of this movement, in my opinion, is that they advocate not only for the indigenous communities but those most excluded. Also, for me, they are men and women of maize because there is another relational sense with the land."[91] The ritual and the political are intertwined in an action that expresses the effect that disembodied discourses of power have on the bodies of citizens.

The issues at stake in this piece have to do with technology and science wanting to become not merely a discourse but the living world itself with all that it entails. The effects of unequal access to technology in a political system that privileges the market has led to problematic "adaptations" that are expected of the indigenous sectors by those in power. George Yúdice explains, "The fact is that the vast majority of traditional groups and other subaltern peoples continue to live under conditions of diminished opportunity. Cultural reconversion—that is, making cultural production marketable—is certainly an improvement over not having sufficient resources for the 'pursuit of life and happiness,' but it is difficult to accept an economic rationale as a solution for cultural production and reception and their role in the construction of more democratic civil societies."[92] The subordination of indigenous cultures to the logic of the international market can be a mode of survival, but it remains at its core a capitalist mechanism for the production of profitable cultural differences. Even if this rationalization could be beneficial for popular sectors of society, the hegemonic groups are the ones who benefit the most, and that makes this a dubious strategy for challenging structural inequality.

For this reason, Luna begins by inhabiting a stage space associated with a concept of nature that is slowly being displaced by technological advancements that seek to control it. Luna's performance places an emphasis on nature that is similar to Haraway's discussion of the topic.

> Nature is . . . one of those impossible things characterized by Gayatri Spivak as that which we cannot not desire. Excruciatingly conscious

of nature's discursive constitution as "other" in the histories of colonialism, racism, sexism, and class domination of many kinds, we nonetheless find in this problematic, ethno-specific, long-lived, and mobile concept something we cannot do without, but can never "have." We must find another relationship to nature besides reification and possession. Perhaps to give confidence in its essential reality, immense resources have been expended to stabilize and materialize nature, to police its/her boundaries. Such expenditures have had disappointing results.[93]

Thus, when Luna takes out a test tube and drinks what is inside and then proceeds to spit out the blood that she drank, nature becomes transmuted by the effects of a technology that seeks to benefit a capitalist system, not humanity or its commonplace: nature. In this sense, modern science becomes the freak itself, with its constant desire to modify everything around it for profit.

To be clear, *NK603* is not necessarily condemning technological advancements as evil; rather there is criticism of science in the hands of corporations that seek economic gain. There is condemnation of the use of science "for the good of the nation," the idea that it is fixing humanity, when instead it is destroying the modes of life of many sectors. After all, the indigenous people that cultivated corn in the Americas depended on science and technology to produce so many varieties. As Luna explains in the same interview, "I don't want to idealize indigenous knowledge, but in terms of science and medicine, this was understood as individuals in relation to the nature around them. What corporations, such as Monsanto, want is to create patents for seeds, and in order to do so they are stealing an ancient knowledge that has developed over thousands of years."Luna refers here to the appropriation of indigenous knowledge in order to create and patent seeds that are more resistant to the environment, and companies such as Monsanto have a fierce reputation for enforcing their patents and suing anyone who allegedly violates them, thus determining who is able to farm what.[94] The long-term effects of this are that whoever provides the world's seeds controls the world's food supply. In the performance, then, the freak is no longer a marginal figure that exists on the fringes of society.

Instead, technology has created a monstrous freak that stems from the corporations that will destroy and contaminate the natural world around them. This is apparent when Luna moves to the second space onstage, dragged by the neck by an invisible hand that holds a metal device (of

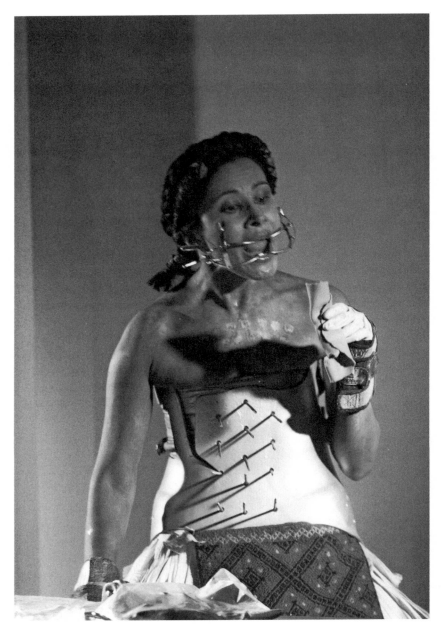

Fig. 13. *NK 603: Acción para performer & E-Maíz*. Violeta Luna performs science and technology. Photo by Julio Pantoja.

course, it is Violeta's hand that performs the actions). With her face covered in the blood she had spit out, she removes the seeds from her chest with surgical instruments. Luna "becomes" modern science as she takes a syringe from the table and pretends to inject different parts of her body, to the dismay of members of the audience, who laugh uncomfortably as she jokes about the possibility of injecting them. Eventually, she does inject her arm, which leads to anxious spasms as she moves back to the table.

The violence of these images, directed at the body, is a clear metaphor for the effects of unfettered technological advances, and for the dogmas espoused on the economy and the benefits of neoliberalism derived from an uncritical use of technology. The inversion of the notion of normalcy is completed in the performance as the artist, continuing with her violent, robotic movements, returns to the table and places a metal clamp in her mouth (which keeps it open). Excitedly, she takes out a metal bag with the insignia "made in the USA" and proceeds to make tortillas out of the blue substance in the bag. This is a very scatological moment in which saliva drools from her mouth and her movements are almost clownish due to her anxious anticipation of what she is making. She gives these tortillas to the spectators. If this is the result of science, it is far from our imposed understanding of normalcy. It is a loss on the body that Lisa Woynarski exposes as a performance of our own vulnerabilities: "As Luna is poked and prodded, bruised and bloodied, the physical health of her body parallels the loss of biodiversity and genetic manipulation of the maize plants. Her body is implicated in the interventions into the land, in the globalization of rural Mexico and in the loss of heritage and culture associated with maize."[95] This contradiction (the loss of the body/land/nature for economic gain/scientific advancement) lies at the heart of the performance, as Luna aims to challenge the scientific gaze on bodies as simple objects for technological advancement and instead points to the other side of this reality, which is often ignored: the social exclusion and cultural annihilation embodied in the genetic modification of crops. In this way, science is not nature. It is a form of imposed tutelage on those sectors deemed to be "underdeveloped" that tends to exploit and threaten ways of life as individuals confront powerful institutions of "development." Control over technology, then, becomes an enabling practice for class, gender, and racial inequality and abuse.

With this performance, Violeta Luna invites the spectator to question possible ways of resistance against the mechanisms of inscription and subjection that, in the name of science and progress, impose on citizens' bodies violent forms of normalization, invade bodies, and legitimize the most violent actions in favor of productivity and economic gain. As Brunner explains:

> The cycle of traditional opposition between Nature and History—where the first is the embracing and fertilizing mother and the second is the law of the father consecrating his domination—will come to a close in Latin America with the advent of the themes of Modernity. From then on, Nature (and society as well) will be the object of Man's action, yielding to the movements of the market and serving, at most, to condemn a culture that makes headway tearing down gods and forests.[96]

In the face of this reality, Luna pushes us to reflect on the effect of this mass-mediatic vision of the world around us that allows for the erasure of those marginal bodies that do not conform to the aims of science and progress. If the "others" that exist outside the realm of development and progress are not deemed apt to exercise power, Luna exemplifies how it is still possible to rise against the order of eugenics and resist the capture of biopower. This is in line with the "biopolitical monster" that Michael Hardt and Antonio Negri described: the multitude and their revolutionary desire to resist exploitation and its normalizing forces.[97] Within biopolitics, notions of abnormality are redefined as discourses of power expand to include elements that can benefit the economic expansion of corporations (such as genetic manipulation in this case), so that what was once considered unnatural and excessive becomes natural and normal. Luna's performance seeks to denounce the normalized monstrosity of this technocracy, which subjects certain sectors to a rationality that justifies their exclusion. The freak, then, is exhibited as scientific knowledge that has dispossessed many sectors of the ability to survive; it has returned to that monster of the past that goes against nature (as was discussed in chapter 1).

There is a clear attempt in this chapter to question the possibility of the figure of the freak as a semiotic sphere of the other that can be normalized for economic profit (as is the case with Luna) while others have the potential for resistance in the face of scientific and political powers of normalization (as is the case with *Vacío* and *De un suave color blanco*). Resistance, then, becomes something more than a struggle—it is an attempt to establish a right to live and exist. These performances provide a new ontology that seeks to change the paradigm, even if it is perceived as a superficial change in the fugacity of a performance or theatrical piece. Nevertheless, it is ontologically potent as it has the possibility of modifying the consciousness of the artist and spectators. The institutionalized system of political power (in this case the neoliberal state) has transformed the imaginary of difference into a vice, a stain, a violence that cannot be tolerated. The law, medicine, and technology (as integral parts of the state) deem it necessary to suppress any form of bodily or behavioral difference that would reveal the gaps in their discourse. The freak, then, is a figure to be feared because it has the potential to expose the falseness of normativity. The performances analyzed in this chapter use this figure to decenter a discourse of political violence inflicted on the marginal body in its various forms in order to contrast the neoliberal system of oppression with a politics of enfreakment.

THREE

The Savage Exotic

Gender and Class in the Construction of Freakery

I am often surprised at the ease with which assumptions about one's person are made in our societies. At the age of eighteen I became pregnant and had a child. This was a great scandal for my intellectual, middle-class parents, especially because the father was from a poor section of Mexico City with no education and an equally "undesirable" family. He was by no means the ideal partner in life that my family envisioned. I was shocked when my mother, an intelligent academic, insisted on telling everyone she knew that of course I would be getting married, yet there was no mention of who this "husband" would be—it was too embarrassing for her to explain. Everything became even more devastating when, seven years after this incompatible marriage took place, my husband ended up in prison (for six years). I was never to speak about this, and his existence was quickly forgotten in my family: in their minds these types of things only happened to uneducated and objectionable individuals. Obviously, my story is more complicated and nuanced than what I quickly reference here, but I want to discuss it because it allows me to reflect on the crossings of gender and class. Reactions to my trajectory in academic circles have been paternalistic at best and pitying at worst. (Is it because I am a Latin American woman? Are they assuming I must come from the sort of low-class background that leads to teenage pregnancies? I had a husband in prison?!). What is obviously clear to me is that my background is not compatible with the expected persona of the professional scholar, and this has been made abundantly clear over time.

These biases are even more complicated by moral expectations in Latin American circles, where categories of class and gender continue to be unmovable and definitive. A woman should not be part of scandals, and much less a woman in academia (or in any form of public forum). For a recent example, one should look no further than Dilma Rousseff, the impeached leader of Brazil, and the media's reactions to her based solely on her gender. Often described as an "unbalanced" woman, a week after her impeachment the weekly magazine *Veja* published a profile on Marcela Te-mer, the wife of Michel Temer, the man who would soon become interim president of the country. This piece became an outrage as it pushed the political and mediatized misogyny of the country to the forefront. Marcela, forty-three years younger than her husband, was described as "bela, re-catada e do lar," meaning beautiful, demure, and "a housewife." The impli-cations are clear: women (particularly women of a certain social class) should behave as beautiful objects to be admired and not intervene in the public sphere. Immediately, outrage over this classist and prejudiced view of femininity spilled through the media, especially as many leftist politi-cians viewed the outing of Rousseff as a sexist act in a country with very low rates of female political representation.[1] As a *Forbes* article explains, "[M]any of the more liberal Brazilians fear [that] Sunday's vote [for the impeachment] veered the country in a morally conservative direction; they see the *Veja* headline as further evidence of that."[2]

Even though Latin American countries have elected more women to power than most other countries in the world,[3] the power afforded to these women is based on misogynistic assumptions. The stereotypical and in-grained binomial image of women as either sexual beings whose only use is for pleasure or respected mothers (and thus figures of power) provides a powerful archetype that is worthy of scrutiny and praise. Jean Graham-Jones has extensively examined the role of feminine icons, or "femicons," in Argentinian culture to explain the role that figures such as Eva Perón have had in embodying the cultural, political, and social anxieties of a na-tion. Femicons like Perón have such a lasting impact that there is a ten-dency by the national imaginary to conflate all women in power with this one single figure (the benevolent, saintly Evita, of course, not the militant one). In particular, Graham-Jones focuses on Cristina Fernández de Kirch-ner (Argentina's twice-elected female president) to show the power of ico-nography on the national stage and the ways in which women have trans-formed and used it. Kirchner's "is not a secondary elaboration or a double performance, yet she evinces an awareness of an icon's dual function as cultural agent *and* cultural product. Cristina is not Evita, nor does she the-atrically embody Evita, and, through her careful actions, biting wit, and sheer political longevity, she has resisted the international media's reduc-tivist attempts at, one again, equating any Argentine woman of weight with the country's premiere femicon."[4]

Given the abundance of stories like these, why are societies incapable of crafting new matrices of class and gender that overcome the established categories of normalcy with which we approach our human identity? I explore that question in this chapter. As previously discussed, since Aristotle, women and the feminine have been viewed as a deformation of man. In addition to being the essential other, they are also the root cause of all difference since monsters are produced by the disorders of the maternal imagination. These concepts continue on, almost without alteration, into the nineteenth century, where we find treatises such as Lombroso and Ferrero's *La donna delinquente, la prostituta e la donna normale* (1893), in which the Italian criminologists construct the notion of a "normal" woman from the male model of normalcy, since even the most normal woman carries within her body and soul the stigma of perversion. Women in the twentieth and twenty-first centuries have not fared much better, even as we can appreciate the vast changes that have taken place in terms of rights and equality. And yet the question remains: Why does womanhood continue to be a category that can easily morph into forms of freakness? And why is this even more likely when combined with class within the structures of consumer capitalism? To frame the implications of class and gender in the formation of normative identity, especially as it applies to the performances that will be discussed in this chapter, I turn to J. Jack Halberstam's concept of "gaga feminism." This notion has come forth as a new methodology for analyzing identity politics in a technologically advanced world that refuses to move on from nineteenth-century notions of the domestic and the public sphere: "Gaga feminism will be a way of seeing new realities that shadow our everyday lives—gaga feminists will see multiple genders, finding male/female dichotomies to be outdated and illogical. Gaga feminism is a gender politics that recognizes the ways in which our ideas of the normal or the acceptable depend completely upon racial and class-based assumptions about the right and the true."[5] According to Halberstam, we continue to hold on to these established structures of what constitutes family, marriage, and so on, even as they expand to accommodate more possibilities.

In the case of Latin American identity performance, the disconnection between a technologically advanced world and a dated notion of gender is further problematized as it is played out in the context of politics. Especially as women have been prevented from exercising explicit political power (with very few exceptions, which are often characterized by misogynistic overtones, as we can see in the case of Dilma Rousseff, among others, including Eva Perón) without explicit masculine patronage. In other words, as Lucía Guerra explains, the Latin American woman "looks for herself in a multiple otherness and intends to replace the abstract theorizing by multiple dialogues carrying in themselves a political potential."[6] In this way, gaga feminism provides an alternative path for understanding the multiplicity of identities that compose our understanding of gender, and, in the case of Latin America, it can allow us to take the power away from legitimized and accepted structures of gender identity in favor of a more open consideration of what constitutes the political power of the individual.[7] Performance art, then, becomes a useful tool through which to address these issues, as it articulates different forms of human identity. Noted performance studies scholar Josefina Alcazar takes this idea further: "Performance recovers the body as a space of transgression and resistance, as a place where social hierarchies, gender roles, and religious taboos can be destabilized, inverted, or satirized. Performance art, as well as the masquerades and carnivals and festivals, is a space where one can question the established order. In these events the social order and the rules are suspended momentarily, the body invades the social stage and you turn the world on its head."[8] In the context of violence and discrimination based on gender and class, I am particularly interested in the ways in which performance practices can become avenues for producing political expressions that, at the very least, become a form of protest and evidence for the manifestation of ideas that might otherwise remain invisible (as unspeakable horrors).[9] Are theater and performance able to aesthetically transform political ideas into creative images that lead to awareness and social action? I find performance to be a connector through which to understand how Latin American culture (in this case) produces—and is produced by—ideologies of race, sexuality, class dynamics, and national identity. David Román has noted that "performance produces an opportunity for a critical reappraisal of official culture and makes space for other modes of understanding."[10]

In this chapter, I look at three performances that allow for new and more nuanced understandings of class and gender. These artists treat gender as unstable categories that are culturally constructed without any essential traits to define masculinity or femininity, especially as they relate to class consciousness. I am particularly interested in the intersections between class and gender in Latin American cultures that have entered the twenty-first century through an unstable neoliberal paradigm, which has ultimately led to radical changes, from the rise in state-sponsored violence and narcoviolence, to increased national debts and an ever-widening income gap, as well as weakened democracies. Halberstam explains why these intersections are significant, as they allow us to understand new possibilities of gender identity that multiply as individuals react to societal and political changes: "[I]f we could actually see . . . gender categories as saturated with contradictions, as discontinuous across all the bodies they are supposed to describe, then we could begin to notice the odd forms of gender, the gaga genders, that have multiplied like computer viruses in late capitalist cultures."[11] These discontinuous identities relate to freak identity if one considers the historical composition of freak shows as representing what the audience (or society at large) was not: bodies that were excluded from mainstream society because of their difference. Thus, Halberstam's notion of gaga brings to the forefront the differences that constitute human identity while revealing the inconsistencies in the power structures that suggest nothing more than the fears and anxieties that plague modernity as we question how to define ourselves and relate to each other. Gaga, then, provides me an entryway through which to get past the prescriptive ideals of heteronormativity and move into the Latin American context of class and gender dynamics.

Considering that the instability of gender remains a contested notion for much of Latin America's popular imaginary (where issues of machismo dominate the understanding of male and female "roles," especially as they relate to class), it is necessary to begin dismantling these old-fashioned notions and bring to light the already existing "odd forms" that are abundant but overlooked or erased from the national consciousness. In an era that has categorically changed our understanding of the body as it relates to power structures, we can no longer depend on a dual gender as a classification of self, as Halberstam asserts: "[N]ew affiliations between bodies, sex, and power remind us that the categories of being that seemed to specify and define human nature over one hundred years ago have quickly become rather inadequate placeholders for identity."[12] Latin American performance artists are actively working to dismantle this order.

I approach the work of Brazilian theatrical dance troupe Primeiro Ato, under the artistic direction of Suely Machado, with this in mind. Their performance *Geraldas e Avencas* (2007) takes on the standardization of beauty as a form of aesthetic dictatorship that seeks to erase all forms of difference.[13] In particular, Artistic Director Machado sought to question the use of the word *perfect* to describe people as she raised awareness that there are imperfections in all and thus the expectation of achieving perfection has led humanity to a deformation of the self. Following the analysis of this piece, I look to the work of Mexican performance artist Katia Tirado as a way of further focusing on issues of class. Tirado's *El brillo en la negrura de sobrevivir* (The Brightness in the Darkness of Survival, 2014) is a site-specific piece that can take up to eight hours to complete. In it Tirado narrates to two tattoo artists the personal histories of the cleaning staff, security guards, cooks, and other "blue-collar" workers of the space in which the performance takes place (in this case, the CENART [National Center for the

Arts] in Mexico City). The tattoo artists then turn these into visual microstories that they tattoo on pigskins, which, in the end, are fried and eaten as
chicharrón by the spectators. I close this chapter with the performance piece
Piedra (Stone, 2013) by Guatemalan artist Regina José Galindo. A site-
specific piece as well, Galindo takes on the violence inflicted on women by
a society that devalues their bodies, especially the bodies of women marginalized by poverty in an industrial economic complex that seeks to benefit from their work and their bodies.

With these three pieces, I want to trace an analytical pathway that leads
from the heteronormative freak show of "perfect" femininity and masculinity to the enfreakment of the working-class woman for the purposes of
exploiting her body and labor. In this way, using performance practices as
embodied politics, it can be possible to discern and discuss some of the
major issues that plague Latin American social practices and ideologies.
This is especially important in an era marked by technological advances
that continue to modify our bodies and minds, and not always for the bet-
terment of the individual. Globalization and neoliberalism continue to
trace what Roger Bartra refers to as imaginary networks of political terror,
and "these imaginary networks constantly generate polar myths about normality and marginality, of identity and otherness, and they crystalize in
simulacrum closely linked to the processes of critical dislocation typical of
postmodern societies."[14] The political processes that characterize much of
Latin America have stimulated the division of normalcy and marginality as
all sorts of individuals are characterized as abnormal, liminal beings that
"threaten with their presence—real or imaginary—the stability of the hegemonic political culture."[15] Bartra continues to explain how this has led to
the perception of "democratic superheroes of normalcy," which seek to
fight the dangerous abnormal enemy in a battle that, even as it is filled with
a high content of allegorical and imaginary narratives, is no less real or
threatening. In addition, women and the lower classes appear to be the
major threat to this "disruption" of democracy as established governments
aim to strengthen the legitimacy and cohesion of society. Therefore, it is
essential to consider the effect of this imaginary network on the formation
of gender identity as the relativism with which society approaches difference continues to expand in a vicious cycle of violence.

A BEAUTIFUL FREAK SHOW: PRIMEIRO ATO'S *GERALDAS E AVENCAS*

Founded in Belo Horizonte in 1983 by four dancers from different backgrounds (classical dance, modern dance, jazz, and theater), the primary

purpose of Primeiro Ato was to create a dance company in search of a more open language for performance that focused on a collaborative process of creation. The members of Primeiro Ato wanted to create art that responded to many possibilities and to bring dance to the street, stages, schools, and any other place where they could reach vast numbers of people. Currently under the direction of one of the founding members, Suely Machado, the company continues to search for performative actions that construct new models for the stage that will awaken the spectator's consciousness about the world around us. Its method is based on the creation of emotions though carefully crafted gestures rather than showcasing virtuoso dance moves. As Machado states, the thread that connects their performances is, above all, "that they speak of human essence, [and that] we present situations necessary for humanity to consider. All our performances are a reflection on the world in which we live. My project is to touch people, to touch their hearts." [16] Thus, dance becomes a moment of transformation, a tool for human communication concretized through the bodies of the dancers onstage.

The theatrical representation of the dancer's body as a stand-in for preconceptions of beauty and perfection becomes the main critique of the piece *Geraldas e Avencas*.[17] The performance focuses on the "plastification," standardization, and overpowering of an imposed aesthetics of beauty and perfection in modern society. With a cast of seven dancers chosen specifically to comment on the remarkable diversity of Brazilians, the piece seeks to highlight, through dance, a not so obvious notion of beauty and difference. I must also emphasize that Primeiro Ato is also known for working with nontraditional dancers. This means that Machado, as artistic director, actively seeks dancers that range from twenty to fifty-five years of age, of all racial backgrounds, with any type of body. This has often led to their pieces being characterized in the media as "too heterogeneous," as this is unheard of in most dance companies in the world. In a way, the company embraces a categorization of freakness that it has come to embody in the world of dance. *Geraldas e Avencas* consists of a series of scenes on a very simple stage: a white set with a large screen on the back; a second, smaller screen to one side; a series of mirrors on the opposite side; and on the back a ballet bar. There is no cohesive narrative, only an exploration of emotions through movements set to an original soundtrack composed by Zeca Baleiro.[18] The dancers are dressed in neutral tones, with simple outfits of loose pants, t-shirts for the men, and half camisoles for the women. At times, certain body parts are highlighted with different colored balloons inside their clothes. The focus is solely on their gestures and movements.

The exploration of this theme is particularly significant for the world of dance. Like theater, dance is a performative discourse that finds its grounding on the body in movement through space. In other words, politics of the body and representation are at the forefront of this genre and become an inescapable issue, especially in a discussion around issues of gender and feminist criticism. As we approach the piece from this angle, representation and identity are primary concepts for consideration. From this perspective, the artistic practice of dance has traditionally been a space in which hegemonic models of what constitutes femininity (and masculinity) have accumulated, gradually contributing to a politics of representation of the female body on and off the stage. The symbolic construction of the female body of the dancer has been, especially in the western imaginary, the idealized woman—a model of perfection that is certainly unachievable for most individuals.[19] This notion of feminine perfection is also crossed by class consciousness, as ballet established, along with a standard for an aesthetic body, a mode of movement associated with aristocratic elegance, a mode of action on the stage, a mode of feminine costume, and so on that constituted (in particular historical periods) the ideal feminine identity. *Geraldas e Avencas*, thus, along with the premises that comprise Primeiro Ato, disputes this model of dance, for "it is against this idealized model that contemporary dance . . . emerges as a model for renewal in avant-garde dance and against which different trends of modern dance are positioning themselves, and with them the first generations of modernizing matriarchs."[20] In this way, this performance contributes to the development of new critical models that take into account a more diverse and inclusive notion of dance, from a perspective of gender that seeks to dewesternize modern conceptions of this art form and insert it beyond an upper-class consumption that maintains it within an aura of high art.

Geraldas e Avencas begins with the principal dancer, Marcela Rosa, coming onstage dressed in a tight pencil skirt, a half camisole that displays her taught abdomen, and one high-heeled shoe on her foot. She has two red balloons inside her camisole on top of her breasts. With a big smile, she addresses the audience, welcoming it to the show with a simple "Good evening, thank you for coming." The audience responds, and she continues to repeat herself, causing laughter, until her words become a mechanized message that begins to break down. Her movements become automatic, her words lack order, and she seems disoriented. Eventually, other dancers come to the stage. They also have balloons that emphasize certain parts of their bodies: hips, buttocks, and breasts for the women and shoulders for the man. They all compete to be the center of attention, showing off their plastic attributes. The scene ends with the dancers standing before the mirrors, which further distort their images, admiring themselves. With this opening, the performance brings to the forefront a questioning of the manipulation of beauty and the contemporary "cult of the body," which aims to create so-called perfection by any means possible. An idea that closely follows Umberto Eco's perception of beauty as something that can also be morally repugnant. Thus, the dancers' bodies appear as grotesque deformations that reflect the invalidity of established norms of beauty. Additionally, as Ileana Diéguez has established through her work on liminalilty, a grotesque aesthetics can prove to be a very powerful tool in performance, as it acts as a disorganizing agent that destabilizes and problematizes the established canon of beauty. Through the aesthetics of the grotesque the body is configured as a space of hybridity, allowing for the emergence of that which has been hidden and degraded as social "dirt" and "ugliness."[21] Thus, artistic conventions that rely on such aesthetics constitute a subversion of hegemonic conventions, as the corporeal becomes a distorting mirror for established patterns of the "normal." The notion of beauty that we see before us is an exaggeration of established parameters: big breasts, protuberant buttocks, lots of makeup, and wide shoulders for the man. The dancers appear to be aberrant Barbie dolls (freak Barbies) consumed by their appearance.

The appearance of these bodies onstage offers an incisive critique that points to the intersectionality between the politics of representation and a subjugated feminine body. Standardized beauty is revealed as a cruel regime that seeks to control the bodies of individuals in search of a goal (perfection) that can only be achieved through consumerism and self-regulation. The dancers appear as automata that lack control over their own bodies (or whose control is breaking down) as they attempt to bring a focus to their bodies. The primary referent here is cosmetic surgery as a modern cultural institution that fetishizes the body under the guise of a normalizing function. As Garland-Thomson explains, "[C]osmetic surgery, driven by gender ideology and market forces, now enforces feminine body standards and standardizes female bodies toward what I have called the 'normate'— the corporeal incarnation of culture's collective, unmarked, normative characteristics."[22] In the performance, though, the cosmetic goal of creating an unmarked body that fits into the "normal" is transformed into bodies of excess that appear ridiculous. The dismantling of normalcy is evident: modified bodies that are meant to appear as a sculpted ideal of neutral, regular, nonparticular (deracialized and deethnicized) feminine identity become an exercise of mutation.

Fig. 14. *Geraldas e Avencas*. Dancers Ana Virgínia Guimarães, Thiago Oliveira, Danny Maia, and Luciana Lanza. Photo by Guto Muniz.

This idea is particularly relevant in the context of Brazilian society, as "Brazil has just surpassed the U.S. as the place with the most cosmetic surgeries performed in the world, even though it has fewer people and collectively less disposable income than the U.S."[23] As many critics have pointed out, in Brazil cosmetic surgery has become a status symbol a lucrative industry that capitalizes on a particular image of beauty that is being pushed on society.[24] Thus, bodily alteration becomes entangled with class politics: "While a history of marginalized people would need to focus on the body in pain and as the subject of violence, disembodiment has typically been a privilege accorded to those who are wealthy and powerful enough literally to 'forget' their fleshy origins."[25] The modified body, then, as a normative practice, serves those who have the means to "unmark" their bodies, whereas the unmodified body appears as unnatural and abnormal. As a "cult of the body," cosmetic surgery veers away from feminist attempts to increase the acceptance of difference and diversity of all body types and instead implants an idealized form as the normative referent for beauty. In the performance, the "out of control" bodies that first appear on the stage provide a lens through which to consider the effect that these hegemonic aesthetic forms have had on individual agency. In a country that considers cosmetic procedures to be investments, the actions in the performance call out the image of beauty that is being sold: the issue is not a "right to be beautiful" but a questioning of the image that is sold as accepted beauty.[26]

The "plastification" and marketing of beauty is clearly a feminist and class issue, and this policing of women's bodies becomes more significant on Brazil's current political stage. Since the impeachment of Dilma Rousseff, which almost all feminist media outlets agree was sexist and discriminatory, the future of women's rights in Brazil seems bleak. Of particular importance is the issue of violence against women, an endemic issue with widespread acceptance in society. There is a moment in *Geraldas e Avencas* that speaks to this issue, as it associates violence with the "cult of the body" I have discussed. Rosa, the principal dancer, comes onstage wearing a flesh-colored two-piece suit. It makes her appear nude. She carries a large, folded poster in her hands, and as she opens it, it reveals a beautiful model posing in sexy lingerie. She places the poster in front of her body, exposing several holes that have been cut out: her eyes, one breast, the hip, and the shoulder. The accompanying music starts with a very soft and sensual melody, as Rosa performs slow movements that exhibit the model's "damaged" body instead of her own. She begins to "inhabit" the poster as she sensually inserts her fingers into the holes in the eyes, a leg into the hip, one arm into the shoulder, and another into the hole on the breast. As she becomes this poster, the lights change to a reddish color and the music becomes more aggressive and loud. Her sensual movements are transformed into violent fits that shake her entire body. The sexualized female body becomes a macabre dance that seeks to expose an intrinsic social violence on feminine identity.

The aggressiveness of this dance reveals the violence that accompanies a societal "cult of the body" that not only controls the aesthetics of feminine identity but is often accompanied by political control over the female body. For example, in an article in *The Guardian*, Ani Hao explains that in Brazil:

Prior to the impeachment, politicians on all sides had passed a raft of bills chipping away at women's rights, including a bill to define personhood from the moment of conception, and another to define "family" in the constitution as the union of a man and woman and their child. Other bills were introduced to prohibit the discussion of gender in the National Education Plan, and to further criminalise legal abortion for victims of rape. There were moves to make it difficult to access emergency contraception, and to increase the penalty for abortion in the wake of the Zika virus.[27]

Fig. 15. *Geraldas e Avencas*. Dancer Marcela Rosa. Photo by Guto Muniz.

Hundreds of women across Brazil have gathered to protest against sexist bills that continue to restrict female agency in a society that is willing to limit the rights of women and leave them unprotected against the countless cases of violence and rape across the country. Thus, the female body is left vulnerable to violence as the media and politics present it as something on which negotiations that benefit a patriarchal system can happen. Woman is made into a freak as her body is exhibited as a receptacle on which fears about traditional family values, sexuality, identity, and so on are inscribed. In other words, she needs to be controlled. This idea is very close to what Luce Irigaray describes when she states that women who live under patriarchal capitalism become objects of exchange by and for men: a mere commodity. Women, therefore, have no inherent value other than their appeal to men: "[I]n order for a product—a woman?—to have value, two men, at least, have to invest (in) her."[28] With her sexy, freaky dance on the stage, Rosa inserts her body into a projected image of feminine sexuality for consumption. The image is then dismantled, as desire becomes aggression, in an effort to denounce not only an oppressive patriarchal system but also a neoliberal system that only seeks to gain economic power from desired female bodies.

The sexualized body as a marketing tool creates narrative models that look to function as regulators of desiring subjectivity. This establishes an

economic social order that controls the methods through which we are supposed to react to sexual desire. In other words, the market decides what
constitutes the ideal vehicle for sexual fantasies, sexual reproduction, sexual dysfunction, and so on. Paul B. Preciado (Beatriz Preciado) has fittingly
explored this idea and points out:

> The new global corporations produce nothing. Their only goal is the
> accumulation and management of patents in order to control the (re)
> production of bodies and pleasures. This politics of *copyright*, which
> oversees the sexualizing of production and the conversion of life
> into information, is what I've called *pharmacoporn politics*; its pur-
> pose is to transform your ass and mine, or rather, your desire and
> mine, into abstract profits. Your clitoris and my cock are subjected to
> the same fate as an ear of corn, given the way that multinationals
> employ genetic engineering to produce new transgenic strains
> whose seeds will be infertile. In the same way that the multination-
> als are currently controlling world production of corn thanks to the
> privatization of germoplasms, but are also busy—and this is
> primordial—transforming the entire planet into potential consum-
> ers of the new transgenic seeds (which are themselves infertile), the
> pharmacopornographic industry is striving for the exponential con-
> trol and production of your desiring body.[29]

Similar to what Violeta Luna proposed in the previous chapter, the "pharmacopornographic industry" is transforming the natural order of things
into a man-made plasticized reality that presents itself as the imposed normal. Because of this, *Geraldas e Avencas* turns to an intervening image of
womanhood with this paper cutout figure, which is partly made of real
body parts, to present the audience with the violence that is contained
within this manifestation of desired femininity. As the music rises to the
point of being almost a cacophony of instruments, the dancer's movements
become more mechanical and forceful. It is an aesthetic contradiction that
moves from the sensual to the abhorrent, signaling the often overshadowed
violence that is enclosed in marketed images of female beauty. In this way,
the performance provides a reversal of aesthetic normativity: society
praises certain manipulated bodies as referents for perfection while other
physical differences are removed as marked, freak bodies. Perfection becomes a freak difference that threatens female bodies.

This sort of violence is counterposed in the performance with scenes
that explore beauty beyond body politics, even as it continues to provide a

critique of human relations. In one of the final scenes in the piece, a male and a female dancer appear onstage and perform a very soft and tender dance. They are dressed in neutral colors as a soft bossa-nova-style lullaby plays. Their movements are contained close to the floor, as they elegantly drag their bodies across the space, maintaining very deep eye contact. Their movements appear as if they are grounded on the floor, possibly a reference to being close to the earth, to their origins. The aesthetic narrative tells a sort of love story in which the man and woman take turns cradling each other's bodies. This sort of dance technique is typical of Machado's choreography, as she explains: "The aesthetic message must be subtle, with minimal movement that has deep meaning. My technique includes a body that speaks through gesture, using art as a tool to get somewhere specific." The gestures in this scene show a very loving acceptance of each other as they perform a dance in which each literally supports the other's body.

Halfway through the scene, the pair of dancers is contrasted to a second couple that comes in. This female dancer has the red balloons on her chest and buttocks, and the male dancer moves seductively around her. They are standing, make no eye contact, and he constantly touches different parts of her body. The female dancer moves in a mechanized way, with very stiff limbs, appearing almost like a zombie, a dead body on the stage. Instead of supporting each other's bodies, the male dancer carries her body around the stage. The first couple exits, and the music transitions to a more festive sound. Two more female dancers appear in the background, with their own sets of balloon breasts, and the choreography becomes an exaggerated set of "tropical" movements that borders on the ridiculous. The contrast between these two couples is at the center of the piece's prevailing message. They reflect human relations based on the physical and the spiritual, exalting the possibilities for a better world. Machado explains: "In the pursuit of perfection people maim their bodies and even invalidate themselves to have a perfect body, which is impossible. I have a scene that references paths to happiness, like a self-help book. You can change everything about your appearance, but your soul is not there. Just as an imperfect body can dance, we want to show that anything is possible. The pursuit of perfection will maul your essence."The scene with the first two dancers provides an example of the utopic vision that Machado imagines as a possibility.

It is further developed through the following scene, in which a male dancer appears alone and climbs on the ballet bar at the back of the stage. As he dances, the lights project a set of wings on his back. He is performing as an otherworldly angel that could be associated with the soul (What happens to the body after death?). A second male dancer comes in and performs very close to the ground, under the first dancer. It is a very moving image of the possible connection that must be established between body and soul, a connection that seems to be impossible in the modern world. At the same time, there is an emphasis on the importance of the body itself, which, as Jean-Luc Nancy explains, is necessary to understand the "revelations" of the divine: "Why, then a body? Because only a body can be cut down or raised up, because only a body can touch or not touch. A spirit can do nothing of the sort. A 'pure spirit' gives only a formal and empty index of a presence entirely closed in on itself. A body opens this presence; it presents it; it puts presence outside of itself; it moves presence away from itself, and, by that very fact, it brings others along with it."[30] In a society that constantly wants to manufacture and transform the body, there is the possibility of losing the interbody connections that are at the core of a functioning social system. Humanity's difficulty in dealing with imperfection can only lead to isolated bodies that lack the capacity for interaction and connectivity. How can a body "bring others along with it" when it is impossible to maintain a relationship of equals among bodies in a system that privileges certain ideals above others? This does not imply that *Geraldas e Avencas* seeks to erase bodily difference to find a utopia of sameness. On the contrary, there is a revalorization of what constitutes difference. As Machado explains, "There is an appreciation and theorization of difference. For me, difference—or what is considered an aberration or a social, ethnic, educational failure—is not difference. It is a wealth. If my artistic philosophy is to reflect on the world in which I live, how can I abolish differences, anomalies, and counterpoints?" This scene in *Geraldas e Avencas* presents a body that seeks to establish a connection to its soul in order to then be able to fulfill its functions in society as one of many different bodies. Interestingly, Alex Dias, a fifty-something dancer who would be considered too old to perform by traditional dance standards, is the dancer who performs with wings. Thiago Oliveira, a dancer who suffered a serious accident that affected his face and body, accompanies him. Together they present an ideal moment of the integration of body and soul that leads to the possibility of a reconfiguration of perfection as it implies an acceptance of difference in order to achieve an ideal state of being.

It is, indeed, a utopic moment, which is at the core of almost all the pieces that Primeiro Ato has developed throughout their history. The company's mission is to provide a space for shared experience and hope, even if it is only for a fleeting moment of performance: "I want to lay bare the soul, the human essence, not the body. . . . Baring the soul is not choreography; dance is living at the present time," explains Machado.[31] In *Geraldas e*

Avencas, that ephemeral moment in the dance that allows for the "baring of the soul" is the climax of the piece, after the possible connection between body and soul has been established and there is a renewed sense of hope in human relations beyond the corporeal. In the closing, the final gesture actively points toward a better world. The dancers come together in a circle, holding hands. The sounds of "Flor no quintal" (Flower in the Yard) can be heard, a very upbeat song about the beauty found in nature. The dancers perform delicate movements as they dance in the circle, with smiles on their faces and deep eye contact with one another. Dance scholar Nancy Ruyter analyzes this final scene as the forming of community: "The piece has evolved from the image of the individual artist, drawing attention to herself and challenging the audience to respond, until the unifying movement presented by the seven dancers, who have left behind their fixation with the presentation and individual fame to merge with the group, to form a community."[32] It is a very moving moment that ends the performance. This final scene can be better understood through Jill Dolan's notion of utopian performatives, "small but profound moments in which performance calls the attention of the audience in a way that lifts everyone slightly above the present, into a hopeful feeling of what the world might be like if every moment of our lives were as emotionally voluminous, generous aesthetically striking, and intersubjectively intense."[33] As she further explains, it is an important moment that provides deep pleasure for the audience, which is aware that even if the performance itself cannot change the world, it can "certainly change the people who feel it."[34]

Geraldas e Avencas allows for such an affective moment of constructed utopia as it moves the audience from intense images of despair and violence against the different body to a final moment of community and acceptance. The performance is about hope, which moves it away from becoming a vacuous critique of bodily alterations in a world that values a heteronormative ideal of normalizing beauty over difference. The body in this performance is the stage itself on which social change can be performed. In other words, the body is more than a natural and physiological entity; it is more than an individual's body. Instead it is a social body that moves toward action, a motivated body that can be in touch with the soul and all emotions and can be mobilized toward social transformation. The freak body, in this case, is denounced as a constructed body modeled on a standard practice of normalcy as beauty—a confusion brought on by a capitalist aesthetic in which the body and other commodities are interchangeable and consumerism becomes our core identity. In this way, the colonial and patriarchal model that establishes the norms for a gendered body is dismantled, as the "different" body is no longer the object/receptacle of unacceptable otherness. Instead, difference appears onstage as the only hope for acceptance and the possibility of a better world.

THE ENFREAKMENT OF THE WORKING CLASS: KATIA TIRADO'S
EL BRILLO EN LA NEGRURA DE SOBREVIVIR

Considering the utopic vision that Primeiro Ato offers for a body that is no longer defined by categories of power and domination, it is necessary to further consider the implications that class consciousness has on the construction of the body itself. For this purpose, I turn to Mexican performance artist Katia Tirado and her 2015 *El brillo en la negrura de sobrevivir* (The Brightness in the Darkness of Survival). German cabaret, Butoh, and post-porn performance art (e.g., the work of Annie Sprinke, with whom she has collaborated in the past) heavily influence Tirado's work. Her greater concern is the construction of gender identity, and through performance art Tirado disseminates what she understands as "the female dimension in a phallocentric culture." [35] Katia Tirado belongs to a new generation of performance artists, mostly women, who are associated with cultural spaces such as the Ex-Teresa Arte Actual.[36] Among these artists are Lorena Wolffer, Lorena Orozco, Doris Steinbichler, Pilar Villela, Emma Villanueva, Niña Yhared, and La Congelada de Uva. Unlike past generations of *performeras*, however, most of these artists focus on themes around the body as a vulnerable entity: its relationship with technology, national identity, urban culture, mass and popular culture, violence, and migration. They are a generation affected by major political changes but who cling to a personal politics that relates, in an almost isolated manner, to social change. Performance art scholar Antonio Prieto-Stambaugh elaborates on this.

> Tirado . . . belong[s] to a generation that saw encouraging developments such as the neo-Zapatista uprising, an increasingly vocal, if conflictive, civil society, and the crumbling of the PRI's hegemony. On the downside, those years also saw the institutionalization of neoliberal policies best represented by NAFTA, accompanied by the weakening of national sovereignty understood as the ability to control resources. The general crisis saw symptomatic representation in urban violence at nearly uncontrollable levels, the crippling of public education during the UNAM strike, and the strengthening of drug cartels. These critical issues went nearly unaddressed by the

majority of young conceptual artists who are loath to be labeled as political. And while conceptual performance during the 1970's and early 1980's was often highly politicized, the next generation rebelled against this trend, preferring to adopt an art for art's sake position, or to indulge in actions of esoteric intimacy.[37]

The depoliticization of the new generation of conceptual artists allows for the adoption of an artistic approach founded on images and movement rather than focusing on the word. This is interestingly elaborated in Tirado's piece *El brillo en la negrura de sobrevivir*, where words are literally transformed into images.

In this piece, the artist has collected stories from several of the workers who perform the everyday duties of the space in which the performance will take place. For the performance I attended, the space was the CENART in Mexico City, where Tirado told the stories of a security guard, maintenance personnel, and a secretary.[38] Tirado stands in a small performance space outdoors, dressed in an apron with nothing underneath. Two tattoo artists, Victoria Martínez and Adrián Velicu, sit near her with their work materials. Throughout the performance, Tirado narrates the stories to the two artists, who proceed to create images on "quilts" made of pigskin on which the individual stories take on new life. Tirado hangs the skins using a needle and a thick thread, which unites them, creating a partition on the sides of the performance space. She call this process and the ensuing piece *Variaciones sobre Xipetotec* (Variations on Xipetotec), a reference to the Aztec god of regeneration. As Tirado explains, this god "spends much of his time on earth borrowing the skin of others to hide his own flayed and bloody body. . . . He represents fertility and sacrifice. With the skin of those sacrifices they would then make tamales so that everyone could eat. Ritual anthropophagy" (quoted from the program notes).[39] The ultimate end of the performance is cooking the skins to make *chicharrón*, which is then handed to the audience to consume, or, as Tirado explains, "It is a civic ritual of collection and consumption of memories translated and represented by the tattoo artist to turn them into an anthropophagic image."

The various elements of this provocative performance require a sociopolitical reading of class, memory, and representation in the consumption of bodies by the social order. I claim that the stories of the individuals that are read throughout the performance create an image of the working class as the urban masses located outside capitalist relations precisely because they are unable to create a decent living following the norms established by a neoliberal system of production. Hence the working class is perceived

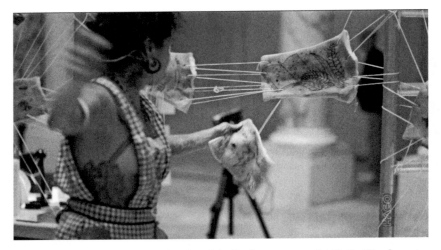

Fig. 16. *El brillo en la negrura de sobrevivir*. Performance artist Katia Tirado puts together the quilt made of pig skins.

by the social order as a damaged body, often made visible though the illness, starvation, and physical injuries brought on by economic hardship. The vision of the working class that this performance offers responds to the particular understanding of class and social stratification that pervades in Mexican society, which can be interpreted following what Zygmunt Bauman describes as "human waste," the outcasts produced by postindustrial, globalized capital. The stories of these individuals are the "hidden" stories of society, those whose work does not benefit their own individual lives but a system that consumes and rejects them. In the performance, there is an acknowledgment of the fluidity that juxtaposes bodies damaged by a failed economic system with freakishness—dehumanized bodies that are relegated to isolation and the loss of self. Tirado's performance seeks to transform this perception by bringing the stories to the forefront of a communal action that reconstructs the forgotten, marginalized body of the working-class individual into an artistic form that nourishes all those present.

Katia Tirado's relationship with the freak body is one of positive dissidence against a power structure that seeks to control behavior and physical appearance. As Tirado explains, the importance that she places on freak aesthetics is directly related to imposed normativity as an equation of power and the regulation of power: "To me, what constitutes the freak is

what comes out of those regulated parameters imposed by power structures. And in that sense, all of my art is freak, because everything I've done
tries, at least if not to fracture, to destabilize those regulations." Thus, her
artistic trajectory is characterized by the constant of bodily deformations
and interventions that seek to destabilize the "normal" body as represented
by established norms. In the case of her own concerns, those normative
standards respond to the imperialist powers established since colonial
times, such as Catholic religion and western cultural values. Tirado focuses
on the poetics of the body as a space that is often repressed and controlled
for the purposes of implanting the normativity that is conceived and or-
chestrated through the imaginaries of hegemonic power.

Examples of this freak aesthetic can be found throughout her work: *Ex-
hivilización/Las Perras en celo,* in which she recontextualizes Mexican wrestling through a "phallic" match between two savage beings (Tirado and a
collaborator, who appear naked in the ring wearing wrestling masks, with
their vaginas connected by a tube); *Lady Luck,* which presents a modern-
day, multilimbed Kali to address the relationship between chance, fortune,
and the body; and many other examples. In this particular performance,
Tirado confronts the audience with the words of individuals that are denied entry into the hegemonic discourses of Mexican society: the working-
class individuals. According to 2013 data from Mexico's statistics institute,
INEGI (Instituto Nacional de Estadística y Geografía), the middle class is
not quite as large as some had thought. It encompasses 39.2 percent of the
population (others have argued that at least half the population is middle
class). The figure represents a four-percentage-point increase from 2000 to
2010, which does not sound like very much, although it may have been
depressed by the impact of the 2008–9 global financial crisis. Only 1.7 percent of the population is considered upper class, while 59.1 percent is lower
class. This doesn't necessarily mean that the lower classes live in poverty,
but they are more likely to sink into poverty when adversity strikes. The
individuals whose stories Tirado narrates fit into this 59.1 percent, and so
their stories are plagued with instances of resistance to a capitalist society
that constantly dehumanizes them.

Tirado calls these stories "Historias de resilencia" (Stories of Resilience)
because of the "ability for adaptation of a living being to a disturbing agent
or an adverse condition or situation."[40] For example, there is the story of
René, the head of maintenance at the CENART. In his interview he told
Tirado that his presence is indispensable because of his ability to listen to
others and create conflict resolution.

> Everything started when he was a young man working at the Museum of Popular Art, he says that constantly seeing the *alebrijes*, fantastic animals that are invented, gave him the idea that everything can be created in this life and that just as they invent *alebrijes* that do not exist, people can invent solutions that do not exist anywhere but the imagination. If one observes enough what happens around and if one takes into account equally all that are involved, this can happen.[41]

René's utopic vision of dealing with conflict is a hopeful image that belies the tragic economic situation Mexico faces today. As a matter of fact, it continues the political machinations that aim to provide a false sense of hope by pushing the working class into the cliché sentiment that with hard work everything is possible. Yet Tirado's performance aims to be a "reliable source" for those voices that remain hidden but are what make institutions such as the CENART function. She is not trying to present her own perspective on the state of the people who work at the CENART but to transmit their feelings and emotions. Therefore, the pride that René feels at being a source of counsel to his fellow workers and his family is the story that he wants told. Of course, there is the central problem that what the audience encounters in the performance is Tirado telling a story that has been filtered through her own imaginary to be plastered as an image filtered through the tattoo artists. René's own physical presence is nowhere to be found.[42] Nevertheless, that is the point. The only way we hear the voices of the marginalized is through a multitude of filters that create an image for consumption. As consumers, we don't want to hear about those whose hard work creates the product; we are more concerned with the marketing strategies that lead us to desire that product. As Argentine cultural critic Beatriz Sarlo has explained, the rules of the market have created a false sense of unity in acquiring objects while furthering the sense of class division.

> These days, the subject in a position to enter the market with enough money to participate as a consumer is a type of *collector in reverse*. Instead of collecting the things themselves, she collects the acts of acquiring things. . . . At the opposite pole from collectors in reverse are those excluded from the market, who range from those who can at any rate dream of imaginary consumption to those so excluded that poverty pens them in, confining them to the most minimal of fantasies.[43]

Following this logic, Tirado has a clear purpose: to interrupt the machines of power in order to clutter the political map of the possible. René's story is a clear indication of this: if the political and economic system will not help his immediate community, he will do anything within his means to step in and disrupt the obstacles placed on the working class by a disinterested political system. It doesn't solve the problem, but it makes the problem evident.

The story of Ana María is an elaboration of this idea. Ana María is a secretary at the institution who talks about how her role as caregiver to her family has extended into that of an improvised nurse to those around her. Because most of the people within her circle have limited resources, she has taken upon herself the task of finding out which generic medications are just as good as the name-brand competitors. Now "she is regularly consulted by patients who know her and ask her to assist them and recommend which cheaper drugs are effective. She clarifies that she does not prescribe medication, but with the prescriptions of doctors she only facilitates access to medicines." This particular story is noteworthy because it emphasizes the negotiations that are often made in relation to gender and class. It is very much in line with Chela Sandoval's *Methodology of the Oppressed*, where she defines people living in today's late capitalist, postmodern society as "citizen subject-agents" who have the capacity to work toward establishing a more equal and democratic society. After all, in a democratic society, it is difficult to speak of the voice of the people when the dominant discourse that rules that society is neoliberalism. Therefore, how can one speak of democracy when multinational corporations control the means of production, exchange, publicity, transportation, and communication, which is in turn reinforced by control of the press, advertising agencies, and marketing propaganda. Thus, Sandoval's notion of "decolonial love" helps us understand the political struggle against the structure of dehumanization as a form of positive desire, as expressed in the simple actions told in the stories of *El brillo en la negrura de sobrevivir*. Although Sandoval is inspired by the raw, limitless, and transformative feeling attributed to idealized romantic love, the Barthesian formulation of love that Sandoval adopts and elaborates is a politicized, social, and revolutionary love. She writes:

> Romantic love provides one kind of entry to a form of being that breaks the citizen-subject free from the ties that bind being, to thus enter the differential mode of consciousness, or to enter what Barthes perhaps better describes as "the gentleness of the abyss." . . . It is a

coming to a utopian nonsite, a no-place where everything is possible—but only in exchange for the pain of the crossing.[44]

Love as social movement is the nonsite beyond the individualized bliss of romantic love. It is the no-place that is precisely outside of, or at least not subject to, the laws of discourse that direct agency and blind possibility. Indeed, the pain of the crossing to this nonsite—through stages of nonbeing to being to oppositional being (in all its myriad forms) and sometimes back—is the pain that Sandoval deciphers in the political histories of oppressed subjects. It is a pain whose intricacies have produced even more intricate modes of survival, resistance, knowing, and being.

The fact that René and Ana María's testimonies are also captured by artists onto pigskins furthers the symbolic impact of the piece, as several levels of artistic hierarchy function within the performance to exemplify the power structures that control the economic system in the country. In addition, the act of tattooing onto the skins becomes an almost bloody celebration of others' lives, a translation of a lived life onto an image. Even though tattooing is not commonly thought of as an artistic practice, for Katia Tirado it is an important part of her identity as a performer.[45] It is the integration of art on the body in a way that escapes hegemonic control as she transgresses and reinvents her physical self. She observes in her personal performance notes that the body "is a territory of affirmation of identity." Her assertion is in line with the space that tattoos occupy in the modern world—no longer a taboo but living art in the name of self-expression as a counterculture. It is through these markings on the skin that expressions of cultural and individual identity are often expressed (and read). In other words, contemporary individuals "are symbolically illustrating that they are in control of their lives as well as negating the importance of the body in mass culture."[46] Tirado uses tattooing as a performance practice that helps her to defy the classism that separates high art from popular culture. In other words, she attempts to nullify the classist ideas that separate the genius quality of high art from the utilitarian and entertainment qualities associated with popular culture.

I find this particularly interesting because of the associations it produces, especially in Mexico, of the working class with Marx's lumpenproletariat. In Marxist terms, the lumpenproletariat is defined by its location outside the relations of production. Among the numerous outcasts that Marx identifies as its members are vagabonds, pickpockets, gamblers, escaped galley slaves, ragpickers, tinkers, and beggars. That is to say, this class comprises "that whole undefined, dissolute, kicked-about mass that the Frenchmen style 'la Bohème.'"[47] It is clear, then, that the lumpenprole-tariat is an unproductive force, and its members make a living by means of what they can obtain (by begging, stealing, or somehow procuring) from the rest of society. In that sense, there is a clear parallel with how Mexican society today views their majority: as pariahs that should be cast to the bot-tom of the economic ladder because they have not been able to make the system work for them. The fact that they create their own system of pro-ductivity outside the norms makes the lower classes even more dangerous. Furthermore, unlike the proletariat—a modern class that emerged out of the Industrial Revolution—the lumpenproletariat has existed in all modes of production since there have always been outcasts excluded from rela-tions of production, whether they were ancient, feudal, or capitalist. This underlines the idea of the lumpenproletariat as a remnant that will not go away and refuses to die.

It should be recognized here that Marx's distinction between proletariat and lumpenproletariat is no longer as clear-cut as it may have been when he formulated it. In late capitalist society the boundaries between these two classes have become blurred, and the points of reference that define them have changed. Notions such as permanent employment and industrial work (which defined the proletariat) and the reserve army of labor (a func-tion fulfilled by the lumpenproletariat, who could be called in to replace workers) have disappeared. Zygmunt Bauman furthers this idea.

> Where the prefix "un" in "unemployment" used to suggest a depar-ture from the norm—as in "unhealthy" or "unwell"—there is no such suggestion in the notion of "redundancy." No inkling of abnor-mality, anomaly, spell of ill-health or a momentary slip. "Redun-dancy" whispers permanence and hints at the ordinariness of the condition. It names a condition without offering a ready-to-use ant-onym. It suggests a new shape of current normality and the shape of things that are imminent and bound to stay as they are.[48]

Bauman is here referring to the new ways in which the lumpenproletariat is expressed in our globalized and postindustrial society—what he calls elsewhere "liquid modernity," in which the "society of producers" has given way to the "society of consumers" and where those who are inad-equate consumers no longer have a social role to fulfill. This leads to the appearance of what Bauman calls "wasted lives," a concept that acquires great significance in the Latin American economic scene if one considers the notion of underemployment. Underemployment, which is defined as the situation of an individual who works less than thirty-five hours a week but wants to work more, is a category often omitted from the statistics of employment. This can be explained by the scarcity of data on underemployment and by the fact that labor statistics treat it as employment, and thus its numbers may not create as much expectation as those of unemployment. Either way, it expands the concept of waste to members of the middle class who cannot find work in their chosen professions (or not enough hours to work) and often take jobs identified with the working class.

That is to say, capitalism not only produces vast quantities of industrial and commercial waste but also waste in the form of humans: the outcasts, the pariahs, and the excluded who have been pushed outside the fields of production and consumerism. A view of the lumpenproletariat as waste may not be a particularly novel idea, since it is already inherent in Marx, who used the term *refuse* to categorize this class. But Marx was expressing his negative views about a class he often saw as opposed to communist revolution. Bauman is describing what he sees as the negative consequences of the changes in industrial production and the organization of labor that have taken place over the past three decades. In other words, waste is not defined by the intrinsic qualities of an object (in this case, a class of people) but is a matter of appreciation. Thus, the new global order produces entire categories of people who are defined as "superfluous" to the system.

The notion of the freak that takes hold in Tirado's performance is directly related to the idea of the working class as waste. The individuals are not treated as freaks by Tirado, who tells their stories and projects them as symbols on a quilted skin, but their bodies are enfreaked by a social and economic system that marginalizes them because of their inability to function "properly" within consumer society. In the performance, the tattoo artists are recovering these "wasted lives" and transforming them into a permanent image onto a skin to be consumed by those who are seeing and hearing the stories. At the same time, there was an additional element of consumption in the performance at the CENART: the primarily middle- and upper-class audience that came to see the performance and was consuming the stories of the marginalized. The CENART is an art school that caters primarily to the middle and upper classes (as those are the privileged majority that can devote their studies to the fine arts in a country fraught with unemployment), and the spectators that attended this performance were primarily students and scholars of performance art. For this reason, there was an awareness of their unfamiliarity with the individuals' stories and lives—a recognition of the prominence that was given to people who did not have this acceptance in "real life." Tirado's performance, then, "pone el brillo," or "makes bright," the existence and lives of those who have been obscured on the margins of the social order. Because their stories *are* being told in their own words (even as they are spoken by Tirado), people like René and Ana María are subverting their categorization as "waste" by insisting on the validity of their lives.

In a way, one could say that Tirado is using their particular invisibility and erasure as a way to make the lives and experiences of others on the margins visible. It is a sort of transference of perceived waste into appreciated existence. Through an ephemeral act of performance Tirado establishes a direct connection with those on the margins, and in doing so she creates an equation that forces those who are watching to experience a fleeting connection or at least to recognize how much society (and in turn, ourselves) makes invisible the validity of others' lives. It is an exercise in the affinity of survival in a neoliberal system that continually claims and destroys the possibility for existence outside consumerism. Tirado artistically develops perceived lives of misfortune from a place that generates power and seeks to represent a completed cycle. The tattoos on the skins are that: they condense in an image a lived experience or lived cycle, marking its completion. That is the purpose of Xipetote *within* the tattoos: Katia Tirado is borrowing skins, using the skins of others to navigate the world.

CIRCUITS OF INVISIBILITY: *PIEDRA* BY REGINA JOSÉ GALINDO

As we have seen thus far, the body is a repository of metaphors, and within its function of global exchange, its limits of fragility and destruction, the body serves as a way of dramatizing the social text. Olivier Mongin, in his important study on film and modernity, has said that there is currently "an economy of images of violence . . . [in which the subject] observes an imaginary violence in a laboratory, a violence *in vitro* which does not concern him or her."[49] This position, which is in dialogue with Susan Sontag's notions concerning war photography (in *Regarding the Pain of Others*), refers to media consumption of images based on the suffering of the other. The image consumed may cause pain and sometimes elicit compassion. Yet, as images of violence are adjusted to the expectations of a market economy (which allows viewers that are sensitive to the phenomenon of violence the possibility of not having to *deal with it* closely), our protected emotional responses become a mechanism of convenient defense against this violence. In other words, Sontag warns us that we have become, "citizens of modernity, consumers of violence as spectacle, adepts of proximity without risk."[50]

Within the economy of representation, the brutalized body has a complicated yet privileged place. Much of the complexity that makes representations of violence move and disturb the viewer—but from *far away*—seems to come from the ambiguous status of the body as *vulnerable* and deserving of special care. This idea, though, also exists within an ambivalence regarding our contemporary understanding of the body. On the one hand, the body has more than ever acquired a status of universal protection, in large part by the declaration of the right to personal integrity as fundamental, which is in line with human rights discourses.[51] On the other hand, as expressed by Judith Butler regarding the War on Terror, "[S]ome lives are grievable, and others are not; the differential allocation of grievability that decides what kind of subject is and must be grieved, and which kind of subject must not, operates to produce and maintain certain exclusionary conceptions of who is normatively human: what counts as a livable life and a grievable death?"[52] This ambivalent dichotomy, in which the body is protected legally but certain bodies continue to be consistently and systematically violated, no doubt conditions the generation and reception of texts in the economy of images of violence. What determines the value of a body, especially a body that has been dismissed as abnormal, becomes the central question for the performance with which I engage in this section. *Piedra* (Stone), by Guatemalan performance artist Regina José Galindo, deals in particular with the social abuse inflicted on the female body and working-class and indigenous women in particular. It was specifically created for the 2013 "Encuentro" of the Hemispheric Institute of Performance and Politics in São Paolo, Brazil.[53]

Adding to an established history of misogynistic violence are neoliberal practices of commercial expansion that promote the displacement and systematic rape and violence against women (especially indigenous women) as multinational conglomerates seek to use land and resources in Latin America for economic gain. Thus, in this constant search for wealth, as Saskia Sassen has observed in reference to the "survival circuits" of the global south: "Prostitution and migrant labor are increasingly popular ways to make a living; illegal trafficking in women and children for the sex industry, and in all kinds of people as laborers, is an increasingly popular way to make a profit."[54] For the purposes of this section, I want to consider the ways in which performance activists (such as Tirado in the previous section and Galindo in this one) have engaged politically, socially, and culturally with this widespread issue, which tragically connects women (in particular) throughout the world in a web of economic exchange. Precisely because the voice of the victim is not heard through the language of the state and economic capitalism, the aesthetics of performance can provide the conceptual structures through which to hear those voices, even when those aesthetics are dependent on something as basic as producing a moment of awareness in the spectator. The performance piece by Galindo allows for a more abstract reflection on the subject of violence inflicted on women. In terms of the ethics of spectatorship to leverage justice, the spectators of Galindo's piece can simply watch the performance, leaving the piece without a concrete space for reflection in the immediate moment.

In Galindo's performance the artist's body remains motionless, covered in charcoal, like a stone. Throughout the thirty-minute performance she never moves, even as two male volunteers (fellow artists Galindo had contacted who agreed on the choreography of the piece) and one improvised female audience member (an unexpected participant) urinate over her still body. The performance begins when a small, thin woman (Galindo) covered in charcoal from head to toe walks through the outdoor patio where the spectators have gathered. She stops in the middle and curls into a ball on the hard floor. As she bends down and rounds her back, knees and elbows cuddled against her ribs, an assistant covers the last piece of visible skin (the soles of her feet) with charcoal. The aesthetic choice of using charcoal to cover her body is, of course, a reference to the violent abuses of the mining industry in Brazil, as well as many other Latin American countries, where often the most exploited victims of this colossal industry are female laborers trapped in a structure of violence and economic ambition that affects their health and livelihood.[55] Completely covered with coal, the body of the artist remains motionless, her face buried in the palms of her hands. The spectators around her, who at first brought out cameras and other recording devices to capture one of her always intense performances, remain quiet around her, awaiting some action.. Yet the artist remains motionless.

This series of actions forms part of Galindo's overall performance poetics regarding the suffering of the female body. In a poem written as part of this performance (which is not recited but included in the documents that accompany the performance and are accessible through her personal website), she states:

I am a stone
I do not feel the blows
The humiliation

The leering stares
The bodies upon my own
The hate.
I am a stone
Upon me
The history of the world.[56]

Working with these metaphors, Galindo is able to produce a very literal performance (regardless of its aesthetic abstraction) about violence and pain, humiliation and exploitation. The purpose of her piece is quite obvious, as she explains when talking about her performance:

> The history of humanity has remained inscribed on the bodies of Latin American women. On their bodies—conquered, marked, enslaved, objectified, exploited, and tortured—one can read the terrible stories of power and struggle that shape our past. Bodies are fragile only in their appearance. It is the female body that has survived conquest and slavery. Like a stone, it has stored the hatred and rancor of memory in order to transform it into energy and life.[57]

It is only through the figurative (and poetic) transformation of woman into stone that she can narrate the history of violence against Latin American women (and women in general). Considering the multitude of instances of violence in her own country of Guatemala, Galindo was particularly inspired in this piece by the ways in which pain can be somatized as a form of social criticism. This is especially true if one is to consider that the constant violence in her society, though directed primarily at men's bodies, has a different dialogue when it is conducted though the bodies of women. Galindo's performance represents the most common scenario of violence: "When one conducts an analysis [of the situation], the point is that men are always shot, and the murdered bodies appear the next day with a mercy shot. Women, on the other hand, are always tortured before they are murdered, and that always equals sexual violence."[58] The bodies of women, then, suffer an additional humiliation: they are marked by rape to prove that they are a surface on which to describe a systematic practice of pain and injustice in a failed political and social globalized project of economic expansion. In the genocidal war of Guatemala, rape became a crucial weapon in the desecration of the indigenous community, as well as a symbol of superiority and a form of torture before the assassination of women.[59] The use of rape in instances of state violence adds to the annihilation of the individual, as Jean Franco explains: "Rape followed by execution *performs* expulsion from the human by first reducing subjects to a state of abjection when the 'I' no longer is sovereign and then disposing of them as so much rubbish."[60] This idea is connected to the notion of "social dirt" analyzed in chapter 2. Such extreme forms of violence practiced on indigenous women are possible because the female body is transformed into rubbish. As the Peruvian critic Rocío Silva Santiesteban has described, the *factor asco* (disgust) allows for acts of extreme violence as it separates those who feel disgust from those deemed impure and therefore dangerous elements in society.[61] The stigmatized body of the indigenous woman is treated as rubbish, and this implies that it must be ejected from the social order. It is an undesirable (abjected) body. In the performance, Galindo aims to represent the tension found in those moments of humiliation and to take that pain to an extreme in order to annihilate the individual and only leave a body to be disposed of.

As a radical practitioner of body art, Galindo uses her own body as a tool for social and political action. She has often described her work as a way to construct a "human bridge" between people and places, oftentimes using spaces that carry a significant weight of violence and abuse. Caroline Rodrigues argues, "Her body is not the end of any given performance but becomes a device for enabling tactics of transversalism, facilitating connections between history and contemporaneity, artist and audience, public space and art space."[62] Galindo, at least for a moment, is able to resignify or denounce the actions on these spaces through her performances, which allows for a more empathic understanding of power, life, and death. In *Piedra*, Galindo links a history of environmental and indigenous exploitation with a colonial structure of dominance and abuse against the bodies of women. As previously discussed, the ghost of colonialism haunts the various exercises in cruelty that have characterized the period of modernity in Latin America. To understand the effect of modernity in Latin America, it is important to grasp that, as the philosopher Enrique Dussel has explained, the Spanish conquest was the event that inaugurated modernity as it gave Europe the advantage over other civilizations: "For modernity, the barbarian is at *fault* for opposing the civilizing process." Furthermore, Dussel describes modernity as an "ambiguous course by touting a rationality opposed to *primitive*, mythic explanations even as it concocts a myth to conceal its own sacrificial violence towards the other."[63] The inheritance of the Conquest, then, is a long-standing history of fear of the other and in particular the indigenous woman, who can continue to procreate the barbarian race. This is in line with Rosi Braidotti's use of the monster to understand female marginalization: "Monsters are linked to the female body in scientific discourse through the question of biological reproduction. Theories of conception of monsters are at times extreme versions of the deep-seated anxiety that surrounds the issue of women's maternal power of procreation in a patriarchal society."[64] In the context of the modern Latin American state, woman is, then, alien to modernity. In *Piedra* the tragic narrative of a colonial tradition (in this case Brazil, though it can be extended to many other countries) rests on the abused body of one woman. Throughout the performance, her body does not move, and ten minutes after the start a man, who appears as part of the group of people that has accumulated around the artist (though he is one of the aforementioned artists who is part of the performance), breaks off and walks toward her. He unzips his pants, pulls out his penis, and proceeds to urinate on that motionless black body.

This is, obviously, a very shocking and violent image: the stream of urine draws grooves and channels down the charcoal, which sticks to her body, dripping down to her face and falling off her fingers. The absolute silence around the action itself (which extends to the audience members, who only observed without outward expressions of emotion) forces the question of how to communicate or make visible trauma and abuse if language is taken away. As spectators of this action, we are only left with the sensorial: a communicable experience of trauma. This is an experience of pain and humiliation that elicits a sense of subordination by an artist who is complicit with the submissive positionality of Latin American women as perceived by most of society. Galindo's piece is problematic precisely because it reproduces scenarios of violence through a performance practice that is later justified by the reflection from the audience. Even though Galindo's point of departure is to denounce violence through a violent act itself, the issue of spectatorial ambiguity remains. This leads to the question Is a horrible act represented or repeated when it is allowed to happen without resistance—especially when witnessed by a group of people who become a "public"?

The pain and humiliation present in the performance remind us that a misogynistic society has taught us that women are conquered through emotional and physical pain or, as Veena Das explains, "[P]ain is the medium through which society establishes ownership of individuals."[65] Thus, *Piedra* connects with the spectator through a voyeuristic relationship established around the action itself. We are witnesses to the pain and suffering of the artist, while the temporal demands of the performance make us aware of the options we have as we choose to remain present or not during the piece: to

Fig. 17. *Piedra*. Regina José Galindo and participant. Photo by Julio Pantoja.

stay might imply enduring, in a way, "along with" Galindo. The cruelty we are actively experiencing acts as a signifier of a Latin American reality, and the vulnerability of her body (which appears to have no agency before the actions thrust on it) has an obvious effect on the observers.

In *Piedra* the performance itself is not the artist's body but the action that this body allows on it. As it lies there, exposed, it loses any form of control or agency, and this opens the way for the spectator to be exposed as well. We stand around this vulnerable body in silence, unwilling to intervene (because we are aware of the role of the audience as observer) but receiving the impact of such an action. At the same time, one must recognize the possibility of identifying with both sides, and this raises the question If one identifies with the woman/stone while at the same time recognizing a possible identification with the man who urinates on her body, what imaginary mechanisms are mobilizing this identification (in relation to issues of abuse and power)? Does this imply competing scopic regimes that we strive to mediate in order to maintain a sense of morality? Is it possible for audience members to reflect on issues of accountability and justice in relation to the witnessing of violence?

In this sense, the performance constitutes a marker of that which is most horrific in society (violence and trauma), but it appears through an abstract image to achieve a different effect on the observer: to make the audience a witness. Or, at the very least, the performance allows for the possibility of questioning our reactions to the piece as witnesses who are concerned with the action before them. This is in line with Giorgio Agamben's notion of the *potentiality* found in the witness for the possibility of commitment and responsibility.

> [T]estimony is the disjunction between two impossibilities of bearing witness; it means that language, in order to bear witness, must give way to a non-language to show the impossibility of bearing witness. The language of testimony is a language that no longer signifies and that, in not signifying, advances into what is without language, to the point of taking on a different insignificance—that of the complete witness, that of he who by definition cannot bear witness.[66]Thus, at the very least the performance brings out the possibility of responsibility from the audience as witness. As difficult as it is to gauge audience reaction in this piece, the silence, stupefaction, and clear discomfort of those around Galindo at the Hemispheric Institute performance showed a shared intentionality as all were clearly affected by the piece and those around them sharing in

the same moment. *Piedra* forces us to face the pain of other lives, to think of another, and, as Ileana Diéguez observes, "[I]f, even without being direct victims, we start reflecting from within the experience of pain, we may realize that, under current conditions, the impossibility of thinking of ourselves or imagining ourselves as separate from the victims is actually intensified."[67] In other words, we cannot readily choose between identifying or distancing ourselves, and this ambivalence produces the critical effect of the piece.

Ten more minutes pass, and Galindo continues to lie perfectly immobile in the same position on the ground. A second man steps forward from the audience (again a fellow artist who is part of the piece) and urinates on her body. The clear lack of concern with which these men urinate on her points to the widespread apathy that is often found with regard to the safety and care of a woman's body. This theme is also a major concern within Galindo's artistic oeuvre. In *Piedra* the female body is represented as a stone precisely because both are objects conditioned (by nature and society) to withstand violent acts. Galindo chose the parallel between woman and stone precisely because she wished to negate the individual (as the act of violence does) but not the live body itself. And a stone is a natural object characterized by its resilience. Even as this body in the performance is in a completely submissive position, what allows it to continue is the resilience with which it faces the humiliation and violence imposed on it. The ease with which a man (whether it be within the performance or outside it) is able to contaminate the female body through an apparently superficial action, such as emptying his bladder, is held in parallel to the everyday violence that the female body encounters as it functions in the social order. This violence emphasizes the unconscious nature of the everyday actions that drive a repetitive structural violence.

Thus, this "stone woman" is, at the same time, an ancient and natural structure (a timeless part of nature), and it performs as a disposable object of inherent exploitation. Galindo's body becomes an emblem of disposability, as useless as a stone on the road. Even more so, this performance in Brazil carries an additional connotation: these disposable bodies also include the workers in the huge industry of coal mining, which is the largest, nonrenewable energy resource in the country and the leading cause of water and land pollution. Besides the environmental damage brought on by multinational corporations that seek to find ways to augment their economic gains by exploiting foreign lands, there is the tragedy of women being raped and killed for protesting the expansion of these conglomerates.

The two issues are tied together, as women are often the primary victims of sexual violence in efforts to conquer through economic expansion. *Piedra*, by means of a simple yet poetic action, manages to capture a local and global crisis: the harmful effects of coal mining on the environment, the plight of the exploited workers, and widespread structural violence against women that economic exploitation perpetuates.

Galindo has said that the history of violence has been recorded on the bodies of women, and this notion is complicated toward the end of the performance by an additional performer. The action of men urinating on the female body aligns femininity with nature and the bodies of men with the processes of violence and exploitation. Ten minutes after the second man has urinated on Galindo's body, a third figure steps forward. This time it is a woman who approaches the artist, plants her legs on either side of the stone/body, and urinates. It must be pointed out that this third volunteer was an unexpected participant, as she was not a part of Galindo's performance but someone from the audience that decided to participate. In the original piece, a third man should have urinated on Galindo's body, but he was unable to because of this unknown woman's interference.[68] The piece was carefully timed, so Galindo herself was not aware of this until after the performance, though she admits that it made it more interesting. The participation of this unknown woman reconstructs the argument around a male body perpetrating violence against a female body and at the same time implies that women are complicit in intrasexual violence. With this, Galindo's criticism folds back on itself to question the ways in which women enact violence on the bodies of other women.

The unexpected participation of this woman also raises important issues regarding agency and control in the piece. As an artist, Galindo has the agency of choreographing the elements of the performance. Yet this unscripted moment stripped her of her agency as she was left to experience an instance outside her control. Galindo's form of artistic agency was complicated through the act of this woman from the audience for a single moment. After a pause, Galindo slowly got up and walked past the audience. The spectators were left behind. They watched her walk away, leaving a trail of urine in her wake. An important part of this performance was its framing: Galindo chose to assume the position/identity of a stone at the beginning, but unlike a real stone she was able to get up and walk away from it in the end. This action appeared to indicate the strength and agency of women in spite of the violence done to them. Of course, one must acknowledge that Galindo's performance allowed for the possibility of having this violence inflicted on her in a momentary way by her own choice, whereas women who are subject to violence do not have that form of agency and protection. Women and stones share the ability to take abuse from their environment and survive continuous wear. Galindo's *Piedra* presents the images of women who suffer from an abject abuse for the purpose of reorganizing the vectors of power between the victim and the victimizer while at the same time emphasizing the durability of the female body and spirit.

In our everyday lives, we are constantly bombarded with images that show physical violence, which clarifies how we are less protected as citizens, especially those who have been declared as "less than" by a system that capitalizes on normative practices of utilitarian, productive bodies. By placing political action as its central objective and presenting the vulnerability of the body, the three performances examined in this chapter make it possible to perceive an instance of healing through the recuperation of agency in the traumatized body. Whether it be by creating a utopic instance of acceptance (*Geraldas e Avencas*), by borrowing a skin onto which to etch the image of a life obscured by society (*El brillo de la negrura*), or by emphasizing the abjected body's power found in resistance (*Piedra*), these performances provoke the audience to reflect. Thus, for a moment we are made aware of our own vulnerability. As spectators, we are forced to recognize our impulses for staring before acting, especially when it comes to nonconforming bodies or behaviors. Garland-Thompson observes that the voyeur's compulsion to stare at extraordinary-looking bodies does not take into account the violence perpetrated on disordering bodies. The woman/freak will be subjected for life to the "perversity and the anxiety of being a staree."[69] She will endure the dominant "ocular intrusion" that is put into practice in freak shows where "staring validates our individuality, calls out our differences from others. Sameness does not merit stares."[70] Indeed, all the artists featured in this chapter bounce the hegemonic gaze back to the audience in order to effect an alternative way of seeing the other. They showcase "inappropriate/d" bodies whose difference challenges audience complicity with the logic of the same and the other and the normalization of the medical gaze on damaged or nonconforming corporeality.

It is true that the law, as well as the Universal Declaration of Human Rights (1948), says many things, but actual politics and economic crises establish a different reality. Besides creating policies, none of the international organizations that we assume protect human rights [United Nations (UN) , United Nations Educational, Scientific and Cultural Organization (UNESCO), Office of Transition Initiatives (OTI)] engage in much concrete action to avoid violations. It is because of this reality that theater and performance are and will be a necessary tool to expand and share these experiences of pain and shame. These instances of performance are one of the few means that remain in force to carry out the notion of community as defined by Ileana Diéguez, where she says: "The representations of the absences, the staging and theatrics of pain, the performativities displayed by the *communitas* of mourners, are all forms of action for life, symbolic practices that emerge in the public space to make others visible, striving to give them a symbolic body against all the projects of disappearance and annihilation of individuals."[71] We live our lives before a sinister and contradictory message, which pushes us to become stronger and more "independent" consumers through neoliberal politics, while those bodies that do not conform are transformed into more vulnerable and unprotected citizens, not by the law but by a permanent state of exclusion. The artists whose work I analyze in this chapter are displaying politics through their own bodies as a possible way of creating dissent within neoliberal practices of exclusion. Their use of the body is in line with Francine Masiello, who asserts:

> (Neo)liberal rule was never a disembodied process. . . . [I]t is not surprising in this respect that a large number of Latin American social movements insist on the body as a point of departure to defend human rights and economic advancement; that powerful activists congregate today around issues of sexual choice; that informal sectors reveal a high female component, with housewives unions in barrios placing successful claims on democratic rule through negotiation with the market.[72]

As she urges, society will need to bring the gendered body as "an originating point of discourse, community, and action" to any discussion of the violent effects of neoliberal development. This appears to be the precise point of departure in the works studied above. Neoliberalism has extended and emphasized a period of cruel and violent exclusion for women, especially poor women, in a system that only seeks to capitalize on their bodies. To leverage justice for women under these circumstances is a difficult task, but these performances do that work through their insistence on public complicity and responsibility for these crimes against women and, indeed, against humanity.

| Violence and Politics on the Freak

The Perversion of Citizenship

In her seminal book *Cruel Modernity*, Jean Franco states, "Neither cruelty nor the exploitation of cruelty is new, but the lifting of the taboo, the acceptance and justification of cruelty and the rationale for cruel acts, have become a feature of modernity."[1] I find this phrase to be of special significance in the context of this book because the lifting of this taboo is what has allowed certain individuals to be marginalized from the social structures that contain citizenship to the point of physical elimination. We have seen this happen time and again in the twentieth century in Latin America: a continual threat to the lives of women, people of color, queer people, those whose ideas do not fit within the status quo, the mentally ill, the disabled. This process begins with their categorization as noncitizens who are deemed to be unproductive members of society and, therefore, constitute a threat to the evolution of the nation. Enfreakment enters into the construction of marginalized individuals when their identities are dehumanized through a discourse that seeks to exhibit their differences as categories for disenfranchisement and, potentially, destruction.

This idea was particularly salient in the second half of the twentieth century in Latin America, a period that was characterized by a series of repressive dictatorships. These regimes sought to exterminate those sectors of society that threatened the ideal of the modern nation accepted by those in power in Latin America and modeled by North America and Europe. As José Joaquín Brunner has explained, there is a great danger to this singular conception of modernity.

> In the case of Latin America . . . the motor of modernity, the international market, provokes and then reinforces an incessant movement of heterogenization of culture, employing, stimulating, and reproducing a plurality of *logics* that act simultaneously, becoming interwoven. Logics that, from a Eurocentric and Enlightenment point of view, we could properly call modern, such as those of seculariza-

tion, formal rationality, bureaucratization, individualization, futurism, alienation, etc. Logics of the collective imaginary, at the same time shaped by a local historical memory (which is itself sometimes varied and contradictory) and by the seductions of the mass media, as occurs with the telenovela. Logics of identification based on economic, social, and cultural positions; social logics of differentiation in a world where consumption distributes, at the same time, signs of status; sacrificial logics of giving, expenditure, and fiestas, which, by themselves, do not manage to resist the commercializing force of the market; political logics of articulation and mobilization, which are not immune to the internationalization of militancies; renewable modern logics of terror and fear in a universe of the disappeared, torture, state and private terrorism, and of the marks left on society by repression.[2]

Here Brunner warns that modernity and its requisite logic rejects the cultural heterogeneity of each nation. Hence, as Gino Germani theorizes and Brunner paraphrases: "Modernity generates serious problems of normative integration that weaken or make impossible democratic governments, leading to catastrophic solutions in the guise of authoritarian regimes of total resocialization."[3] During the period of military dictatorships in Latin America, the efforts and anxieties produced by the need to represent modernity led to authoritarian regimes that sought to produce an integration of the nation that also removed any undesired heterogenetity.

The 1960s in Latin America began with utopian dreams ushered in by the Cuban Revolution and the postwar economic boom that made a consumer society possible. The hopefulness that was felt throughout the continent quickly dissipated as right-wing rulers (for the most part, under the auspices of US counterinsurgency experts who trained and promoted those who would be in control) began to dominate the political landscape. Particularly in South America in the 1960s and 1970s, bureaucratic-authoritarian regimes like those in Chile and Argentina attempted to use the power of state institutions to enact a fundamental reordering of society. Long-term military governments, with changing leadership in most cases, controlled eleven Latin American nations for significant periods from 1964 to 1990: Ecuador, Guatemala, Brazil, Bolivia, Argentina, Peru, Panama, Honduras, Chile, Uruguay, and El Salvador. Military governments, though inevitably authoritarian, enacted varying economic, social, and foreign policies that allowed for the implementation of a neoliberal economic system that continues in various degrees in the present. They had staunch supporters and intense opponents, and in every case, a large proportion of the population died under these regimes, particularly the rural and indigenous communities, as well as left-leaning Marxist youths. The exercise of cruelty in this era was disguised through the discourse of power that called for a modern nation free of individuals who would detract from this vision. Thus, the continuous "problem" throughout the century was the ways in which repressive governments and discourses of power constructed "normalcy" as a required identity for the appearance of a modern nation, and that utopian normalcy associated with progress, in turn, constructed those who did not fit this model as a "problem."

As Jorge Larraín suggests, by "the end of the 1980s . . . the project of rapidly advancing to modernity, even at the cost of identity, was becoming dominant in Latin America."[4] Larraín goes on to argue that "the stage that opens up after the end of dictatorships [in the 1980s] continues with, and accelerates, economic and political modernization under the influence of an already consolidated neoliberal ideology"; the result is that "concerns about [Latin American autochthonous] identity recede as neoliberal optimism gets the upper hand everywhere."[5] All sorts of cruel practices have occurred across Latin American history in the name of modernity, including the wars on communism, which have often led to the genocide of indigenous communities, as neoliberalism has allowed for the practice of casual violence in the name of market production. The indigenous populations of Peru and Guatemala have been especially suppressed, as they were deemed to be primitive individuals that prevented modernization. The extermination of a group based primarily on its ethnic identity as an exercise of state control is an idea that was clearly explained by Foucault as a form of biopower: "[R]acism develops primo with colonization, that is to say with colonizing genocide. When it is necessary to kill people, kill populations, kill civilizations, how can one debate on the basis of biopower? Through the themes of evolutionism, through racism."[6] Furthermore, racism becomes the condition that leads to the acceptance of violence inflicted on the other: "It introduces a division between peoples, between my life and the death of the other on the basis of biological difference; the death of the inferior race (the degenerate of the abnormal) is what will make life in general healthier: healthier and purer."[7] This is an extreme form of biopower that justifies the eradication of certain groups that threaten so-called national progress, and in Latin America this has often been associated with indigenous populations as a legacy of colonialism's fear of the other.

As discussed in chapter 2, the stigma imposed on certain sectors of society that would label their members' physical appearance and/or behavior as abnormal has a long tradition in western thought and the value it placed on eugenics, especially throughout the nineteenth century. As Lennard Davis has thoroughly discussed, the issue at hand with eugenicists is their tendency to extend what they consider to be "undesirable" traits across large groups of the population that do not necessarily have any connections. In other words, the "unfit" can be described as "the habitual criminal, the professional tramp, the tubercular, the insane, the mentally defective, the alcoholic, the diseased from birth or from excess."[8] If one extends the sphere of influence of such thought to the Latin American context, "undesirable" traits were transferred to indigenous populations, as this evolutionism is an ingrained form of racism established since the Conquest, which bequeathed to modernity a long-standing fear of the "savage" population.[9] Modernity and civilization were equated with westernized forms of whiteness, and thus the indigenous became the enemy. In the case of countries like Chile and Argentina, where the indigenous populations had already been decimated and the modern enemy was the "lefty" subversive, the process of their dehumanization as threats to the modern state would encompass modes of "moral" thought. Marxist youths became an unfit body that threatened the nation with their moral deviations, which could only pervert the social order. In other words, "[T]here are strong reasons for viewing the atrocities of the 1980's as more than the escalation of long-standing discrimination. Or, rather, long-standing discrimination became harnessed to the cause of modernization, underscoring the value of whiteness or, as Bolivar Echeverría terms it, *blanquitud*, that is, not whiteness as such but the iconic ideal of capitalism's new man."[10] This era shows a society increasingly threatened by ethnic and racial difference, as well as any form of political dissent.

What has been made clear throughout this book is that the principal concern of the modern Latin American state is to secure the comfort of those it deems normal, meaning those who have the power and economic security to maintain the status quo. As a social and political configuration, the normal appears intrinsically as a synonym for progress and an ideological consolidation of the power of capitalism. In other words, "[T]here was an iron-clad civility for the privileged few, and violence against the underprivileged masses was a routine affair."[11] Thus, the simplest way to exclude those who do not fit into this model is by marginalizing their status as citizens and exhibiting their identities as freaks whose very bodies do not fit into the political corpus. This means that their bodies and/or behaviors are deemed erratic and abnormal, and thus in need of control, even if this means the use of cruel methods: "The anxiety over modernity defined and represented by North America and Europe all too often set governments on the fast track that bypassed the arduous paths of democratic decision making while marginalizing indigenous and black peoples. States of exception and states of siege not only justified the suppression of groups deemed subversive or alien to modernity but also created an environment in which cruelty was enabled in the name of state security."[12] The fear over the indigenous and the "subversive" citizen (communist, hippy, homosexual, etc.) revealed the anxiety felt throughout most of Latin America at being considered the underdeveloped, peripheral third world. In order to become part of the technologized first world, the clear solution seemed to be to get rid of those sectors of society that embodied those stigmatized traits, such as rebellion, primitiveness, and traditional values.

Another thing that has been emphasized throughout this book is the power of theater and performance as forms of resistance. Theater and performance use the bodies of those exhibited onstage as a tool for reversing the normative gaze that has enfreaked the bodies of those who do not fit within the social order. With this in mind, I turn to three plays grounded on the history of violence in Chile, Argentina, and Peru. I start with *Gemelos* (Twins, Teatrocinema, Chile, 1999), an adaptation of a short novel by Agota Kristof about two boys who feel and think in identical ways. After the war (a fictional war) begins, they are abandoned and forced to survive though a process of reeducation that will allow them to deal with the horrors and violence of war. I begin with this play because it allows us to focus the discussion on an abstract notion of war and violence while clearly specifying humanity's capacity for cruelty. *El barro se subleva* (The Mud Revolts, Norman Briski, Argentina, 2013) is a play about one man who wants to change the world by any means possible, even if that means violence. This performance allows me to center my analysis on the utopia of revolution that has failed the contemporary individual, who now finds only disenchantment in the ideals of a past that has only produced further isolation and marginalization. This plays presents the revolutionary idealist of the past as the repository of contemporary fears. What happens when there is no hope left? *Halcón de oro: Q'orihuaman* (The Golden Falcon: Q'orihuaman, Ana Correa and Rodolfo Rodríguez, Peru, 1995) tells the story of an encounter between an Andean priest and a young ex-military man who has been sent to an insane asylum to face his own demons. This final performance provides the element for a possible purification and recuperation of memory for the purposes of creating a better world. They are the final words of hope for creating a notion of citizenship that values difference as a cure for violence. These performances deal with state violence and question a period in the history of each nation in which certain individuals were deemed to be different (because of political views, social behaviors, physical appearance, etc.) and thus made to disappear from the social order through violent means. In other words, certain bodies are disposable because in the economy of national conformity they represent a surplus value that must be eradicated for the benefit of the nation. Freakness, then, becomes something more than stigma, as it leads to the removal of the individual from society and leaves a lasting impact on future generations that have been violently taught the price of not fitting in.

I do want to emphasize that these performances are works in which memory plays a large part in understanding the impact of individual dissidence. Cultural and literary critics have often coincided in categorizing a majority of the productions of the last few decades as a culture of memory. As Beatríz Sarlo has indicated, this is a particular sort of literary (and dramatic) production whose function is directly related to the moral, affective, political, and intellectual needs of the present.[13] Even though Sarlo is quite critical of this sort of literary production as an unquestioned source of truth, my particular concern with memory and theater is the ways in which it can address collective forms of remembrance as political resistance, especially in a neoliberal system. Andreas Huyssen considers the prevalence of memory in cultural production as a response to "the capitalist culture with its continuing frenetic pace, its television politics of quick oblivion, and its dissolution of public space in ever more channels of instant entertainment [that] is inherently amnesiac." Because of this, "[O]ur obsession with memory functions as a reaction formation against the accelerating technical processes that are transforming our *Lebenswelt* (lifeworld) in quite distinct ways."[14] It is important to consider that the period of military dictatorships in Latin America was characterized by severe repression, which provoked a dependence on memory as a form of testimony (photographs, diaries, letters) in the place of "history." Writers such as Eduardo Galeano have theorized this process by questioning why the past must been relegated to "history," to something merely known. Instead, Galeano argues, the past — even the past that was never experienced by anyone living today — should be remembered. The plays that compose this chapter do not provide a revisionist history or pretend to champion an individual memory as absolute truth. Rather, they appear as a clear effort similar to what Sandra Lorenzano has suggested, that "if economic neoliberalism has counteracted any labor or social development in the region," or if "social fabrics have unraveled with profound losses in human and civil rights," then "memory is one of the only remaining spaces of resistance."[15]

I'm interested in these three performances because they represent a bridge between those who lived the atrocities of the dictatorships and members of the newer generations who continue to explore the significance of this history in their own lives, which were not directly affected. I find this to be a process similar to what Diana Taylor posits in *The Archive and the Repertoire: Performing Cultural Difference in the Americas*, in which she seeks to find ways for the past to count as the experience and identity of people in the present. To that end, Taylor argues that performances are "vital acts of transfer, transmitting social knowledge, memory, and a sense of identity."[16] For Taylor the "repertoire" turns events in the past into memory because it "enacts embodied memory," which in turn requires "presence: people participate . . . by 'being there,' being part of the transmission."[17] Since the viewer participates in a performance—as Taylor argues, by "being there"—we can purportedly move from thinking of ourselves as learning about something in the past to thinking that knowledge is "transmitted 'live' in the here and now" and thus "experienced as present."[18] The idea is that spectators who experience the transmission of this knowledge through a performance can then reperform it. By reperforming it, people can think of themselves as not only remembering things but also embodying them. This is an interesting notion to have in mind as we approach the performances in this chapter, especially as these particular companies and artists have a long history of political dissidence in their own countries and have had to figure out in these performances how to incorporate their past lived experiences into a present political paradigm.

Teatrocinema, for example, was founded in 1987 (toward the end of the military dictatorship in Chile) under the name La Troppa and has continued into the present, reconfiguring it repertoire and method and including a new generation of performers. La Troppa first performed the play *Gemelos* in 1999 and later it was recovered by the new collective (now called Teatrocinema) as a way of exploring new visual forms on the stage in order to narrate the horrors of the past. In this way, there is a certain artistic value to be found in the intergenerational encounter that the play provides as it was transformed from the perspective of one collective to the other: from the past to the present. There must be a difference to be found as the play was created in the midst of an authoritarian regime and then re-created under a neoliberal democracy. Yet *Gemelos*, in its present production, is grounded in the meeting of both perspectives. This becomes a process similar to what theorists such as Pierre Nora and Maurice Halbwachs have already posed regarding memory, that through the process of narration a collective memory is assembled in the course of remembering and narrating. The same can be said for the other two plays. In the case of *El barro se subleva*, we have playwright Norman Briski, who was forced into exile in 1975 after receiving death threats from the Argentine Anticommunist Alliance. He wrote this play in 2012 in close collaboration with Eduardo Misch, the solo actor in the performance who is an active militant from a younger generation. The final product is a performance of intergenerational memory that "reconstruct[s] the past, to negotiate between private and public histories, and to imagine a present and a future that are informed but not overshadowed by the past."[19] *Halcón de oro: Q'orihuaman* is directed by Ana Correa, one of the founding members of the collective troupe Yuyachkani (discussed in the first chapter), which has publicly denounced the atrocities committed by the military in Peru. This particular performance is an effort to come to terms with the present situation in the country. All three productions constitute an effort to consider the continuous effects that result from the demonizing of the individual in the collective memory of a nation that was often complicit, or at the very least aloof to, the cruelty on the ground.

It is useful in this analysis to turn to Marianne Hirsch's exploration of the nature of postmemory: "Postmemory characterizes the experience of those who grow up dominated by narratives that preceded their birth, whose own belated stories are evacuated by the stories of the previous generation, shaped by traumatic events that can be neither understood nor recreated."[20] Hirsch notes that the children of trauma survivors experience not the "events" but only their "representations."[21] However, rather than concluding that the children of trauma survivors merely learn about or know the traumatic event (or experience its effects secondhand), or that the "obsessive repetition" of media-driven representations of traumatic events "distance and protect [them] from the event," Hirsch argues that their repetition "retraumatize[s], making distant viewers into surrogate victims who, having seen the images so often, have adopted them into their own narratives and memories, and have thus become all the more vulnerable to their effects."[22] Thus, for Hirsch, postmemory actually "connects the second generation to the first, *producing* rather than *screening* the effect of trauma that was lived so much more directly *as compulsive repetition* by survivors and contemporary witnesses."[23] The three plays in this chapter, then, constitute an effort to show that the memories that are echoed in the performances are by no means historical truth but the remnants of a lived experience and the experience transmitted by others. The result is that the act of learning about the traumatic experiences of others through representation is reconceived as the experience of trauma itself. This idea is further problematized in the performances because the plays are not trauma themselves but a retelling of a history of trauma. In other words, audience members are not directly experiencing trauma but encountering a representation of the historical trauma of others in order to incorporate it into their own experiences and identities: an echo of trauma. What I find most interesting in these (re)conceptions of the past in the present is that the performances narrate through characters that escape notions of normalcy, whether it be through their physical appearance or their behavior. This is important because the act of remembrance is to be found in the voices of those marginalized by a system that sought their destruction. In the words of Chimamanda Adichie, "The premise for empathy has to be equal humanity; it is an injustice to demand that the maligned identify with those who question their humanity."[24]

Through all this (the violence, the medicalization, the stigma, the dirt, etc.), how can we understand the idea of citizenship, its denial and its granting, within these parameters of identity construction? These plays deal with the modern reality of the Latin American state: the control of the population and its everyday behavior through extreme fear. The pervasive image of freakish behavior and individual bodily difference in these plays are useful indicators of how those in power sought out hateful images of ethnicity and political dissent to mitigate their own fears about the other. The degrading and dehumanizing images of marginalized individuals presented by those in power, then, reinforced hierarchies that kept the "white" capitalist "new man" on top while degrading and literally disappearing the threatening other. As long as the "rebel" was a dirty *indio* or an out of control communist, the construction of the "enemy" was meant to dehumanize any individual that was not accepted by a political system that relied on an authoritarian mode of government. Thus, the notion of enfreakment to be found in these plays functions as an allegorical figure that broadens the term as it stands for a means of condemning whatever is deemed to be "dangerous" difference through the gaze of those in power. I find the juxtaposition of these three plays to be particularly significant as it allows my analysis to move from the general notion of violence inflicted on the innocent and the eventual corruption of the individual produced by unhinged cruelty (in the case of *Gemelos*) to the disparate hope of the disenchanted revolutionary who can no longer adapt to the cruelty of neoliberal violence (*El barro se subleva*) and finally to the moment of finding forgiveness in a world that has destroyed the humanity of the individual who is not in power (*Q'oriwaman*).

UNHINGED VIOLENCE AND ADAPTATION IN *GEMELOS*

Teatrocinema is a Chilean theater troupe that goes back to 1987, when it was founded under the name La Troppa by three artists: puppeteer Jaime Lorca, performer-designer Laura Pizarro, and writer-director Juan Carlos Zagal. In 2005 it was renamed Teatrocinema to highlight the way its diverse artists unite theater and cinema, which has been a constant innovation in their productions. The play *Gemelos* was originally performed in 1999 while the company was still La Troppa, but it has been reintroduced into the repertoire of Teatrocinema to continued acclaim.[25] It tells the story, from a child's perspective, of two twin brothers who must struggle for survival during an unnamed war that is very much evocative of World War II. The use of a child's perspective is a useful tactic for a story such as this, as actor-director Zagal explains: "The reality is very hard, very brutal. So, we decided to take this reality to the stage from the perspective of a child, with his life of toys, of puppets. It is a different way of facing such a violent reality."[26] *Gemelos* is a free adaptation of Hungarian author Agotha Kristof's novel *The Notebook* (1987). The use of a text that was not written for a theatrical performance is typical of this company; it would rather work with novels, short stories, or even a specific statement made by a character in a narrative. The lack of a specific theatrical text gives the artists the liberty to research and develop their own personal images.[27] The play is performed by three actors (Laura Pizarro, Juan Carlos Zagal, and José Manuel Aguirre) on a miniature stage made of carved wood that constitutes all of the spaces in the play, from the grandmother's house to the outdoor spaces in the small town in which they live. This small stage is reminiscent of puppet theater, with its plush red curtain, a connection that is emphasized by the acting style of the twins onstage. Also the connection between film and theater is emphasized through this miniature set and the use of puppets that are easily manipulated to create changes in perspective, so that a character seen in a sort of long shot, profiled against the horizon (as a puppet), reappears in close-up almost instantly (as the actor). Or an iris effect that recalls silent movies is used to whisk us briskly between scenes.

The performance begins with a silent set of actions that present the mother and father, a middle-class couple who seem to be entrenched in the rites of society: the father falls in love with the beautiful mother (the mother appears turning like a music-box ballerina), they get married (the father puts a ring on the mother's finger), and they have children (they appear onstage with two clay sculptures of heads, onto which they place two identical hats). Immediately, the twins are signaled as something different

Fig. 18. *Gemelos*. Actors Laura Pizarro as the Grandmother, and Juan Carlos Zagal and José Manuel Aguirre as the Twins. Photo by Montserrat Q. Antequera.

when the father states, "[T]his is not normal. They think together, act together. They live in a world apart. In a world all of their own."[28] Their concern is that an individual must have his or her own life, and the twins refuse to separate. But the world of this play has no place for selfhood, only for sameness. Of course, individuality stops being a concern for the parents when the boys' father goes off to war and their mother, unable to support them, takes them to live with their bitter, cruel grandmother in the countryside.[29] This crone, a sort of antimother, starves and beats the boys, emphasizing from the beginning that she will "teach them how to live." They react to her abuse by conducting their own course of self-discipline, reeducating their hearts and minds to ignore physical hardship and remain obstinately indifferent to the ridicule and abuse they receive from the locals. As the ugly truths of the war slowly encroach on their lives, however, the boys gradually carve their way into their grandmother's heart, eventually learning to manipulate and even dominate her.

To fully grasp the meaning of this play, it is useful to first contextualize it within the history of modern Chile. The play (as well as the short story on which it is based) occurs in an unnamed country. Not knowing precise details can be anxiety provoking for an audience, but this contributes to the overall effect of the play as a parable for violence and division. Even though the visual referents onstage signal that the action occurs in a European country during World War II, which is a useful generalization for understanding the cruelty of unfettered power, there is also a clear metaphor of the process of annihilating difference that was endured between 1973 and 1990 in Chile. The eternal war that occurs onstage can quickly be associated with the violent genocide that occurred in this country during the military dictatorship. As a company, Teatrocinema belongs to a generation of Chilean theater artists who carry within their imaginary the Pinochet dictatorship as a constant referent. Even though their artistic production doesn't directly critique the social and political system in place during the dictatorship, there are clear situations that cast a glance toward the violence lived. Therefore, themes such as power and cruelty acquire great significance in their performances. The military dictatorship in Chile was unique because of its strong implementation of the neoliberal system, the first country in Latin America to do so. In addition to the violations of human rights, the military dictatorship "forced the privatization of public life, controlling individual success, as well as a passion for consumerism, all proposed through fear and force. . . . Thus, in the '70s, when the anticommunist impetus in Latin America was in the air, the neoliberal system was imposed as a response to the specific problems of Chile's economy."[30] As most researchers point out, the neoliberal system was adopted in Chile through violence, torture, and genocide as a means of controlling the middle class economically. Even with the transition to democracy, the neoliberal system continues on, "leading Chile to a greater crisis than [in] the previous years and to wider social segregation, since many peripheral classes in the economic system were, in the late 1990s, in an even worse labor and economic situation."[31] Even though the artists of Teatrocinema (as La Troppa) created this piece in the context of the new democracy, they continue to confront the legacy of the oppression that dominated their childhoods.

Furthermore, *Gemelos* brings to the forefront the effects of abysmal divisions in class and labor that continue to exist in the democratic present. As we find out by the end of the play, while the twins learn to survive amid great violence and poverty, the mother has remade her life, married another man, and had another child, maintaining the perceived comforts of her middle-class existence. The grandmother and the children, though, learn to manipulate and transform their oppressed existence and violent

surroundings with great success, to the point where the twins refuse to return to their mother's home. This unexpected siding of the children with
the grandmother proves to be part of the poetics of action that characterizes
most of this company's productions: "[W]e chose the actions that are the
least obvious, symbolic actions that speak a hermetic discourse, initiatory,
of the hidden history in any story."[32] The world that appears onstage has
no baseline for normalcy; thus the spectator is given no moral direction,
and this disorientation is mirrored in the actions of the characters. In order
to destabilize the expected relationships in the symbolic order of power
(mother/sons), the twins form a stronger bond with the cruel grandmother,
who, despite her cruelty, teaches them a new moral order of survival and
gives them a place of belonging through her harsh educational process of
survival under the most difficult of circumstances. The grandmother, thus,
becomes the mother figure who will lead the twins to reach "autonomy
and integrity as adults and not as children-who-lack."[33] Within these circumstances, then, the central issue for the children is how to retain their
humanity in this reality and, even more problematic, how to become a citizen of a world order that seeks to destroy any sort of perceived difference,
be it physical or moral.

One of the main adversities the twins face is their isolation (whether
self-imposed or inflicted by society and family) in the world. The first instance is their removal from the family home and the long journey to the
grandmother's house. This long passage from the city to a rural village
(represented in the background by a small hill and windmill) is accentuated onstage through the use of lights, which transform the scene from day
to night, as well as the modality of the actors. It is the first time we hear the
twins speak, and as they slowly walk in place, their soft voices carry overtones of exhaustion. After explaining that they have been walking for a
very long time, they describe the grandmother's house, which is "on the
other side of the village, far from the train station. Here there are no street-
cars, or cars, or buses. Only some military trucks." This new environment
comes as a shock to the twins, who are by no means ready for physical labor or prepared for the isolated house and the grandmother who doesn't
want them. They have been abandoned by their mother, who says they
must stay there as long as the war continues, an exchange of one type of
violence for another as they are left with a woman who calls them "sons of
bitches" and has no use for children. Of course, as children, the twins are
fully unaware of their situation; their main concern is the chaotic state of
the grandmother's house and the grandmother herself.

This situation is handled with comedic elements, especially when the twins sing about their newfound state. In this scene, as occurs throughout the play, it is really the actors' precise, stylized performances that capture and hold one's attention. They wear half masks that recall commedia dell'arte and move in an angular, mechanized way that makes them resemble eerily ambulatory marionettes who have somehow removed their strings. Both actors (Aguirre and Zagal), as the twins, speak in contrasting voices, often in unison, to suggest their deeply entrenched emotional interdependence. In this funny musical interlude, they complain about the dirtiness of their clothes (the grandmother won't wash their clothes like their mother did in the city), the lack of soap or clean water, the smell inside the house, and the disgusting state of their grandmother, who cleans her snot as she cooks, driving the twins to refuse her food. The pettiness of their concerns (emphasized by the silly song) about the lack of pulchritude and order in the house points to their inability to recognize the violence that led to their isolation in this space. At this point, their own comfort takes precedence over any instance of abuse, to the point that it is also difficult for them to find any empathy for the cruel grandmother, who is also an abused, marginal individual. The twins are unable to grasp the innate cruelty of their isolation and apply it to the grandmother as well.

In the beginning, this lack of understanding further separates them from the grandmother. The exchange between the daughter and grandmother at the beginning of the play clarifies that their mutual hatred stems from the fact that the daughter abandoned the grandmother after the grandfather's death. There are specific moments in the play that allow the spectator to understand the depth of the grandmother. For example, as she unpacks the suitcases of the twins (or ransacks them, as she is going to sell all their belongings), she stops to smell the contents as she cries. It seems as if the relationships in this family conform to a chain of abandonment and rancor. In addition, the twins' unsuitability for life in this village produces further resentment in the grandmother, who can find no use for them. Her life, as explained by the twins, who observe her closely, consists of strapping her wheelbarrow to her neck and walking "to the market without stopping and without putting down her wheelbarrow, not even once. Upon her return, she continues working. All day, every day, all her life." Their lack of adaptability leads the twins to be further isolated from the grandmother, who can't tolerate their ineptitude for hard work.

The differences between the grandmother and the twins at this point are critical for understanding their evolution. Onstage, the twins maintain their mechanical movements and concordant voices; they always seemed to be enveloped in slowness, which is emphasized by the dreamlike quality of the music.[34] The grandmother, on the other hand, is characterized by her shrill snarl and a mesmerizing witchiness that translates into abrupt movements. To the twins, she is an absolutely savage and primitive being: "Grandmother never washes herself. She doesn't use underwear. When she wants to urinate, she stops wherever she is, separates her legs and pees under her skirts. Obviously she never pees inside the house." This portrayal of the grandmother is paramount for understanding the transformation of the twins throughout the play. At the beginning, her savageness leads the brothers to isolate themselves further into their own world, away from this cruel woman. She doesn't fit the paradigms of the traditional social order to which their parents have made them accustomed.

The grandmother is the "original freak" in the play. By this I mean that she is the abject other whose perceived difference will "contaminate" the brothers. To the townspeople she is nothing more than a witch, removed from the confines of the town. Even to the brothers, as I have pointed out, she is nothing more than a savage beast when they first encounter her. If she is to be a maternal figure, then she represents a "monstrous mother" to these children. This perception of the grandmother by those around her continues the western tradition of woman as subhuman disorder. In the words of Rosi Braidotti, when it comes to womanhood, "it is as if 'she' carried within herself something that makes her prone to being an enemy of mankind, an outsider in her civilization, an 'other.'"[35] The grandmother goes even further with this, as she doesn't behave according to the normative image of mother/womanhood either, as described by the brothers. Onstage she appears in a mask that exaggerates her features, with a big nose and hunched back. Her costume is a drab, ample brown dress that covers her body from head to toe. She makes accelerated, curt movements, very different from the twins' mechanized movements. The actress, Laura Pizarro, gives life to a shrill, violent being that is so complex that one, as spectator, cannot simply hate this character. She represents survival amid chaos, and this quickly becomes apparent to the twins, who must "enfreak" themselves to become like her if they wish to survive.

Pain becomes the tool for surviving in the cruel and hostile world they now inhabit. The war and its atrocities are meaningless to the twins; the only reality they have is life with their grandmother, and they can neither comprehend nor control this scenario. Thus, they create their own measure of control for survival: exercises carried out to avoid the harmful influences of the external world by creating an apathetic consciousness that is immune to harm and pain. For example, the twins decide to accustom themselves to hard work in order to toughen their bodies. They carry heavy loads in the burning sun and repeat over and over "this is not heavy" and "the sun doesn't burn." They do the same with insults, repeating the most offensive words that have been hurled at them to each other until "little by little, words lose their meaning and the pain they cause softens." Words, thus, are themselves deformed as they lose their meaning. The entire reality that surrounds the twins has to change in their perception, as they gradually become the automatons that were already foreshadowed through their movements onstage. Their physical behavior (mechanical movements), then, fits their mental and moral state, as they grow accustomed to the new order of things. This is taken to the extreme in another exercise in which they hit one another until they can "endure pain without crying." As they explain to the grandmother "[E]ventually we no longer feel any pain. It is another who burns, another who cuts himself, another who suffers Grandmother." This idea brings much discomfort to the audience, as one does not know how to interpret some of the action onstage (this became apparent in the performance by the scattered laughs and gasps one could hear during these uncomfortable scenes). The performance has a lack of evaluation (positive or negative) for all events. The twins' "objective" voice establishes a sort of normalization of perversion.

The narrative that is being created by the twins, then, becomes the creation of a new ethic, a new morality that fits their need to adapt. They seek a narration devoid of judgment, evaluation, and feeling. Their acts, though, are not simply subordinate to the will to survive. Their relationship with the character of Harelip, an outcast little girl who lives nearby and whom the boys decide they must protect, expresses a moral agenda of rebellion against injustice and the atrocities that surround them. Harelip looks like a rag doll; she has a colorful dress that has seen better days and a wig with hair made of wool and she constantly sucks her thumb. A mask with visible stitching covers her face. She first appears onstage attempting to carry a bucket of water, but the other town children (represented by puppets that pop up and down) constantly spit in her bucket. The twins decide to protect her as another exercise. Harelip is an example of corrupt innocence; she is an oversexualized child (there are hints that the town priest has sexually abused her), who is constantly making references to sexual acts. She is an extreme of the pain that the twins have experienced—a broken child who has only known pain and acts accordingly. She is alone in her painful experience, as her mother is blind, deaf, and mute (again, represented by a doll onstage), whereas the twins have each other. Harelip only recognizes, and thus seeks, abuse because it is the only form of "play" she knows. It is as if for those who have no rights, those on the margins of a cruel system, the

Fig. 19. *Gemelos*. Actors Laura Pizarro as Harelip, and Juan Carlos Zagal and José Manuel Aguirre as the Twins. Photo by Montserrat Q. Antequera.

only way to survive is to get "used to" the violence that surrounds them. The twins appear to conform to this notion, but their behavior also shows an agency in their rebellion that protects those around them.

The twins' benevolence toward Harelip stands in contrast to the violence they display toward those they consider to be the abusers, such as the priest. First they blackmail him and demand that he give them money or they will tell everyone what he has done to Harelip. Eventually, they plant a bomb in the church, which almost kills the priest's maid. The questions that come to mind here is Is the twins' violent behavior an example of "acceptable" violence? In their journey from helpless children to active individuals, are they approaching a sort of "perverted" citizenship through which they acquire selfhood in a system of oppression? The twins act using the same rules followed by those in power: violence as a form of action. They "come of age" through cruel methods (leaving behind their bourgeois childhood), and their actions seem to question the existence of only one acceptable form of violence (when it is exercised by those in power). Their cruel methods are reminiscent of those of the grandmother, whose cruelty is the cruelty of survival in a system that has dehumanized her. It is a never-ending cycle of violence and punishment that is also contrasted with empathy and benevolence by those on the margins. As explained by Jaime Lorca, a founding member of the company, the twins demonstrate "a complex spiritual purity . . . [for] they possess a relentless ethic, a sure and coherent way of reasoning for the horrible world in which they have to live."[36] Their evolution resembles the instances to which Achilles Mbembe refers when he states:

> To live under late modern occupation is to experience a permanent condition of "being in pain": fortified structures, military posts, and roadblocks everywhere; buildings that bring back painful memories of humiliation, interrogations, and beatings; curfews that imprison hundreds of thousands in their cramped homes every night from dusk to daybreak; soldiers patrolling the unlit streets, frightened by their own shadows; children blinded by rubber bullets; parents shamed and beaten in front of their families; soldiers urinating on fences, shooting at the rooftop water tanks just for fun, chanting loud offensive slogans, pounding on fragile tin doors to frighten the children, confiscating papers, or dumping garbage in the middle of a residential neighborhood; border guards kicking over a vegetable stand or closing borders at whim; bones broken; shootings and fatalities—a certain kind of madness.[37]

In the case of *Gemelos* the result is the institution of a peculiar social order as we observe a series of ethical deliberations that take place between the grandmother and her grandchildren in an unexpected and adverse situation: survival in the midst of genocide.

The twins have evolved through a process of adaptation that culminates with their abandonment of all ties to the bourgeois system that has failed them. This is made clear toward the end of the performance with the imminent return to school. At this point, the twins have established a deep connection to the grandmother, rejecting their mother in the process. A letter arrives demanding that they report to school. None of the characters sees any purpose in this, and so they concoct a plan to evade it. The characters onstage reenact a scene in which they tell what happened when the school authorities came and the grandmother told them that the children were deaf and blind, as well as mentally ill. They are removed from school "because of [their] disability and psychological trauma." With this metatheatrical act, the twins become completely marginalized. What constitutes abnormality in the eyes of the state becomes a state of liberation for these characters.

From this perspective, the twins act together as one transgressive character that observes and denounces the arbitrariness of a political system that abuses and removes those deemed "inept" or of no use to the state. Their actions show an awareness of the abuses of those in power and recognition of the injuries suffered by the outcasts but without any empathy or emotion about what they observe. The voices of the children are the only testimony we, as spectators, are offered, and the shrunken dimensions of the production are an apt miniature world from which to experience this tale from the point of view of two boys caught up in the brutalizing march of history. The well-known horrors of World War II blend with disarming ease into the other nightmares the twins must survive. *Gemelos*, then, manages the unusual feat of allowing us to experience familiar sorrows from a distinctive, slightly disorienting new perspective. The cruelty that has surrounded their lives and their actions around this evoke Antonin Artaud's concept of cruelty, which complicates the meaning of the word: "Cruelty is above all lucid, a kind of rigid control and submission to necessity. There is no cruelty without consciousness and without the application of consciousness. It is a consciousness that gives to the exercise of every act of life its blood-red color, its cruel nuance, since it is understood that life is always someone's death."[38] Perceived through this lens, the supposed cruelty acted out by the twins becomes an ethical catalyst for change, for the impulsion of acting out. They must be completely expulsed from the system that oppresses them in order to insert themselves back into it as conscious individuals. The conclusion of the play is precisely that: after the grandmother's death, the "impenetrable" twins, who have no emotions or expressions (only a mechanical, unison voice and presence), break with their mechanized being and go their separate ways. They emerge as individuals who, even as they have been declared abnormal, have more humanity than the cruel enactors of the horrors around them.

THE PERVERSION OF UTOPIA: NORMAN BRISKY'S
EL BARRO SE SUBLEVA

Violence and anger toward those in power are common threads in Latin American theater that looks back at the various instances of human rights violations that have occurred across the continent. During the decades of the 1970s and 1980s it was a pervasive theme that impacted not only the creation of theater but also the artists, who were often blacklisted and highly censured. When critics think about the artistic representation of military repression and its aftermath in Latin America, they usually consider the theater of Argentina. There are many brilliant playwright and directors who were intimately affected by what happened, from Griselda Gambaro to Eduardo Pavlovsky and Ricardo Monti, as well as more current artists who continue to explore the effects of violence on society (Lola Arias, Rafael Spregelburd, Claudio Tolcachir, and many others). Yet an often overlooked figure in Argentine theater is Norman Briski, who is best known for his work as an actor on stage, in television, and on film, working with leading figures such as Carlos Saura, Luis Puenzo, and the Swedish director Stig Björkman. While he is well known for his acting prowess, scholars rarely consider his contributions as a writer and director.

Briski is a sort of freak figure himself, one who understands that his desire for a more just world is often overlooked as a political position of the past. A devoted militant who advocated leftist Peronism, in the 1960s he founded Grupo Octubre, which specialized in assembly theater in neighborhoods and towns around the country. Briski was forced into exile in 1975, in the midst of the military dictatorship, and he returned to Argentina with democracy. He was imprisoned in the 1980s for a brief period because of his militant past. His embodiment of political enfreakment was furthered when he founded Teatro Calibán in 1984, a very small theater space where he stages his own productions and gives classes to this day. As Briski explains, he chose this name because "Calibán was the one who can't but could; he is a character who is searching for his freedom: who will grant it to him or what must he do to get it?" [39] Briski's ideals of justice and freedom are engrained in his method for producing theater. Teatro Calibán does not receive government funding, and it creates artistic works under the motto that creating important theater does not require money. It is possible, then, to guess which are the ideas that Briski intends to rescue in his play *El barro se subleva* (The Mud Revolts), a title that refers to the tango "La última curda" (The Last Drunkenness); the mud that revolts is the revolution born from below, the legitimate, the popular.

When I saw this play for the first time in Buenos Aires, I was with two Argentinian friends. We went to an isolated theater, where you have to walk down a long, narrow hallway to get to the space, a small venue with classrooms and a theater. This was during the second season of the performance.[40] There was a medium-sized audience of mostly young adults, and we entered the dark space of the theater, where a bright yellow tape with the word "danger" separated us from the space where the work would occur. The immediate danger referred to a pit in the floor, which separated the stage from the audience. As it would be made clear later, *danger* also referred to those who dare to take a different look at the social and political scene that unfolds around them. *El barro se subleva* is a very complicated play, and I left the theater with more questions than answers, but I was taken aback when my two companions stated with equal conviction that this play could only have been written and staged by Briski, for only he maintained such clear political conviction in the contemporary neoliberal disaster that is Argentina after 2001. I was very fortunate to be welcomed into Briski's house a few days later to interview him, and when I asked him about this comment his simple reply was, "I guess it is because in general, intellectuals kept outside the popular struggles. The only ones who can talk about these issues in a molecular sense are Pavlovsky and myself, as well as Gambaro." Briski was referring to his lived experience in the militant front, and the idea of understanding the issues on a "molecular" level is a common theme in the play itself, since the main character is described as a man who was *genetically* born to believe that the world should be different. Like Briski.

As previously stated, the Argentinian military dictatorship tends to be the "common place" for the study of authoritarian regimes in Latin America, a focus on a single event that narrows the enquiry to the exercise of cruelty in Latin America. Yet the Argentinian Dirty War is a political marker of an explosion of violence during a tumultuous period that covered much of the continent. Nevertheless, as Jean Graham-Jones explains, this moment cannot be understood as a static period of violence in time as "the repression did not begin with the coup of March 24, 1976. Militarism and authoritarianism have long been a part of Argentine life and consequently have directly influenced the country's artistic production."[41] The appalling result was the some thirty thousand people who were disappeared when the military took over the government and eliminated all perceived opposition.[42] This was the time when Norman Briski went into exile after receiving death threats for his political work. There is much written about this period, but I am more concerned with the return to democracy and the establishment of a neoliberal agenda that continued to impose a casual violence without limits, as this is what the play reacts to: the destruction brought about by capitalist imperialism.

The Argentine postdictatorship era began in 1983 with the democratic election of Raúl Alfonsín. During this period, tremendous changes were carried out that promoted the defense of human rights violations committed during the military dictatorship. However, the economy was in crisis due to hyperinflation and the devaluation of the national currency. The election of Carlos Menem in 1989 ensured changes to this situation. However, the country underwent an abrupt change in the governmental organization that was based on a neoliberal model that privatized the public sector and was headed by private and foreign companies. At the same time, the export and import sector was deregulated and foreign exchange parity with the dollar was carried out. The policy of privatization left many on the outside, since these were measures that made employment precarious, leading to bankruptcies and closures of factories. After all, the cost of economic transformation was to be assumed by the people while a neoliberal image was granted to the foreigner. As early as 1998 it became clear that most of these changes were fictitious and that both financial strength and parity were impossible to maintain. The cost of transforming the state was the reduction of social programs, which accentuated the social inequality exacerbated by the neoliberal model. It was to be expected, then, that in 2001 the crisis of this neoliberal model would give way to a new economic crisis in the country. The country burst into protests, and this social outburst spelled the end of the neoliberal model, which had all along been shown to be a failure.[43]

This is the reality to which *El barro se subleva* is responding, the new horrors that continue to eradicate the marginal sectors from a system that has continually failed them: from the literal disappearance of individuals to the death and torture brought on by an authoritarian system of the past to the inability to survive in the precarious situation of the present. It is the continual removal of those who do not "benefit" a system of power, a cycle explained by Saskia Sassen as expulsions of the global economy: "Historically, the oppressed have often risen against their masters. But today the oppressed have mostly been expelled and survive at a great distance from their oppressors. Further, the 'oppressor' is increasingly a complex system that combines persons, networks, and machines with no obvious center."[44] In an era of neoliberal politics, it has become more difficult to identify the specific power dynamic that is keeping one from fully participating in the social system, and for the character in this play, his oppressor is a capitalist system of imperialism that prevents him from exercising his power as a citizen and convening a community willing to share in his idealism for a revolution of those on the margins.

El barro se subleva is a one-man show with Eduardo Misch as the only actor onstage. He performs the main character as well as the other individuals who pass through his life. It is the story of one man who wants to change the world, or at the very least to create a difference, and who inhabits his social realm with a great sense of justice and the belief that we are all equals. With this sense of justice as his catapult, he is consumed, as if under

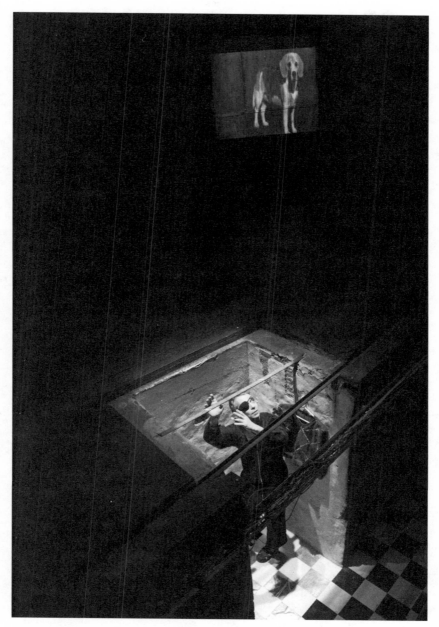

Fig. 20. *El barro se subleva*. Actor Eduardo Misch. Photo by Emmanuel
Melgarejo.

a genetic imperative (following Briski's notion of dissidence occurring at a molecular level), by the idea that the world has to be different. The performance itself is a series of acts that present different instances in his life, from the death of his dog (his only companion) to his relationship with a girlfriend, his time in jail for a minor infraction, and his experiences as a street vendor. It all occurs on a black stage, with a wooden wardrobe at the back. Its doors constantly open and close and are covered with mirrors that reflect the action onstage and the audience that observes. It is a vertiginous event that provokes observers from the moment they enter the space. After crossing the pit that separates it the stage, the audience has to climb to its seats on the steps in front of the stage. It is a dark space that is almost confining, with two sets of bright lights on either side of the stage.

This is a complicated play, which presents the audience with an individual that I read as a freak because of his moral imperative. He is marked as a different body because he refuses to behave in a normative fashion. The performance is further complicated by the fact that it requires a critical apparatus that is acquired through Briski's published novel *Nagasaki de memoria* (Nagasaki from Memory). This novel completes the play. It narrates this individual's journey before the action in the play as he travels to Nagasaki as a guest for a memorial commemorating the bombing and becomes disillusioned by the commercialization of the memory of this event. In the novel, Briski describes this character as an intellectual who has studied all of his life and suddenly realizes that this academic consciousness is of no use to him, for "his education will not bring any social change and his intellectual consciousness does not bring change, reason, or strength. Intellectual reason is not enough." Thus, he drastically changes his life and moves himself to the margins of society to create change from the bottom—the mud. The series of acts that comprise the play are short and delirious episodes that appeal more to the emotions than the intellect, leading to an all-encompassing message clearly stated by Briski: "Revolution is not accomplished with everyone knowing about it. It is a thing of contagion, of companionship, of 'if you go, I will go too.'"

This man's expulsion from the social system is directly linked to his embodiment of freakness: his idealism is reconstructed by the social order as insanity or perversion. He doesn't belong to the social order (as perceived by those who benefit from this power structure) because he believes in the possibility of a more just system and is willing to act against the prevailing political/economic order. His freak identity is established at the beginning of the play: in the second scene, he comes onstage on stilts and dressed in a reindeer outfit. He is selling Christmas cards, appealing to the great icon of capitalism: Santa Claus. But the cards he sells have different icons on them; he sells cards with images of Ché Guevara, Marx, and others. He tries to sell a card to a small boy and is taken aback because the child doesn't recognize the people on the cards. The child's father attacks the man, accusing him of harassing his son; the man tries to tell the father that he only wanted to sell his cards, but he ends up punched and battered. This is all, of course, acted out by Misch as all the characters. The man's idealism makes him a freak because he is a threat to the norm imposed by capitalist interests in this era of consumer culture.

As a street vendor who sells Christmas cards with revolutionary figures on them, this man constitutes a clear imbalance to the capitalist logic of consumerism. This is one of the foundations that allows for the stability and continuation of the dominant discourse on the part of the neoliberal system. By promoting the consumption of goods, dominant discourses, through the mass media, manage to control the market for symbolic goods. The market for symbolic goods operates from the institutionalization of an entire symbolic repertoire, that is, the mythification of certain images and objects. The image represents the possession of the object, and in turn the object of consumption is constituted as a sign of economic status. This man is playing with those symbols and values by attempting to resignify the economic mythification of Christmas and transforming the images that "sell" this holiday. In addition, the images of Marx and Ché have also been transformed as they have become a consumer good. Capitalist industrial society works through the consumption of these objects, and, as Umberto Eco asserts, "Therefore, the *Suger* of our time, who create and spread mythical images destined to be rooted in the sensibility of the masses, are the laboratories of the great industry, the advertising men of Madison Avenue, which popular sociology has designated with the suggestive epithet 'hidden persuaders.'"[45] Are Marx or Ché equally revolutionary when they are stamped on a Christmas card to be bought by a consumer? Is Christmas a revolutionary act when you celebrate it with Marx? These are some of the questions that stem from this man's actions as he attempts to exert some control over consumer culture, an action that is quickly overturned through the beating he receives. This violent action puts him on display as he is attacked on the street in a reindeer outfit, tripping on his stilts, claiming that he just wanted to sell cards. He is a freak who doesn't belong to the system and threatens to destabilize it with his idealism.

But this man perseveres. Through the different episodes of the play, it is evident that the forms of social organization that we produce and reproduce every day (such as buying a Christmas card) can become absurd and

irrational; instead his delusions end up being more lucid than the hypo-
thetical "normality." The same can be said for technological advances,
since science plays a crucial role in this man's idealism and disillusionment
with the modern world. This is an overarching theme in both the novel and
the play, where it seems as if science has a connotation of hope, but it turns
out to be the opposite. Science and its achievements collaborate more with
corporations and the atomic bomb than with the people they are supposed
to help. It is another source of disappointment. The man onstage faces this
as he attempts to perform almost ridiculous acts using technology. For example, he tries to hang a banana from a remote control helicopter. This action could mean many things, from the dropping of a bomb to the use of
drones, but the man is unable to make the helicopter work, and he asks
himself, "Why? Maybe because of my age. The peremptory . . . that holocaust . . . The miserable poverty of my resources to change courses. Idealist
burps?"[46] The possibility of using technology as a weapon fails for him, and
so he has to come up with alternatives for emancipation. This man wants to
come up with solutions, and this makes him different from those around
him, as the actor Eduardo Misch explains: "He is almost like a man-bomb;
he wants a different society, and he is seen by society as a serial killer, a
terrorist, a murderer, an individual that frightens those around him."[47] The
man perceives his role to be an ethical one; he must fight for justice, and so
he must remain marginal from those who do not share his vision. His constant fuel is to come up with an alternative that will allow him to modify
his reality, and this sense of justice makes him a subversive individual in
the eyes of society. With such an enormous enemy in imperialism, he can
only be marginalized as he constantly fails the battle. Most might consider
him to be insane, a freak, because it is easier to categorize him that way. But
he is a reasonable man who doesn't want to scare anyone (as established in
the scene with the reindeer suit); he just has to tend to his own hatred as he
finds this to be the catalyst that will allow change.

This hatred is a complex mechanism for his own revolution, a character-
istic that stems from Briski's own beliefs: "I have great respect for the potentiality of hatred to battle injustice." For the character in the play, the
hatred he feels toward injustice begins with his experience in Nagasaki. "It
was the photograph of a woman from Nagasaki," he tells his girlfriend in
the performance, "twenty years after the bomb, and her face only had one
eye, and the other eye was in the middle of her forehead. That eye couldn't
see, but it had an eyelid with long eyelashes. That's why a feeling of re-
venge was born within me . . . I decided to focus my actions in a vengeful
manner, without any irony."[48] This photograph (which also happens to be

the photograph on the program that the audience receives) is an injection of reality for this man. When he sees it he realizes that everything he knew as an intellectual solves nothing, and so he has to rely on hatred as a motive for revolutionary action. The idea is complemented by the novel, in which he experiences a further awakening when, while in Nagasaki, he goes to a freak show, which transforms him.

> A gloomy circus . . . A red-lacquer actor comes on the stage . . . And here the horrifying thing, of which I did not know anything. Quasi people walk naked before my eyes. Some with small platforms with wheels . . . ropes that tugged from outside the scene. Fright. Legs and arms bound by I do not know what vertebras, inverted feet, ears in the belly, deformed faces with one eye . . . What was I seeing? These weren't the mutilated bodies that preserve certain nobility. This was a genetic revolution, the most feared image, the creative impossibility of reaching the only spectacle of warning.[49]

His naïveté toward the catastrophic reality of the aftermath of the bomb, an idealization of the devastation, is transformed as he observes this sideshow of deformed bodies as entertainment for tourists. The revolutionary awakening he experiences after encountering those freakish bodies is better understood through the work of Mikhail Bakhtin, for whom the ambiguous body was also the foundation for free expression and political action.[50] The deformed body represented a utopian union of separate selves into a communal, grotesque body. This is an "unfinished and open body," an important aspect because it "is not separated from the world by clearly defined boundaries; it is blended with the world, with animals, with objects. It is cosmic, it represents the entire material bodily world in all its elements. It is an incarnation of this world at the absolute lower stratum, as the swallowing up and generating principle, as the bodily grave and bosom, as a field which has been sown and in which new shoots are preparing to sprout."[51] In a similar fashion to what is spouted by this man, Bakhtin advocates the dissolution of established hierarchies of power in favor of a shared humanity. Hierarchies represent the normate, "that which represents stable, immovable, and unchangeable being, not free becoming."[52] The freak body, though, is a transgression that transcends this unchangeable normativity through its unpredictability. This is the same transgression found in social revolutions; it incites liberation as it transcends the limits of individuality, denouncing the falseness of normate hierarchies and inciting wonder as the freak challenges normativity. The man in *El barro se subleva* is transformed by the bodies he encounters in Nagasaki and attempts to eliminate the ideal of the normal as the path to political freedom. He has to separate himself from the vertical hierarchies of normativity and fight oppression through recognition of his own marginality.

In the play, this man is coming to terms with his disillusionment in his own intellectual defeat after experiencing those moments in Nagasaki. His conversations with his girlfriend exemplify this change in perception: while she goes on analyzing their relationship through an almost incomprehensible theoretical discourse, he narrows down the conversation to the need for action, culminating in the description of the photograph. Intellectual discourse does not produce action because it belongs to the educational establishment. The photograph of a deformed body inspires him because it is a body that is the product of violence and war. This allows him to embrace his own difference as the most coherent path; he finds rationality in the abnormal. Anger and fear are the constants that move him forward, and in the performance these are the sentiments that catapult the action and are transmitted to the audience. The performance begins with an act of defeat. The man steps onto the stage from inside the wardrobe, carrying his dog (a medium-sized dog made of papier mâché) and places him in a small pink bathtub. As he bathes the dog, talking lovingly to him, the dog bites him in the eye. There is an immediate blackout. When the lights come on again, we see the man with an eye patch at the dog's funeral. I refer to this action as an act of defeat because the dog was this man's only family, his best friend. The dog bites him because there has to be a drastic end to all forms of idealized relations and familial bonds. Idealization acts as a central element of defeat—and defeat moves this man toward action in his disillusionment.

There are two pivotal scenes that move the character's disillusionment with the modern world forward. Toward the beginning of the play, we find this man sitting on the stage, his feet hanging into the pit below. He has a handful of cables in his hands, which he is unsuccessfully trying to connect. He mumbles to himself, stating that he is "fed-up with meetings, with psychotic fear, with illicit associations."[53] It becomes clear that this man views the world through a different lens and that this has isolated him. "I don't wait for anyone," he says, primarily because he doesn't understand it: "I don't trust the Internet . . . it's cybernetic communism. No one can declare their love with cellular orthography, so fast, so precocious."[54] He can't find his place in this world, where there lives, "the genocidal hero, killing immigrants with bank transfers."[55] His militancy stems from the thirty thousand deaths of the violent past, which can get lost in this modern "superficial liquid." Graham-Jones addresses this imposition of the past into the present in her discussion of theatrical productions in Buenos Aires post-2001. As she explains, many of the productions after the economic crisis "kept the ghost of repression alive" as they attempted to deal with the situation.[56] She quotes Monica Viñao's description of the country as a land of the economically disappeared and explains, "In reciting a term usually reserved for the 30,000 Argentines who were abducted and killed during the 1976–83 military dictatorship—that is, the *desaparecidos*—Viñao recalled the not-so-distant past of the late 1960s and early '70s when Argentina possessed an active Left, later violently repressed under the military regime."[57] The man in this play is attempting the same, precisely because the "ghost of repression" continues to exercise violence with impunity through the form of a neoliberal system. He is proclaiming the need for a revolution from the "mud that revolts," that is, from below. Only when the mud revolts can you shape new shapes, and he claims, "we are in the mud that revolts. I need to convince myself that I even crazy I can, crazy to believe that I have the master key. Explicit connections, 'communicational communication,' they do not work. It's from behind, below, surreptitiously. Without party, without members, by chance . . . just because."[58] A few more words, and the sound of an explosion leads to a blackout. The audience realizes that he was attempting to create some sort of bomb, but even in that he is unsuccessful. Yet we are reminded that his attempts are always in the search for hope in a better world, even as he continues to fail.

This intentional act of creating a bomb can be contrasted with the final scenes of the play. First the man appears with a giant tractor tire inside the pit, as he rolls it along he talks to the ghost of his dog (a projection on the stage) and tells him, "Now I understand everything, they asked me to straighten the world . . . Who asked me! . . . Because for me we are all equal . . . those of us who are alive . . . Why do they honestly fight us? Because their love is only a love for their herd. It is a love for territory. And that makes them think that they are the owners of history. And history belongs to whoever wants to tell it."[59] Nevertheless, it is impossible to idealize this man and his search for justice because his situations are always ridiculous. He moves from this scene to a space in the pit that the spectator can quickly understand as a prison cell. But this is not how he expected to land in prison. "I always imagined being a heroic prisoner,"[60] he says, but he is not the romanticized and idealized image of the political prisoner. Instead he is there because he ran a red light while riding his bicycle. Even his imprisonment is a failure: it isn't for a great cause but for a simple infraction. But his disillusionment and failure do not mean defeat. As Briski explains, when individuals want to create structural change they must always expect failure: "Do not worry about winning the battle, you worry about doing the battle." What is perceived as abnormal behavior, to persist in fighting for a lost cause, constitutes his freak identity, but this is also what allows him to continue with his cause even while imprisoned: "[H]ere it is thanks to insanity that one doesn't feel any pain."[61] It is indeed his personal tragedy that he must always be alone and searching for a community of similarly minded individuals.

However, there is a paradox that is established with the fact that Misch is also the only individual onstage and that, in turn, he gives life to a story with many characters. The actor inhabits other characters' beings without resorting to exaggerated mimicry, like his girlfriend or his prison companions. He tries to unite with the people of the prison, he creates a group with the prisoners, and still nothing happens. He's trying to change the world and nobody heeds, but he decides to keep pushing. This leads to the question Do the others really exist or are they the product of the unnamed man's fantasy? It is one of the unanswered questions that Briski leaves, and it is not of little importance if what this man wants is social change. Briski has often stated that the purpose of theater is not to solve problems but to lead to an assembly of people who can question together what they see: "[T]he best plays are the ones that lead to an assembly when finished." Therefore, this man raises questions that are posed to the audience. Are we this man's community? Are we willing to come to the assembly?

A TIME FOR HEALING: *HALCÓN DE ORO: Q'ORIHUAMAN*

The sense of hope for justice stirred in the *El barro se subleva* continues and is expanded within the framework of the play at the center of this final section: *Halcón de oro: Q'orihuaman* (The Golden Falcon: Q'orihuaman), another solo performance directed by the Peruvian artist Ana Correa and performed by Rodolfo Rodríguez, based on a short story by Rodríguez.[62] This short performance of around forty-five minutes delivers a strong and powerful study of the effects of war on the individual. As previously discussed, the multiplicities of cultures and languages that compose Peru have led to a history of discrimination (social, racial, and gender) and overt racism. A long history of colonialism has contributed to the marginalized condition of the indigenous populations over all others. Multiple groups have suffered under the most adverse conditions: from the virtual slavery of the colonial period to the extreme poverty and precariousness brought on by over thirty years of highly unscrupulous neoliberal and neoconservative policies in modern times, along with the terrible consequences of the armed conflict (often referred to as a civil war) between the Shining Path and the Peruvian state between 1980 and 2000. Both sides produced terrible forms of violence, from the terrorism of the Shining Path to the antiterrorist activities of the government. The result was years of violations of basic human rights that caused tens of thousands of deaths and disappearances. The majority of the victims were indigenous individuals who did not participate in the armed conflict but lived in the territories of battle. The Truth and Reconciliation Commission (TRC), appointed by the Peruvian government in 2000 to investigate what occurred, estimated that this war probably caused sixty-nine thousand deaths. According to the TRC, three out four victims were of indigenous or rural origin.

The effects of this war continue today, more than a decade after the TRC's report, as numerous mass graves are still being discovered with hundreds of bodies awaiting identification. However, very few of these cases have been legally processed. As a nation, Peru has been unable to come to terms with the aftermath of this long period of violence since there has not been a legal process that establishes culpability on either side. The military has not recognized its responsibility and continues to cover up its role with euphemisms that extend from a language of "excesses" to the dismissal of violence as having occurred in "isolated cases" in which it committed crimes in defense of the state. Meanwhile, the leaders of the Shining Path, faced with the great number of their victims, responded that they had calculated that their victory would cost a million lives. *Halcón de oro* inserts its narrative into this history of cruelty. As the program notes explain, this is "the story of a young ex-soldier held in an asylum during dark times and his relationship with an Andean priest, who through a series of different tests will help him to recover his memory and lead a life of service and healing." This is accomplished in a particular way, since the performance never uses texts or language, and the different actions are dramatically marked through the music arraigned for the play. It is an almost magical space, empty of any decoration other than a metal bed frame and the body of the actor, Rodolfo Rodríguez, which is the sole impulse for dramatic action. What we observe, then, is a true corporeal score, fulfilled with the utmost rigor and precision. Rodríguez, who appears covered with white paint, a shaved head, a naked torso, and frayed military pants, brilliantly interprets the sole character that occupies this empty space. His physical appearance emphasizes the abnormality of his emotional state. It is suggestive that the actor, who is trained as a mime, draws on an unnatu-

Fig. 21. *Halcón de oro-Q'orihuaman*. Actor Rodolfo Rodríguez hangs from the bed. Photo by Fidel Melquiades Carvallo.

ral representation for his physical appearance. From the first instant of the performance, Rodríguez's physical presence emphasizes a different body: the artificial whiteness of his skin, the strange movements of his body (reminiscent of Japanese Butoh), and the visceral expressions on his face. It could be argued that there is an element evocative of freak performance in insane asylums, where audiences once paid to view patients in their cells. Furthermore, his main companion onstage is an old metal bedframe.

The relationship between the character, named Amílcar, and this object—through physical actions and the composition of images—is what gives the audience signals about his emotional—if not mental—state and references about his isolation, loneliness, and madness. In this way, through the symbolic aspect of objects and the great physical feats of the actor, the performance suggests the dark and dense environment of an insane asylum that is also reflective of the repercussions of war and violence on the individual. This solo performance, though, includes a second character that appears and disappears. After a long accumulation of tension brought on by the music and the actor's movements, a second individual appears dressed in a bone-colored dress. This character seems to reference the *ukukus* of religious celebrations in Cusco.[63] This second character is Q'orihuaman, whose interaction with the main character—in his different appearances—reveals his role as a shaman. The link between the two characters generates a ritual atmosphere (at times too cryptic to understand) that promotes the emergence and development of other dynamics of action and energy in the performance. What starts as a dense and dark environment gives way to an enigmatic ritual that triggers the transformation in the character of Amílcar. Overall, the performance is composed of rises and falls of physical and emotional energy—ranging from the use of objects to pantomime and physical actions—that reveal situations that allude to the violent conflict lived in Peru throughout the second half of the twentieth century.

To understand the aesthetics of this performance, it is necessary to further inquire into the artistic encounter that brought together Ana Correa and Rodolfo Rodríguez. In the words of Correa, "From 1992 and 1996, we welcomed Rodolfo Rodríguez, an actor from Cusco, who was eager to share his work and train with us in Grupo Cultural Yuyachkani. As our colleague, Rodolfo accompanied us on a journey in search of a Peruvian theatre identity and a method of working with actors and actresses in times of violence. . . . Our encounter was of two corporeal identities with strongly distinct techniques."[64] Thus, this artistic encounter gave way to the collaboration of two corporeal experiences that stem from different techniques and backgrounds. Rodríguez is an established actor and mime, with more than three decades of experience working with classic and popular pantomime. He performs primarily in open spaces. Ana Correa is one of the founding members of Grupo Cultural Yuyachkani.[65] Her work also centers on the body but emphasizes training in folkloric dance, martial arts, tai chi, and dramatic work with objects. In addition, Fidel Melquiades, technical designer for Yuyachkani who passed away in 2012, joined the two in planning the composition of the objects that create the performance. Their different artistic experiences inspired a performance that explores the intersections between ritual and body as a necessary instance for remembrance and healing of the continual scars and trauma produced by political violence in Peruvian society. Immersed in a space without clear temporal or geographic references, the protagonist represents one of the many anonymous soldiers who faced real and symbolic death to endure the pain caused by political violence.

Halcón de oro: Q'orihuaman premiered in November 1995 after a long process of exploration and collective creation. Nevertheless, it closed after nine performances. Fifteen years later, in 2010—after Peru had witnessed the public hearings of the TRC; the flight, capture, and trial of the fugitive ex-president Fujimori; and the difficult path that has been initiated toward redress and justice for the victims of the war—the creators of *Halcón de oro* regrouped and began, at last, to share a long anticipated tour around the country and continent. The play developed from a short story by Rodríguez, based on the life of Benito Qoriwaman, an Andean high priest from Cusco, and his relationship with a young man who had gone insane though drug use, whom he healed and converted to be his student. Thus, the play interposes one character from mythology and the reality of ancestral worship and another that emerges from the contemporary practice of derision and death. It is difficult to establish a clear narrative for the performance, but in general terms it is divided into three major actions. In the first part, Amílcar evokes emotional states brought on by his confinement, such as oppression and anguish, through a series of interactions with the metal bed in the empty space. A strong white light comes and goes, keeping his body in the shadows as he falls on the bed or hides beneath it. In the second part, he faces personal and cultural memories with the help of Q'orihuaman. These memories are embodied through characters performed by Amílcar using a skirt, jacket, headscarf, and a golden mask that the shaman bestows on him. They include figures such as the archetypal mother, carrying her child and dancing with delicate, circular movements that refer back to the cyclical time of the Andean cosmovision. In the final action, the ex-soldier strips off his clothes in a purifying ritual led by this spiritual shaman through which he purges all trauma in order to acquire a new sense of identity grounded in his cultural individuality. This narrative and performative structure completes a cycle that progresses throughout the play. The cycle could be described as the creation of (1) context/density/accumulation, (2) ritual/transformation, and (3) detonation/memory. Thus, following this logic, the performance leads to an energetic climax followed by calm so that Amílcar can reconstruct a cycle for new processes of transformation and memory.

The element that stands out the most in this performance is the lack of language. By avoiding any reference to verbal language, the play relativizes the centrality of Spanish as an instrument of a political-legal rationality that historically has excluded other languages and forms of knowledge particular to indigenous communities. This is why the musical soundtrack is a crucial element of the piece. It combines various soundscapes, such as melodies featuring different styles of Peruvian pan flutes (zampoña, antara), to construct atmospheres in which ethnicity and the affective bond to it are consti-

Fig. 22. *Halcón de oro-Q'orihuaman*. Actor Rodolfo Rodríguez. Photo by Gloria Pardo.

tuted as fundamental elements for the reinvention of a sense of identity. In this way, the actor uses his body as an articulating axis from which to enunciate what legal documents tend to silence: the perspective of the protagonists who lived this internal violence. In other words, the absence of words refers to the silence of those voices whose testimony was ignored by the media and official authorities in their attempt to write an official history that would exculpate those involved in human rights violations.

This absence of language must also be understood in relation to a complex sociohistorical context that required the search for other languages with which to narrate the effects of the war. This is an idea that goes hand in hand with *Gemelos* and the use of a child's perspective to narrate moments of extreme violence. For example, Amílcar takes in his arms the skirt that had previously been bestowed on him by Q'orihuaman. He rocks it in his arms as if it were a child. Then he drops it to the ground, where it becomes a body. Through his elaborate movements it becomes evident that Amílcar opens the body, removes the heart and eyes, and violates the body. He then appears to stack bodies, falls to the floor, becomes entangled in the skirt, frees himself, and runs to the bed frame, which has been standing upright. He climbs the frame, and standing erect, high on the bed frame, he speaks the only words of the play: "Apu Kallahualla."[66] Amílcar is an accomplice in this war and also a victim. What makes him a freak is not his racialized body but the trauma involved in how he was forced to act in order to survive the violence of war. There can be no doubt as to the effects of this on him, something that is further explained by the Argentine philosopher León Rozitchner, who writes that "[C]rime and murder, whether individual or collective, by the state or by society, although they may be 'normalized' and bureaucratic, are not and can never be banal. . . . The evil that leads one to delight in the murder and torture of another human being can never be, in our view, an indifferent experience for the perpetrator."[67] The moments in which he is able to connect to his indigenous culture are the only moments of clear identity. The excesses of war and the massacres and desecrations of other bodies produced a fundamental change in his core values as a human being, unable to recognize his own vulnerabilities, much less those of others.

Another important structure for the creation of meaning is the metal bed frame. The actor shares the stage with this object, which holds, imprisons, sustains, defies, and eventually elevates him as it hangs from the ceiling. Needless to say, this bed becomes a character, triggering major conflicts. The act of carrying the frame of the bed, for example, and moving around the stage with it evokes those displaced by violence, who had to abandon their individual, family, and ethnic ties. Ana Correa explains that the use of this object stems from their first investigations, when they visited a psychiatric hospital in Lima "in an effort to gain awareness and come into contact with patients, spaces, environments, textures, and furnishings." [68] They found an old iron bed there and decided to use it for scenic exploration, mainly because of the multiple possibilities such an object offered: "In a bed you can make love, be born, sleep, heal, eat, read, write, play, dream, wait/hope, agonize, and die."[69] The bed became the object through which the character's emotional state could be exteriorized.

Amílcar is a very complex character, and necessarily so as he stands with Q'orihuaman, a character of mythological proportions. This drug-crazed youth becomes a social model of the great losses the nation suffered throughout the moments of civil unrest. He has caused violence and been a victim of this violence. As a result, the spectator needs to know what terrible circumstances have caused his anguish and imbalance. Throughout the years of violence, hundreds of peasants, men and women, disappeared or died. The first mass graves were discovered at the same time that rural populations were witnessing the return of traumatized young people from their compulsory military service. The majority of them did not receive the medical treatment that would have helped them reintegrate into society. These ex-combatants had engaged in killing sprees of their fellow citizens, "orgies of collective violence," explains Jean Franco, "that consolidated the executioners as bands of brothers."[70] These "bands of brothers" created their own forms of ritual violence to establish bonds of loyalty and solidarity in the continued cruel acts that characterized this period in history. Violence was encouraged by the state: "The cultivation of sadism and the deliberate defiance of all taboos challenges any notion of the state as the guardian of the human rights of its population. The deliberate destruction of feelings of empathy in its young men would have effects long after the end of civil war."[71] The military had to completely reprogram young men emotionally to hate their fellow indigenous people in order to commit horrendous acts.

For this performance, Correa and Rodríguez did not have to search very far; they came into contact with the recorded testimony of Alberto, a young psychiatric patient admitted to the Military Hospital who had fought in Ayacucho. Alberto related that in order for him to carry out his extermination orders his superiors made him take drugs, converting him, little by little, into an addict. He and his fellow soldiers would enter communities where they would rape and kill by extracting eyes and hearts, cutting off limbs and throwing them in the air, or dumping suspected terrorists out of helicopters. They used these testimonies as the basis for the lunacy of the main character. Amílcar has lost his detrimental band of brothers and gone from the cruel rituals of his military brotherhood to the isolation of a psychiatric ward. And the remnants of the atrocities he committed continue to haunt him. After taking off the mask and tunic that Q'orihuaman had given to him, and after that brief moment of happiness in which he explored the space with these objects, which are remnants of his indigeneity, Amílcar spins the bed, gaining momentum, and places it vertically. Accompanied by uplifting music, he scales the frame and reaches a rope hanging from the ceiling. He entangles his legs in the rope, hangs from the ceiling with a series of beautifully nightmarish movements, and finally lifts the bed (with the help of Q'orihuaman, who immediately leaves the stage) and hooks it to the rope. Amílcar floats over the suspended bed. The music changes to a haunting set of noises and there is only one spotlight focused on the hanging Amílcar with his bed. The noises focus on the sound of helicopters flying as Amílcar fades onto the bed. He remembers all the violence he committed. This is his instability and devastation: an identity forged by war, violence, and hatred toward the perceived enemy, his fellow men and women.

As a soldier, Amílcar was trained to view the indigenous populations as nonhuman, noncitizens that represented a threat to the state. As Primo Levi explains, "[B]efore dying the victim must be degraded so that the murderer will be less burdened by guilt. This is an explanation not devoid of logic but it shouts to heaven: it is the sole usefulness of useless violence."[72] And, as history has shown, war justifies and even rewards such cruel and violent acts. Thus, the "enemy" of the state had to be transformed into a freak, in this case through the implementation of a set of characterizations that "conflated all types of ethnicities and physical abnormalities to make the Other as freakish as possible, to make difference synonymous with disloyalty."[73] In this case, Thomas Fahy is referring to the images of the enemy created in the United States during World War I, but the statement is also applicable to the Peruvian case, where overt racial discrimination was simply an escalation of a long-standing colonial gaze that considered indigenous populations to have no place in the modern state: "It was less problematic to torture, disappear, assassinate, and exercise different forms of violence and extreme cruelty against those who were considered not only different but, more particularly, unreal—those whose lives have been negated."[74] The indigenous populations were denied any possibility of citizenship through a process of enfreakment that removed their identity from a modernizing project for the nation.

This idea that the state has the power to not only marginalize but remove certain individuals from society follows Achille Mbembe's notion of sovereignty: "[T]he ultimate expression of sovereignty resides, to a large degree, in the power and the capacity to dictate who may live and who must die. Hence, to kill or to allow to live constitutes the limits of sovereignty, its fundamental attributes. To exercise sovereignty is to exercise control over mortality and to define life as the deployment and manifestation of power."[75] Following Foucault's notion of biopower, Mbembe extends this idea to his concept of the necropolitical, a state of exception directly related to enmity that becomes a normative state with the right to kill: "In such instances, power (and not necessarily state power) continuously refers and appeals to exception, emergency, and a fictionalized notion of the enemy. . . . In other words, the question is What is the relationship between politics and death in those systems that can function only in a state of emergency?"[76] This he relates to Foucault's use of racism in the divisions of biopower.

> That *race* (or for that matter *racism*) figures so prominently in the calculus of biopower is entirely justifiable. After all, more so than class-thinking (the ideology that defines history as an economic struggle of classes), race has been the ever present shadow in Western political thought and practice, especially when it comes to imagining the inhumanity of, or rule over, foreign peoples. Referring to both this ever-presence and the phantomlike world of race in general, Arendt locates their roots in the shattering experience of otherness and suggests that the politics of race is ultimately linked to the politics of death.[77]

In the economy of biopower, then, the function of racism is to regulate the distribution of death and to make possible the murderous functions of the state. This requires that those others be characterized as a mortal threat to the legitimate citizens of the state, who will be able to live secure and happy lives only when those individuals are eliminated. This also implies that the execution of the other becomes a mechanized and impersonal procedure that acts quickly in its methods of extermination. In the case of Peru, the process of mechanized extermination was apparent as mass graves began to appear and the disappearances of these "stateless" individuals was more extensive.

Halcón de oro deals with the effects of the violent state of exception as a process of resignification through which Amílcar must find a sense of purity and forgiveness. The character must resignify his ethnic identity as he comes to terms with his complicity in the extermination of his own people, and he must find new rituals for community that will help remove his drug use as a coping mechanism and replace it with healing methods to purify his soul. The character of Q'orihuaman, even though he is an ephemeral figure that comes and goes from the performance space, is an integral part of this process. Q'orihuaman is a real person. Rodolfo Rodríguez met Don Benito Qoriwaman (*Qóri* = gold, *Waman* = falcon) as an adolescent when he healed his mother of a rare and serious illness. Don Benito had knowledge of medicinal plants, sacred songs, and the necessary offerings for Pachamama (Mother Earth). He knew how to heal people; he knew how to call their frightened and traumatized souls back from fear and sickness. While he was curing Rodolfo's mother, Don Benito recounted tales from his life. At the age of nine, Don Benito fell off a mountainside and died. The day of his wake an Andean priest arrived, offering to wake him, but only if and when his mother agreed that after reviving him the priest could take Don Benito with him. The mother agreed, and from that day Benito followed the priest and inherited his knowledge. Therefore, the performance is nourished by the presence of this character, who experienced suffering and imparts knowledge to this young man, who was brought up by the violence of war.

Amílcar must be led toward healing. In the final scene, Q'orihuaman appears with two white flags, which carry many connotations. He uses them almost like wings, flying around Amílcar, who takes them and attaches them to the hanging bed. Slowly, Amílcar removes his clothes until he is completely naked. He walks toward the shaman, who has made a circle of coca leaves, enters the circle, and sits. Q'orihuaman washes the young man with water and rose petals and then walks away. Amílcar slowly rises and follows him. The only thing left is the hanging bed with the two white flags. It is possible and necessary to heal from the violence of the past. From this point of view, the ex-soldier's body in crisis interpellates in its silence the official history and evokes the collective memory and the actors involved in it. Healing and reconciliation cannot happen through the official decrees spouted by the state. Reconciliation from that single, official perspective would be tantamount to silencing the voices of the native communities and minimizing the value of the lives of those historically considered second-class citizens. In *Halcón de oro* remembering through the body becomes a ritual that cures trauma and opens the possibility for a just reconciliation with the past.

The three plays examined in this chapter signal the possibility of healing after a history of cruelty. In order to do so, these artists, as well as the artists found throughout this book, depend on the bodies of individuals who have suffered extreme forms of cruelty due to their inability to fit into the normative standards for inclusion. Obviously these are nothing more than theatrical representations. None of the performances and plays discussed throughout the book includes overtly nonnormative actors. Instead, the artists use their bodies to create allegories of enfreakment that exemplify the multiple possibilities found in otherness. Theater, then, is magnifying the freakness to sting the audience into recognizing the brutal exclusion of certain bodies from a system that we all are a part of. The individual that was enfreaked by neoliberalism is ultraenfreaked onstage in order to show the effects of this perceived difference on an individual. In the case of this final chapter, the imposed difference becomes a death sentence, or at least life threatening. For example, *Gemelos* resorts to a process of enfreakment in which the bodies of the actors appear to be almost nonhuman, like puppets or caricatures that are too far removed from a visual recognition of normativity. Their exaggerated difference serves to illustrate the extremes to which society will go to castigate those who do not fit in and the embodied violence that follows these violent practices. *El barro se subleva* and *Halcón de oro* move this discussion forward by progressively showing the range of possibilities that frame discourses of violence founded on normativity, from the exclusion of bodies based on moral figurations to the enfreaked body of those who unwillingly took part in the violent erasure of marginalized communities. These three performances highlight the extreme forms of freakery that are perceived as a threat that must be removed and exterminated. At the same time, the plays allow for instances of hope in recognition of the effects of violence and the possible healing to be found in this process.

Conclusions

When I began to research this book, I thought I would only be writing about the physical aspects of the monstrous and those individuals who have been marked as "weird." This interest probably stems from my teenage days as a punk kid who tried her hardest not to conform to the norm (without really understanding what "the norm" meant, I might add). Yet, as I began to select the plays and performances that I wanted to write about, I began to understand that this book was about more than staging rebellious characters; it was about a legacy of colonial power that pushes us, Latin Americans, to the confines of normalcy according to Euro-US standards. Now, as I finish this book, in the midst of a Trump presidency in the United States, the relevance of denouncing this discriminatory and dangerous gaze is more apparent than ever. A perceived lack of conformity to an established norm is violently impacting all sorts of human interactions across the globe.

This, however, is nothing new: performance and theater have warned us about the dangers of these perspectives over the centuries. A more recent example is the now famous 1992 piece *The Couple in the Cage,* in which Guillermo Gómez-Peña and Coco Fusco warned about the complacency with which societies of power continue to perceive the Latin American identity as an object that embodies difference and danger. In their performance, the artists critiqued the quincentennial celebration of Columbus's arrival in the Americas, and the piece has become a standard from which to discuss racial difference in a postcolonial context. In the piece, Gómez-Peña and Fusco pretended to be "specimens" from a recently discovered tribe of Amerindians and were put on display throughout museums in the United States and other parts of the world. The set of the performance was the cage, which they furnished with "indigenous" artifacts and "modern" goods (e.g., a radio and television). The audience would stand around the cage to observe them (as native people were often displayed in the past), and the two artists would interact with them—posing for pictures, speaking a made-up language, and touching their hair and clothing. The impact of this performance was in the way it played to, and challenged, the audiences' own dehumanizing stereotypes and perceptions of racial difference. This is made especially obvious in a video montage of the performance. In it many viewers responded directly to the authority of the museum space and understood the performance to be a "truth": the exhibition of two native people from an undiscovered tribe. While some were pleased to observe "such wonders," other spectators were outraged at this human rights violation. Either way, the space of the museum provided a set of challenges as a bastion of science and truth. Fusco and Gómez-Peña delved deeper into this confusion by connecting the piece to the "circus freak" category. In a video of the performance edited by Paula Heredia and Fusco, the piece is juxtaposed with documents and photos from the nineteenth and early twentieth centuries to further associate the performance with the freak show. By drawing attention to a history and practice of exhibiting humans (this was very much endorsed by Columbus, who took several Arawak Indians to the court in Spain), Gómez Peña and Fusco defy the continued ethnographic spectacle of bodies that are deemed extraordinarily different (and therefore subject to exhibition and control). In other words, if we extend the significance of this performance to today, the artists force the audience to confront a history that, at least in the United States, has led to a tremendous number of deportations, rampant Islamophobia, a ban on transgender individuals in the military, and a long list of other acts.

Even though there is an exhaustive amount of scholarship on this performance, I must reference it here as a piece that (re)popularized the image of the freak in Latin American performance. Fusco and Gómez-Peña purposely revived the freak shows of the nineteenth century as a critique of the humiliation suffered by racialized bodies through the discourses implanted by coloniality. Closing this book with *The Couple in the Cage* (one of the best-known performances of freakness in academic circles) shows that this common trope has evolved in multiple ways, including the ways I chose to look at the various possibilities that theater and performance create for interacting with the freak body. This trope is so pervasive that theater critic Helen Shaw recently said that what she finds to be most common now is "the move toward what I call the Weird."[1] Shaw continues, "Indeed it's almost rare to see an important piece that doesn't hint at strange forces gathering, that doesn't stretch its hands out to the supernatural, that doesn't use realism for non-realistic ends. Look around. We're in an upwelling of what Yeats called the 'mad abstract dark.' Even writers who hew to realism-qua-realism use the metaphysical to set off their brutal observations."[2] If this trope is becoming a metaphor often used to explore the brutality of our world, how is Latin America different? Will the freak as an allegory become so common as to lose its strength? We must question some of these ideas as we consider the future of this figure.

There are number of plays and performances in Latin America that use the figure of the freak as a means of exploring the history of violent repression and inequality that is part of our identity. It is important to consider this representation as a form of what José Esteban Muñoz termed disidentifications as modes of survival. This book has provided an analysis of how the freak has come to embody a broad range of deviant and nonnormative positions: the queer, the colonial, the abject, the criminal, the neoliberal, and so on. In each of my examples, the playwrights and performance collectives mobilize the freak to flip accepted social norms and values. By disidentification Muñoz means, "The survival strategies the minority subject practices in order to negotiate a phobic majoritarian public sphere that continuously elides or punishes the existence of subjects who do not conform to the phantasm of normative citizenship."[3] The characters in the plays I have discussed access some form of freak identity as either a strategy of survival or a direct method of denouncement. The varied representations of "freakdom" found in Latin American theater point to the immediate necessity of addressing the ways in which the neoliberal machine has exploited those abject (or soiled) bodies to the point of making them disappear from the public sphere.

Throughout *Freak Performances* I have attempted to redefine how difference in Latin America is weighted by the shadows of colonization, from the time of the Conquest to today. Nevertheless, theater and performance continue to encounter and resist these assigned representations. Roger Bartra narrates an episode from 1538 recounted by the chronicler Bernal Díaz del Castillo during a celebration at the *plaza mayor* in Mexico/Tenochtitlan. According to del Castillo, on that day "a forest appeared in the central square of Mexico. . . . In the middle were trees that looked as if they had been felled. . . . And inside the forest were many deer, and rabbits, and hares, and foxes. . . . And there were some thick groves somewhat apart from the forest, and in each one was a squadron of wild men with knotted and twisted clubs, and other wild men with bows and arrows, and they go to the hunt."[4] The idea of the savage has always been crucial to the colonizers' enactments of their power. The history of colonization continues to demand a different other to be publicly and violently performed and into which society can empty all of its fears about enforcing a social order founded on artificial normalcy. This continued legacy is found in the constant effort to invent entire systems of thinking and structures of authority shielded by science, law, and religion in order to avoid any encounter with or provide dignity to those who differ from the norm.

The plays examined throughout this book, however, present the different body as a reflection of the self. Through exaggerated bodies and aberrant behaviors, which are themselves allusions to freak shows, these works capture the physical and psychological horrors of the dictatorship and genocides that characterized the mid-twentieth century in Latin America. They portray a society that continues to be afraid of difference. These performances use freakishness to shatter any naive assumption about war as a glorified act and violence as a part of modernity. Some very specific social factors have contributed to the construction of certain members of society as freaks rather than citizens in these times of extreme violence. These factors continue to persevere in our collective imagination: even as we think that we have transcended those violent times, we continue to see the world in harmful, disabling ways. The plays discussed in this book serve as cultural works that guide audiences into processes of remembrance, recognition, and acceptance of a colonial heritage that not only configure Latin America in the eyes of western modernity as a different body but also permeate our own consciousness to such an extent that we marginalize and exclude those who most represent that imposed non-European difference. The freak on these stages is not only configured by a history of coloniality that stems from the western gaze; it is also perpetuated by a Latin American society that replicates this same process of disfiguration and destruction through a culture of coloniality. It is the colonization of an imaginary.

Notes

INTRODUCTION

1. "Procreamos una cosa bien rara, como nosotros pero con otra cara. Nuestra genética, un laberinto somos igual de distintos." Unless otherwise noted, all translations are mine.

2. Reggaeton is a musical genre that began in the 1980s in Puerto Rico as a new sound that fuses black Atlantic genres (primarily hip-hop and dancehall reggae). Most intellectuals and the general public have considered this type of music, along with the artists, trash. This has been so, explains Frances Negrón-Muntaner, primarily because "reggaeton speaks to what good taste considers garbage—that is, the genre's main subject is sexuality in its most carnal dimensions; and, also, because until now it has been mainly associated and consumed by a 'trashy' group with little social prestige, the Puerto Rican lower classes" (*Reggaeton*. Eds. Raquel Z. Rivera, Wayne Marshall, and Deborah Pacini Hernandez. Durham: Duke UP, 2009. 327).

3. The interview is referenced in Griselda Florez's article "You've Never Seen a Music Video Like This: Watch Residente's NSFW 'Somos Anormales,'" *Billboard*, January 13, 2017, http://www.billboard.com/articles/columns/latin/7655112/residente-somos-anormales-nsfw-video-leguizamo

4. I am borrowing David Hevey's concept of "enfreakment" (The Creatures Time Forgot: Photography and Disability Imagery. London: Routledge, 1992. 53) to refer to the figure of the freak as a social construct and as a practice of othering. As Rosemarie Garland-Thomson states, "Enfreakment emerges from cultural rituals that stylize, silence, differentiate, and distance the persons whose bodies the freak-hunters or showmen colonize and commercialize. . . . What we assume to be a freak of nature was instead a freak of culture" ("Introduction." *Freakery: Cultural Spectacles of the Extraordinary Body*. Ed. Rosemarie Garland-Thomson. New York: New York UP, 1996.10). Robert Bogdan also defines the process of enfreakment as a cultural framing: "'Freak' is not a quality that belongs to the person on display. It is something that we created: a perspective, a set of practices—a social construction" (Freak Show: Presenting Human Oddities for Amusement and Profit. Chicago: U of Chicago P, 1988. xi).

5. Guy Debord, *Society of the Spectacle* (Detroit: Black & Red, 2010), 57.

6. Jesús Martín-Barbero, "Globalización y multiculturalidad: Notas para una agenda de investigación," in *Nuevas Perspectivas desde/sobre América Latina: El desafío de los estudios culturales*, ed. Mabel Moraña (Pittsburgh: Instituto Internacional de Literatura Iberoamericana, 2002), 22.

7. Alberto Sandoval-Sánchez, "Nuyorican Fairy Tales: Allegories of Existence and Bare Survival in Migdalia Cruz and Eddie Sánchez's Theatre," in *Freakish Encounters: Constructions of the Freak in Hispanic Cultures*, ed. Sara Muñoz and Analola Santana. Special issue of *Hispanic Issues Online* (forthcoming Spring 2018, no pagination available yet).

8. Julia Kristeva, *Powers of Horror: An Essay on Abjection*, trans. Leon S. Roudiez. New York: Columbia UP, 1982), 2.

9. Judith Butler, *Bodies That Matter: On the Discursive Limits of "Sex"* (New York: Routledge, 1993), 3.

10. This is not a new idea, and much has been written about the construction of worldviews through cartographic conventions. For more information, see Walter Mignolo, *The Idea of Latin America* (Malden, MA: Blackwell, 2005); Jordana Dym and Karl Offen, eds., *Mapping Latin America* (Chicago: U of Chicago P, 2011); and José David Saldívar, *Trans-Americanity: Subaltern Modernities, Global Coloniality, and the Cultures of Greater Mexico* (Durham: Duke UP, 2011).

11. Of course, on the opposite side of this representation are the utopic engravings of the Dutchman Theodore de Bry, whose multivolume *America*, published throughout the 1590s, is considered to have been a major source of the Black Legend (this refers to historical writings, primarily by other European colonial powers during the periods of conquest and after, that demonized the Spanish Empire as particularly cruel and bigoted against the American natives in contrast to other European empires). In his work he offered visual "proof" of the barbarous Spaniards, whose cruelty was contrasted to the passivity and beauty of the idealized indigenous natives. Nevertheless, as Greer, Mignolo, and Quilligan point out, "Spanish soldiers are seen to become indistinguishable from their Negro slaves as they all toil, with bulging buttocks, up the left side of the engraving." Margaret Greer, Walter D. Mignolo, and Maureen Quilligan, "Introduction," in *Rereading the Black Legend: The Discourses of Religious and Racial Difference in the Renaissance Empires*, ed. Margaret R. Greer, Walter D. Mignolo, and Maureen Quilligan (Chicago: U of Chicago P, 2007), 9. In other words, in order to denounce the brutality of the Spanish, de Bry draws on African imagery as the founding source of violence.

12. Mignolo, *Idea of Latin America*, xii.

13. Ibid., 8.

14. Achille Mbembe, "Necropolitics," *Public Culture* 15.1 (2003): 27.

15. Georges Canguilhem, *The Normal and the Pathological* (New York: Zone, 1989), 32.

16. The discursive transformation of the monster from a creature of mythology to a specimen of science is further developed in the second chapter of this book.

17. Michael Chemers, *Staging Stigma: A Critical Examination of the American Freak Show* (New York: Palgrave Macmillan, 2008), 6–7.

18. Susan Antebi, *Carnal Inscriptions: Spanish American Narratives of Corporeal Difference and Disability* (New York: Palgrave Macmillan, 2009), 27.

19. Tobin Siebers, "Disability in Theory: From Social Constructionism to the New Reality of the Body," in *The Disability Studies Reader*, ed. Lennard Davies, 2nd ed. (Hoboken, NJ: Routledge, 2006), 737–38.

20. Tobin Siebers, *Disability Theory* (Ann Arbor: U of Michigan P, 2008), 5.

21. Rosemarie Garland-Thomson, "Introduction," 1.

22. Chemers, *Staging Stigma*, 7.

23. Ibid.

24. Susan Antebi, "Blindness and Freakishness," *Literal. Latin American Voices* 16 (Spring 2009): 28.

25. Rosi Braidotti, "Mothers, Monsters, and Machines," in *Writing on the Body: Female Embodiment and Feminist Theory*, Katie Conboy, Nadia Medina, and Sarah Stanbury, eds. (New York: Columbia UP, 1997), 62.

26. José Ramón García Menéndez, *Política económica y deuda externa en América Latina* (Santiago de Compostela: Iepala, 1986), 242.

27. Naomi Klein, *Shock Doctrine: The Rise of Disaster Capitalism* (New York: Picador, 2007), 94–103.

28. For more information, see ibid.; and Tomás Moulián *Chile actual: Anatomía de un mito* (Santiago: LOM, 2002).

29. Klein, *Shock Doctrine*, 89–160.

30. Jacobo Schatan, *El saqueo de América Latina: Deuda externa, neoliberalismo, globalización* (Santiago: LOM, 1998), 10–37.

31. According the Joseph E. Stiglitz, the Washington Consensus refers to the set of views about effective development strategies associated to Washington-based institutions: the IMF, the World Bank, and the US Treasury. Their conception was based on three key ideas: a market economy, openness to the world, and macroeconomic discipline. Joseph E. Stiglitz, *Making Globalization Work* (New York: Norton, 2007).

32. Ibid., 36.

33. Lara Nielsen, "Introduction: Heterotopic Transformations, the (Il)Liberal Neoliberal," in *Neoliberalism and Global Theatres: Performance Permutations*, ed. Lara Nielsen and Patricia Ybarra (New York: Palgrave Macmillan, 2012), 5.

34. Mark Bly, "Introduction," in *The Production Notebooks*, vol. 1 (New York: Theatre Communications Group, 1996), xxiii.

35. Jimmy Noriega, "Teatro Travieso and *creación colectiva*: Devising Intercultural Performance in Lima, Peru," *Theatre Topics* 26.2 (2016): 210.

36. Enrique Buenaventura, "El Método de Creación Colectiva," in *Creación Colectiva: El legado de Enrique Buenaventura*, ed. Beatriz Rizk (Buenos Aires: Atuel, 2008), 128.

37. Judith Weiss, *Latin American Popular Theatre* (Albuquerque: U of New Mexico P, 1993), 137.

38. Hana Worthen, "For a Skeptical Dramaturgy," *Theatre Topics* 24.3 (2014): 175.

CHAPTER ONE

1. Antebi, "Blindness and Freakishness," 27.

2. Garland-Thomson, "Introduction," 1.

3. Siebers, "Disability in Theory," 737.

4. John Block Friedman, *The Monstrous Races in Medieval Art and Thought* (Cambridge: Harvard UP, 1981), 111.

5. Francis Bacon, "Novum Organum," in *Francis Bacon: Advancement of Learning, Novum Organum, New Atlantis,* Great Books of the Western World, vol. 30 (Chicago: Encyclopaedia Britannica, 1952), 159.

6. See the work of Rosemarie Garland-Thomson, Rachel Adams, Michael Chemers, Robert Bogdan, Leslie Fiedler, and Roger Bartra, among others.

7. Jacques Rancière, *The Emancipated Spectator* (New York: Verso, 2009), 13. Rancière is obviously building upon the work of theorists such as Bertold Brecht and Augusto Boal, whose theatre aimed to make the audience active participants of the theatrical work.

8. The original title of the play is *De monstruos y prodigios: La historia de los castrati, Libremente inspirada en La historia de los castrati de Patrick Barbier,* text by Jorge Kuri, directed by Claudio Valdés Kuri, Teatro El Galeón, Mexico City, 2000. As a company member and dramaturg of Teatro de Ciertos Habitantes, I have personal knowledge of this production and a unique perspective on the work in relation to the theoretical questions that concern this chapter. My analysis is based on multiple viewings of the live play (it was staged from 2000 to 2010 at different venues), as well as a video of the performance provided by the director.

9. Katherine Zien, "Troubling Multiculturalisms: Staging Trans/National Identities in Teatro de Ciertos Habitantes's *El Gallo,*" *Theatre Survey* 55.3 (2014): 348.

10. The exploration stage is a laboratory process through which the actors explore themes related to the production but do not deal with the play itself. Often they are not even aware of which play they will be performing.

11. Given the enormous success of its previous performance, *Becket o el honor de Dios,* the company had been invited to present this play at the Festival Iberoamericano de Cádiz and the Festival Internacional de Teatro in Girona, Spain. Unfortunately, many of the actors had previous obligations that prevented them from traveling. Valdés Kuri, the director, had already been in rehearsals for nine months with the cast of *De monstruos y prodigios,* and so he asked the festivals if they would be interested in premiering this new play. They agreed, and the play premiered abroad before returning for a full season in Mexico City. For more information on the history of this staging, see Analola Santana, "Vida del proyecto," in *De monstruos y prodigios: La historia de los castrati, recuento de un proyecto teatral inclasificable,* ed. Leonel Sagahón (Mexico City: CONACULTA/Tintable, 2014).

12. Rosalina Perales, "El mundo al revés: Inversión y carnavalización de la historia," in *Discursos teatrales en los albores del siglo XXI,* ed. Juan Villegas and Alicia del Campo y Mario Rojas (Irvine, California: Gestos, 2001), 175.

13. The creation of the conjoined twins, the main narrators of the play, stemmed from a set of misunderstandings and artistic creativity. Originally, Claudio Valdés Kuri and Jorge Kuri (who is of not related to the director) decided that the narrator had to be Ambroise Paré because of his historical significance for the play's theme. They had invited Mario Iván Martínez to play this role, but this was all done in a very informal manner and Mario Iván had

commented that he had many different commitments. Valdés Kuri and Kuri had assumed that he wasn't interested in the role, and so they began working with a different actor, Hernán del Riego. One month after the start of the rehearsal process, Mario Iván contacted them about beginning rehearsals, and so all of the sudden they had two actors for one role. The playwright and the director decided that the only solution was to put two heads on Ambroise Paré and name the other one Jean.

14. The background story that Valdés Kuri and Kuri envisioned for this character (who is two people who act as one) is as follows. "[T]his being was the child of a French woman and an Italian man, two countries that were always in conflict, so that one head leaned toward intuition and the other always tried to impose the use of reason" (Claudio Valdés Kuri "Genealogía de monstruos: Concepción y proceso de creación." *De monstruos y prodigios: La historia de los castrati, recuento de un proyecto teatral inclasificable.* Ed. Leonel Sagahón. Mexico City: CONACULTA/Tintable, 2014. 17).

15. Claudio Valdés Kuri, "Del director sobre la puesta en escena," *Gestos* 16.31 (2001): 115.

16. Jorge Kuri and Claudio Valdés Kuri. "De monstruos y prodigios: La historia de los castrati." Gestos 16.31 (2001). 139.

17. Terry Eagleton, "Bakhtin, Schopenhauer, Kundera," in *Bakhtin and Cultural Theory*, ed. Ken Hirschkop and David Shepherd (Manchester: Manchester UP, 2001), 229.

18. Chemers, *Staging Stigma*, 297.

19. Kuri and Valdés Kuri, *De monstruos y prodigios*, 141.

20. It is important to emphasize that all the actors sing live onstage, as well as playing different musical instruments: the harpsichord and the violin.

21. Garland-Thomson, "Introduction," 5.

22. This centaur, the embodiment of bestiality in humanity, is an obvious reference to Chiron, the wise son of Kronos, who learned the medical, musical, and divining arts from Apollo and Artemis. He is in obvious contrast to the wildness and savagery associated with centaurs in Greek mythology.

23. Kuri and Valdés Kuri *De monstruos y prodigios*, 120.

24. Bogdan, *Freak Show*, 35.

25. Kuri and Valdés Kuri, *De monstruos y prodigios*, 119.

26. Ibid., 120.

27. Ibid., 121.

28. Garland-Thomson, "Introduction," 3.

29. Roger Bartra, *Wild Men in the Looking Glass: The Mythic Origin of European Otherness*, trans. Carl T. Berrisford (Ann Arbor: U of Michigan P, 1994), 16.

30. Kuri and Valdés Kuri, *De monstruos y prodigios*, 133.

31. Ibid., 134.

32. The centaur, as a literary figure in Latin America, has a clear precedent in the work of Rubén Darío. He devoted many of his works to this figure, particularly "Coloquio de los centauros," in which Quirón the centaur is posited as a prophet, unveiling the enigma of nature made possible by his androgynous condition. As Ángel Rama explains, the fascination of the fin de siècle Latin American modernists with animalization, such as the centaur, had to do with

anxiety about the changes wrought by modernization: "The appearance among the poetic modernizers of a constellation of images that translate that instinctive, unbridled, animal energy that tortures and kills corresponds to a period of the acidic expansion of capitalism in Western societies." Ángel Rama, "José Martí en el eje de la modernización poética: Whitman, Lautréamont, Rimbaud," *Nueva Revista de Filología Hispánica* (NRFH) 32.1 (1983): 112.

33. Kuri and Valdés Kuri, *De monstruos y prodigios*, 119.

34. Ibid., 120.

35. Musician and actor Edwin Calderón played Professor Galuppi. Calderón, a gifted opera singer and pianist, also played the harpsichord (which he had to learn) throughout the performance.

36. Kuri and Valdés Kuri, *De monstruos y prodigios*, 129.

37. Carlos Jáuregui, *Canibalia: Canibalismo, calibanismo, antropofagia cultural, y consumo en América Latina* (Madrid: Iberoamericana, 2008), 541.

38. David Gerber, "The 'Careers' of People Exhibited in Freak Shows: The Problem of Volition and Valorization," in *Freakery: Cultural Spectacles of the Extraordinary Body*, ed. Rosemary Garland-Thomson (New York: New York UP, 1996), 45 (emphasis in the original).

39. Kuri and Valdés Kuri, *De monstruos y prodigios*, 132.

40. Ibid., 146.

41. Juan Villegas, "De monstruos y prodigios: La historia de los castrati y la decadencia de la cultura y la estética de occidente," *TEATRO/CELCIT* 19–20 (2002): np.

42. Umberto Eco, *History of Beauty* (New York: Rizzoli, 2004), 239.

43. Elizabeth Grosz, "Intolerable Ambiguity: Freaks as/at the Limit," in *Freakery: Cultural Spectacles of the Extraordinary Body*, ed. Rosemarie Garland-Thomson (New York: New York UP, 1996), 57.

44. Kuri and Valdés Kuri, *De monstruos y prodigios*, 154.

45. Garland-Thomson, "Introduction," 3.

46. I want to point out the two actors who played this role at different periods throughout the eleven-year history of the performance. The first was Kaveh Parmas, an Iranian actor who initially bestowed a sense of the Orient on this character through his singing. Later Gerardo Taracena took on the role. He is an actor of indigenous descent who transformed the characterization of this "savage," granting him an association with the native cultures of the Americas. Thus, this character embodies several renditions of what has historically constituted the monstrous races of those faraway lands.

47. Jáuregui, *Canibalia*, 14.

48. Kuri and Valdés Kuri, *De monstruos y prodigios*, 120.

49. Claudio Valdés Kuri, "Genealogía de monstruos." 19.

50. Within the Latin American context, this is an interesting choice of word. With the exception of Brazil and the Caribbean (and some countries that border the Caribbean, such as Venezuela), the continent has historically avoided any incorporation of blackness into the construction of national identity. Nevertheless, African descent has often been used as a pejorative aspect applied to other ethnic markers (such as indigeneity) and class constructs (e.g., the *cabecitas negras* of Argentina, a term used to describe those with dark hair who are associ-

ated with the lower classes). It is not gratuitous, then, that *De monstruos y pro-digios* would use the term *negro* to address Sulaimán, associating him with all forms of marginalized identity.

51. Kuri and Valdés Kuri, *De monstruos y prodigios*, 136–37.

52. Born in Havana, Cuba, in 1853, José Martí wrote the essay "Our America" while in New York in 1891. This particular work has become a seminal text in Latin American nationalism, as it argues for the rejection of European and US cultural values, whose aggressive imperial power threatened the forging of racially harmonious and politically stable Latin American nations.

53. José Martí, quoted in Roberto Fernández Retamar, *Caliban and Other Essays* (Minneapolis: U of Minnesota P, 1989), 22. Another important Cuban writer, Fernández Retamar wrote the significant essay "Caliban: Notes toward a Discussion of Culture in Our America" in 1971. There he outlines a vision for a revolutionary American culture based in a political and intellectual history that began with José Martí and other intellectual soldiers of the era of independence in Latin America, which had been most recently realized by the Cuban Revolution. Fernández Retamar traces the dialectics of Caliban versus Ariel—as symbols of barbaric versus civilized America—and their conflicting links to Prospero, the character in Shakespeare's *The Tempest* who represents the colonizer. Tracing the evolution of Caliban's symbolism through Columbus's letters, Shakespeare's works, José Enrique Rodó's *Ariel*, and other sources, Fernández Retamar argues that even as European colonizers sought to degrade America by assigning it the identity of Caliban and writers like Rodó have embraced this negative view of the character, American culture must be derived from its Caliban (cannibalistic) characteristics.

54. Ibid., 22.

55. Jáuregui, *Canibalia*, 14.

56. Kuri and Valdés Kuri, *De monstruos y prodigios*, 147.

57. Ibid.

58. Ibid.

59. Fernández Retamar, 14.

60. Claudio Valdés Kuri, interview with the author. Mexico City, June 4, 2015. Unless otherwise noted, all statements from the artist are drawn from this interview.

61. Kuri and Valdés Kuri, *De monstruos y prodigios*, 147.

62. There are many anecdotes that support this statement. For example, the day after a performance in a small town in Mexico, some government representatives asked for a meeting with Valdés Kuri to determine if they should press charges against the person who interrupted the play. In another performance in Venezuela, the woman who interrupted the play was chased out of the theater by some audience members who angrily demanded that she be removed from the space.

63. Rancière, *The Emancipated Spectator*, 13.

64. The musical choices in this section change depending in the city and country of the performance. They range from Britney Spears to Flans (a Mexican pop group of the 1980s) and Mecano (a Spanish pop group).

65. Kuri and Valdés Kuri, *De monstruos y prodigios*, 156.

66. Aníbal Quijano, "Coloniality and Modernity/Rationality," *Cultural Studies* 21.2–3 (2007): 169.

67. Ibid., 171.

68. Dirk Kruijt and Kees Kooning, "Introduction," in *Societies of Fear: The Legacy of Civil War, Violence, and Terror in Latin America,* ed. Dirk Kruijt and Kees Kooning (London: Zed, 1999), 7.

69. Nevertheless, the MRTA, according to the country's Truth and Reconciliation Commission (TRC) report, differed from the Shining Path in the amount of violence committed, as well as its nonclandestine approach.

70. The final statistics provided in the TRC report claim more than thirty thousand dead, eighty thousand displaced, and six thousand disappeared during this period.

71. Hugo Salazar del Alcázar. *Teatro y violencia: Una aproximación al teatro peruano de los '80.* Lima: Centro de Documentación y Video Teatral Jaime Campodónico, 1990, 13.

72. Fujimori ended his presidency by fleeing to Japan amid a scandal of corruption and human rights violations. In 2005 he left Japan for Chile, from which he planned to reenter Peru. This led to his arrest, and he was eventually extradited to Peru for trial. In 2009 he was convicted of human rights violations for his role in killings and kidnappings by the Grupo Colina death squad during his government's battle against leftist guerrillas in the 1990s. He was also convicted of embezzlement after he admitted to giving fifteen million dollars from the Peruvian treasury to his intelligence service chief, Vladimiro Montesinos. Regardless of his verdict and incarceration, he continues to be a popular figure among Peruvians, especially because of his tough stance against terrorism and his economic policies. This fact was especially divisive in 2016, when his daughter Keiko Fujimori ran for the presidency and lost by the very narrow margin of 0.25 percentage points.

73. The state-appointed TRC did not begin its work until April 2002. For more information on this period, see Jean Franco, *Cruel Modernity (Durham:* Duke UP, 2013); and the Peruvian Human Rights Commission's book *Memoria para los ausentes: Desaparecidos en el Perú (1982–1996).* Lima: COMISEDH, 2001.

74. The analysis of this play is based on a video provided by Miguel Rubio Zapata, artistic director of Yuyachkani, as well as interviews and conversations with Ana Correa and Teresa Ralli, founding members of the company, about the specifics of the performance.

75. Francine A'ness, "Resisting Amnesia: Yuyachkani, Performance, and the Postwar Reconstruction of Peru," *Theatre Journal* 56.3 (2004): 400.

76. Luis Ramos-García, ed. "Las Notas de Miguel Rubio: Teatralización en el imaginario social peruano," in Miguel Rubio Zapata, *Notas sobre teatro* (Lima: Grupo Cultural Yuyachkani, 2001), xx.

77. Again I must emphasize that the majority of the victims of the Dirty War were members of indigenous communities who were either killed or forced to migrate to the city in an attempt to escape the violence in the provinces.

78. Slavoj Žižek, *The Plague of Fantasies* (London: Verso, 2008), xiv.

79. I should also clarify that the members of Yuyachkani themselves do not come from the marginalized sectors of Peru. This has been a point of some con-

tention and criticism, as they use elements from indigenous culture to reconstruct national identity.

80. Miguel Rubio, interview with the author. Lima, Peru, June 12, 2012. Unless otherwise noted, all statements by the artist are drawn from this interview.

81. Rachel Adams, *Sideshow U.S.A.: Freaks and the American Cultural Imagination* (Chicago: U of Chicago P, 2001), 2–3.

82. Beatriz Marcos, "Memoria y dramatización del daño," 16, accessed June 1, 2017, https://beatrizmarcos.wordpress.com/2012/07/07/memoria-y-drama tizacion-del-dano-estoy-pensando-estoy-recordando-el-grupo-de-teatro-peruano-yuyachkani/

83. Vladimiro Montesinos was the head of Peru's secret police and central intelligence throughout former president Alberto Fujimori's ten years in office, from 1990 to 2000. In 2000 secret tapes made by Montesinos, the infamous "vladi-videos," were leaked to the press and began to air on Peruvian television. They were secret videos recorded by Montesinos that showed him bribing elected congressmen to leave the opposition and join the Fujimorist side of the Congress. Montesinos was the mastermind behind plots to use Congress, the Public Ministry, and the judicial branch to cover up human rights violations and allow the third reelection of Fujimori. The ensuing scandal led to the collapse of President Fujimori's government. Montesinos fled Peru and was eventually captured in Venezuela and extradited. Subsequent investigations revealed him to be at the center of a vast web of illegal activities, including embezzlement, graft, gunrunning, and drug trafficking. He has been tried, convicted, and sentenced for numerous crimes.

84. Leslie Fiedler, *Freaks: Myths and Images of the Secret Self* (New York: Simon and Schuster, 1978), 24.

85. Ibid.

86. Víctor Vich, *El canníbal es el Otro: Violencia y cultura en el Perú contemporáneo* (Lima: Intituto de Estudios Peruanos Ediciones, 2002), 11.

87. Josefina Ludmer, "El Coloquio de Yale: Máquinas de leer 'fin de siglo,'" in *Las culturas de fin de siglo en América Latina*, ed. Josefina Ludmer (Buenos Aires: Beatriz Viterbo Editora, 1994), 9–12.

88. Ibid., 14.

89. Miguel Rubio Zapata, *El cuerpo ausente (performance política)* (Lima: Grupo Cultural Yuyachkani, 2008), 37.

90. Ibid., 68.

91. Rosemarie Garland-Thomson, *Extraordinary Bodies: Figuring Physical Disability in American Culture and Literature* (New York: Columbia UP, 1997), 17.

92. Ileana Diéguez, *Escenarios Liminales: Teatralidades, performatividades, políticas* (Mexico City: Toma, Ediciones y Producciones Escénicas y Cinematográficas, 2014), 86.

93. Rosemarie Garland-Thomson, *Staring: How We Look* (Oxford: Oxford UP, 2009), 1.

94. Diana Taylor, *The Archive and the Repertoire: Performing Cultural Memory in the Americas* (Durham: Duke UP, 2003), 208.

95. Bogdan, *Freak Show*, 176–78.

96. Bogdan, "The Social Construction," 29.

97. Fiedler, *Freaks*, xviii.

98. Adams, *Sideshow U.S.A.*, 2–3.

99. Leonard Cassuto, "Freak," in *Keywords for Disability Studies*, ed. Rachel Adams, Benjamin Reiss, and David Serlin (New York: New York UP, 2015), 87–88.

100. Debord, *Society of the Spectacle,* 5.

101. Adams, *Sideshow U.S.A.*, 63.

102. I first saw this play in Buenos Aires in the summer of 2013 at the Centro Cultural San Martín. My analysis of the play is based on this performance, as well as a video provided by the director.

103. The quote appears in the program notes along with an explanation for this inspiration.

104. Denise Mora, "*Fauna*: Una indagación sobre cómo el arte puede representar la vida," *Revista Telon de Fondo* 20 (2014): 241.

105. Walter Benjamin, "The Work of Art in the Age of Mechanical Reproduction," in *Illuminations,* ed. Hannah Arendt, trans. Harry Zohn (New York: Schocken, 1969), 223.

106. Romina Paula, *Fauna,* in *Tres obras* (Buenos Aires: Editorial Entropía, 2013), 16.

107. Romina Paula, interview with the author. Buenos Aires, Argentina, May 2013. Unless otherwise noted, all statements by the artist are drawn from this interview.

108. Michel Foucault, "The Masked Philosopher," in *Politics, Philosophy, Culture: Interviews and Other Writings, 1977–1984,* ed. Lawrence D. Kritzman (New York: Routledge 1988), 328.

109. Paula, *Fauna,* 12.

110. Nadja Durbach, *The Spectacle of Deformity: Freak Shows and Modern British Culture* (Berkeley: U of California P, 2010), 153.

111. Paula, *Fauna,* 12.

112. Grosz, "Intolerable Ambiguity," 57.

113. Bartra, *Wild Men,* 3.

114. Ibid., 14.

115. Paula, *Fauna,* 19.

116. Ibid., 20.

117. Ibid., 23.

118. Bartra, *Wild Men,* 18.

119. Paula, *Fauna,* 57.

120. Ibid., 49.

121. Zygmunt Bauman, *Wasted Lives: Modernity and Its Outcasts* (New York: Blackwell, 2004), 19.

122. Ibid., 21.

CHAPTER TWO

1. Roger Bartra, "El trágico viaje de una mujer salvaje mexicana al mundo civilizado," in *Freakish Encounters: Constructions of the Freak in Hispanic Cultures,*

ed. Sara Muñoz and Analola Santana. Special issue of *Hispanic Issues Online* (forthcoming Spring 2018), no pagination as of now.

2. Garland-Thomson, *Extraordinary Bodies*, 74.

3. A recent example can be found in a *New York Times* article that describes the gang rape of at least ten Mayan women in Guatemala at the hands of men who were evicting people (and setting their houses ablaze) from a village for the Canadian mining company Hudbay Mineral, Inc. The article states, "In a 2014 report, the Council on Hemispheric Affairs, a policy group in Washington, concluded that Canadian companies, accounting for 50 percent to 70 percent of the mining in Latin America, were often associated with extensive damage to the environment, from erosion and sedimentation to groundwater and river contamination. Of particular note, it said, was that the industry 'demonstrated a disregard for registered nature reserves and protected zones.' At the same time, the report said, local people were being injured, arrested or, in some cases, killed for protesting." Susan Daley, "Guatemalan Women's Claims Put Focus on Canadian Firms' Conduct Abroad," *New York Times* April 2, 2016. Seven of the ten countries with the highest numbers of female murder victims are in Latin America. For more information, see http://www.mapadaviolencia. org.br/pdf2015/MapaViolencia_2015_mulheres.pdf, where activists say the phenomenon reflects not only high rates of violence, social conflict, and organized crime but also a cultural strain of aggressive hypermasculinity. Although there have been powerful women's movements in the region for a long time, the campaign against gender-based violence has gathered momentum, culminating in the #NiUnaMenos—"not one less"—movement. This campaign gained special momentum in Argentina in 2017.

4. Aristotle, *Generation of Animals*, trans. A. L. Peck (Cambridge: Harvard University Press, 1944), 4.3.767.

5. Ibid., 4.3.775.

6. Garland-Thomson, *Extraordinary Bodies*, 20.

7. Important works on the popular representation and meaning of genetics are Alondra Nelson, *The Social Life of DNA: Race, Reparations, and Reconciliation after the Genome* (Boston: Beacon, 2016); Dorothy Nelkin and M. Susan Lindee, *The DNA Mystique: The Gene as a Cultural Icon* (New York: Freeman, 1995); Jose Van Dijck, *Imagination: Popular Images of Genetics* (New York: New York UP, 1998); and Celeste Michelle Condit, *The Meaning of the Gene: Public Debates about Human Heredity* (Madison: U of Wisconsin P, 1999).

8. Lennard Davis, "Introduction: Normality, Power, and Culture," in *The Disability Studies Reader*, ed. Lennard Davis (New York: Routledge, 2013), 1.

9. Ibid., 2.

10. Armand Marie Leroi, *Mutants: On Genetic Variety and the Human Body* (New York: Penguin, 2003), 15.

11. Ibid., 17.

12. Michel Foucault, *Discipline and Punish: The Birth of the Prison*, trans. Alan Sheridan, 2nd ed. (New York: Vintage, 1995); *Abnormal: Lectures at the College de France (1974–1975)*, ed. Valerio Marchetti and Antonella Salomoni, trans. Graham Burchell (New York: Picador, 2003), 61.

13. Foucault, *Abnormal*, 214.

14. Ibid., 25.

15. Foucault explains that the subjection of the body "can also be direct, physical, pitting force against force, bear[ing] on material elements, and yet without involving violence; it may be calculated, organized, technically thought out; it can be subtle, make use neither of weapons nor of terror, and yet remain of a physical order" (*Discipline and Punish*, 26).

16. Foucault, *Abnormal*, 44.

17. Ibid.

18. Ibid., 52.

19. Foucault, *Discipline and Punish*, 187.

20. Garland-Thomson, *Extraordinary Bodies*, 7.

21. Erving Goffman, *Stigma: Notes on the Management of a Spoiled Identity* (New York: Simon and Schuster, 1963), 4.

22. Ibid., 115.

23. Garland-Thomson, *Extraordinary Bodies*, 32.

24. Ibid., 33.

25. Mary Douglas, *Purity and Danger: An Analysis of Concepts of Pollution and Taboo* (New York: Routledge, 2003), 40.

26. In the last decades we have observed how the legal system, in particular, has used these classifications to enforce "justice" through acts of discrimination that are permitted precisely because a multifaceted individual is reduced to one "deviant" aspect.

27. Douglas, *Purity and Danger*, 41.

28. Abya Yala carries several meanings in the indigenous Kuna language. It is the name given to the continent and the name for mother earth.

29. The analysis of this performance is based on my viewing of the live play at the Festival Iberoamericano de Cádiz (Spain) in October 2012, as well as through videos provided by the company's director, Roxana Ávila. She also provided me with the unpublished manuscript of the play. All quotes from the play are from this source. All translations are my own.

30. Roxana Ávila, "Experiences from the Center of Abya Yala," in *Theatre and Cartographies of Power: Repositioning the Latina/o Americas*, eds. Jimmy Noriega and Analola Santana (Carbondale: Southern Illinois UP, 2018), 189.

31. Barbara Creed, *The Monstrous-Feminine: Film, Feminism, Psychoalanysis* (London: Routledge, 1993), 7.

32. Ibid., 43.

33. Carlos Jáuregui and Paola Uparela Reyes, "La vagina-ojo y otros monstruos gineco- escópicos," in *Freakish Encounters: Constructions of the Freak in Hispanic Cultures*, ed. Sara Muñoz and Analola Santana. Special issue of *Hispanic Issues Online* (forthcoming Spring 2018).

34. See ibid. for a complete study of this subject in the medical sciences.

35. Sample lyrics are "Fueron tus manos o tu boca, / Fueron tus ojos o tu voz, / O a lo mejor la impaciencia / De tanto esperar tu llegada" (It was your eyes or your mouth, / It was your hands or your voice, / It was perhaps the impatience / of waiting so long for your arrival).

36. Roxana Ávila, interview with the author. Cádiz, Spain, October 2013. Unless otherwise noted, all statements by the artist are drawn from this interview.

37. Gayle Rubin claims that every society is organized by a "sex/gender system," meaning "systematic ways to deal with sex, gender and babies" ("The Traffic in Women: Notes on the 'Political Economy' of Sex," in *Towards an Anthropology of Women*, ed. Reyna Reiter (New York: Monthly Review Press, 1975), 168). In other words, the sex/gender system is society's dominant mode of production and a social product in itself.

38. Petra Kuppers, "Bodies, Hysteria, Pain: Staging the Invisible," in *Bodies in Commotion: Disability and Performance*, ed. Carrie Sandahl and Philip Auslander (Ann Arbor: U Michigan P, 2005), 147. For example, during the seventeenth century, when human curiosities were popularly exhibited across European cities, asylums eagerly participated in this moneymaking exhibition by charging people to look at the inmates. As Richard Altick explains this mode of showmanship, "[T]he cells were arranged in galleries, in the manner of cages in a menagerie or booths at a fair, and in each one was a chained lunatic, whose behavior, if it were not sufficiently entertaining to begin with, was made so by the spectators' prodding him or her with their sticks or encouraging further wildness by ridicule, gestures, and imitations." Richard D. Altick, *The Shows of London* (Cambridge: Belknap Press of Harvard UP, 1978), 45.

39. For a thorough discussion of the modern talk show as a continuation of the freak show, see Joshua Gamson, *Freaks Talk Back: Tabloid Talk Shows and Sexual Nonconformity (Chicago: The U of Chicago P, 1998)*; Jack Richardson and Jennifer Eisenhauer, "Dr. Phil, Medical Theaters, Freak Shows, and Talking Couches: The Talking Stage as Pedagogical Site," *Journal of Literary and Cultural Disability Studies 8.1 (2014): 67–80*; and Elizabeth Birmingham, "Fearing the Freak: How Talk TV Articulates Women and Class," *Journal of Popular Film and Television 28.3 (2000): 133–39*.

40. Marcos Rosenzvaig, *El teatro de la enfermedad* (Buenos Aires: Editorial Biblos, 2009), 16.

41. In her essay "Feminism: Modern or Postmodern?" Raquel Olea questions the failure of modernity from the perspective of women. As she states, modernity originated in the eighteenth century with the ideals of liberty, equality, and fraternity established by the French Revolution, which marked "the project of human liberation, the domination of nature by 'man'" in a quest for the construction of a modern society, yet "to refer to modernity from feminism is in fact to mark the absence of women in a social project that included us only ambiguously" Raquel Olea, "Feminism: Modern or Postmodern?" in *The Postmodernism Debate in Latin America*, ed. John Beverly, José Oviedo, and Michael Aronna (Durham: Duke UP, 1995), 193.

42. Kuppers, "Bodies, Hysteria, Pain," 148.

43. For more on the construction of motherhood in Latin America, see Marina Becerra "Maternidad y ciudadanía en la Argentina de principios del siglo XX: Un análisis de la autobiografía de María Rosa Oliver," *Contracorriente: A Journal of Social History and Literature in Latin America 10.2 (2013): 202–18*; América Luna Martínez, "Maternidad y escritura femenina: Una experiencia perturbadora," in *La otredad: Los discursos de la cultura hoy*, ed. Silvia Elguea Véjars (Mexico City: Universidad Autónoma Metropolitana, 1997); and Francisca Noguerol Jiménez, "Driven up the Wall: Maternity and Literature in Con-

temporary Latin American Women Writers," *Review: Literature and Arts of the Americas* 86.46 (2013): 13–19.

44. A useful source for the further study of gender construction and medical discourses in nation building in Latin America is Jorge Salessi, *Médicos maleantes y maricas: Higiene, criminología, y homosexualidad en la construcción de la nación argentina* (Buenos Aires, 1871–1914) (Buenos Aires: Editorial Beatriz Viterbo, 1995).

45. Luce Irigaray. *To Speak Is Never Neutral*. Trans. Gail Schwab (New York: Routledge, 2002),

46. The continuous lyric is "Mama said there'll be days like this. There'll be days like this my mama said."

47. Kuppers, "Bodies, Hysteria, Pain," 151.

48. Ibid.

49. Hélène Cixous, "The Laugh of the Medusa," trans. Keith Cohen and Paula Cohen, *Signs* 1:4 (Summer 1976): 886.

50. Ibid., 880.

51. Homi K. Bhabha, "Postcolonial Authority and Postmodern Guilt," in *Cultural Studies*, ed. Lawrence Grossberg, Cary Nelson, and Paula A. Treichler (New York: Routledge, 1992), 56.

52. Ibid.

53. And, of course, a more poetic reference is found in Chilean poet Pablo Neruda's verses "Me gusta cuando callas . . ." (I like you when you are quiet . . .).

54. Rosemarie Garland-Thomson, "Feminist Disability Studies," *Signs* 30.2 (2005): 1567.

55. Ibid.

56. See, Larry Diamond, Jonathan Hartlyn, Juan J. Linz, and Seymour Martin Lipset, eds. *Democracy in Developing Countries* (Boulder, Colorado: Lynne Rienner Publishers, 1999); Terry Lynn Karl "Dilemmas of Democratization in Latin America," *Comparative Politics* 23.1 (1990): 1-21 ; Karen Remmer, "Democracy and Economic Crisis: The Latin American Experience," *World Politics* 42.3 (1990): 315-35; and Evelyne Huber and Fred Solt, "Success and Failures of Neoliberalism," *Latin American Research Review* 39.3 (2004): 149-64.

57. Beatriz Rizk, *Imaginando un continente: Utopía, democracia, y neoliberalismo en el teatro latinoamericano* (Lawrence, Kansas: Latin American Theatre Review Books, 2010), 1:4.

58. See Martín-Barbero, "Globalización y multiculturalidad"; Eduardo Mendieta *Global Fragments: Globalization, Latinamericanisms, and Critical Theory* (New York: State U of NY Press, 2007); and Néstor García Canclini, *Consumers and Citizens: Globalization and Multicultural Conflicts*, trans. George Yúdice (Minneapolis: U Minnesota P, 2001).

59. The analysis of *De un suave color blanco* is based on my live viewing of the performance in 2009 at the Festival Iberoamericano de Cádiz (Spain), as well as a video of the performance that I recorded with the permission of the artists. Arístides Vargas, the writer and director, also provided me with an unpublished manuscript of the text. All references to and quotations from the text come directly from this version, and all translations are my own.

60. Marcos, "Memoria y dramatización."

61. Lola Proaño Gómez, *Poéticas de la globalización en el teatro Latinoamericano* (Irvine, California: Gestos, 2007), 87.

62. García Canclini, *Consumers and Citizens*, 24.

63. Percy Cayo Córdoba, *Perú y Ecuador: Antecedentes de un largo conflicto* (Lima: Universidad del Pacífico, 1997), 80.

64. Diana Taylor, *Disappearing Acts: Spectacles of Gender in Argentina's "Dirty War"* (Durham: Duke UP, 1997), 124.

65. Ibid., 122.

66. Rizk, *Imaginando un continente*, 88.

67. Ramón del Valle-Inclán, *Bohemian Lights*, trans. Anthony N. Zahareas and Gerard Gillespie (Austin: U of Texas P, 1976), 183.

68. Martin Esslin, the well-known drama critic and Brecht scholar, calls attention to the *esperpento* as "the grotesque or ridiculous" in *The Theatre of the Absurd* (3rd Edition. New York: Vintage Books, 2004), 395. It is not a direct translation, but it depicts a world inhabited by the tragicomical. Anthony Zahareas, the translator of Valle-Inclán's *Bohemian Lights*, claims that the term "refers to things or people who are grotesque, bizarre, ludicrously eccentric, absurd. Valle-Inclán uses *esperpento* strictly in aesthetic terms: it is a style of writing, a manner of representing, a way of portraying," in Ramón del Valle-Inclán, Bohemian Lights, trans. Anthony N. Zahareas and Gerard Gillespie (Austin: U of Texas P, 1976), 38.

69. Elga Pérez Laborde, *A Questão Teórica do Esperpento e sua Projeção Estética: Variações Esperpênticas da Idade Média ao Século XXI* (Brasília: Department de Teoria Literária, Universidade de Brasília, 2004), 171.

70. Arístides Vargas, "Texto Negro," *Revista Teatro/CELCIT* 35–36 (2009): 26–27.

71. Garland-Thomson, "Introduction," 3.

72. Antebi, *Carnal Inscriptions*, 49.

73. Carrie Sandhal and Philip Auslander, "Introduction," in *Bodies in Commotion: Disability and Performance*, ed. Carrie Sandhal and Philip Auslander (Ann Arbor: U of Michigan P, 2005), 10.

74. This does not exclude the Doctor from being a freak body as well. The moment that this character aims to present himself as "normal" there is always something in his tone of voice, movements, or gestures that marks him as different. The ridiculousness of the Doctor is in contrast to the cold and calculating manner with which he handles the naked body/bodies of the Double Woman as he examines her. This notion of the freak as a part of the state discourse is further developed in the next section.

75. Antebi, *Carnal Inscriptions*, 50.

76. Garland-Thomson, "Introduction," 12.

77. Michael Handelsman, "El teatro contemporáneo del Ecuador entre dos milenios: Resistencia y representatividad," in *Antología del Teatro Ecuatoriano de fin de siglo*, ed. Lola Proaño Gómez (Quito: Casa de la Cultura Ecuatoriana "Benjamín Carrión," 2003), 28.

78. René Girard, "From Mimetic Desire to the Monstrous Double," in *Mimesis, Masochism, and Mime: The Politics of Theatricality in Contemporary French Thought*, ed. Timothy Murray (Ann Arbor: U of Michigan P, 1997), 104.

79. Arístides Vargas, interview with the author. Cádiz, Spain, October 2013. Unless otherwise noted, all statements by the artist are drawn from this interview.

80. Beatriz Preciado, *Testo Junkie: Sex, Drugs, and Biopolitics in the Pharmacopornographic Era*, trans. Bruce Benderson (New York: Feminist Press at the City University of New York, 2013), 34.

81. José Joaquín Brunner, "Traditionalism and Modernity in Latin American Culture," in *Latin America Writes Back: Postmodernity in the Periphery*, ed. Emil Volek (New York: Routledge, 2002), 22–23. See also Michel Foucault, *"Society Must Be Defended": Lectures at the College de France, 1975–1976*, trans. David Macey (New York: Picador, 2003).

82. Ibid., 23.

83. Violeta Luna has performed this piece throughout the globe, from Serbia and Slovenia to Ecuador, Guatemala, and Mexico. My analysis of the piece is based on two separate viewings, one at the Encuentro de Mujeres during the Festival Iberoamericano de Teatro in Cádiz, Spain, in 2007, and the other during an Association for Theatre in Higher Education (ATHE) Latino Focus Group preconference event in Washington, DC, in 2008.

84. Violeta Luna website, http://www.violetaluna.com/NK603.html

85. This idea differs from the common associations that theory has provided for the cyborg body. Whereas Katherine Hayles imagines a possible posthuman condition—"My dream is a version of the posthuman that embraces the possibilities of information technologies without being seduced by fantasies of unlimited power and disembodied immortality" [How we Became Posthuman :Virtual Bodies in Cybernetics, Literature, and Informatics (Chicago: U of Chicago P, 1999), 5]—and Donna Haraway famously proposed it as a politically resistant idea of "transgressed boundaries, potent fusions, and dangerous possibilities which progressive people might explore as one part of needed political work" ["A Cyborg Manifesto: Science, Technology, and Socialist-Feminism in the Late Twentieth Century," in *The Transgender Studies Reader*, eds. Susan Stryker and Stephen Whittle (New York: Routledge, 2006), 107], the possibility of technology as tools for new feminist affinities becomes problematized in this performance by racial and cultural marginalization.

86. Paola Marín, "Performance e hibridez: *NK 603* de Violeta Luna," *Gestos* 50 (2010): 198.

87. Gabriel Giorgi, "Introducción," in *Ensayos sobre biopolítica: Excesos de vida* (Buenos Aires: Paidós, 2009), 11.

88. Ibid., 30–31.

89. Donna Haraway, "The Promises of Monsters: A Regenerative Politics for Inappropriate/d Others," in *Cultural Studies*, ed. Lawrence Grossberg, Cary Nelson, and Paula A. Treichler (New York: Routledge, 1992), 297.

90. Violeta Luna, interview with the author. San Francisco, California, February 2015. Unless otherwise noted, all statements by the artist are drawn from this interview.

91. On January 1, 1994, an insurgency was launched in Chiapas, Mexico, led

by a group known as the Zapatista National Liberation Army (EZLN). Thousands of armed indigenous people occupied seven Chiapas towns and declared war on the Mexican government. Their demands—not just for the oppressed and poverty-stricken indigenous communities but for all Mexicans—were clear: equality, democracy, liberty, justice, independence, employment, land, food, housing, health, education, and peace. Under the leadership of the charismatic Subcomandante Marcos, they stood up to a government that had, throughout history, exploited the inhabitants of Mexico's poorest states. In the words of Noam Chomsky, "Chiapas became a symbol of resistance to the peculiar form of 'globalization' that grants priority to capital and the private tyrannies that control it, leaving the interests of people to the side, as incidental" ["Chiapas: Symbol of Resistance," in *Ya basta! Ten Years of the Zapatista Uprising*, by Subcomandante Insurgente Marcos (Oakland, California: AK Press, 2004), 13].

92. George Yúdice, "Postmodernism on the Periphery," *South Atlantic Quarterly* 92.3 (1993): 552.

93. Haraway, "Promises of Monsters," 296.

94. According to US Department of Agriculture data, since the 1980s Monsanto has become the world leader in genetic modification of seeds and been granted 674 biotechnology patents, more than any other company.

95. Lisa Woynarski, "Snapshot—Ecological Health in Violeta Luna's NK603: Action for Performance & e-Maiz," in *Performing Health and Wellbeing*, ed. Veronica Baxter and Katharine Low (London: Bloomsbury Methuen Drama, 2017), 231.

96. Brunner, "Traditionalism," 12.

97. For Hardt and Negri, "[T]he monster is not an accident but the ever present possibility that can destroy the natural order of authority in all domains, from the family to the kingdom," *Multitude: War and Democracy in the Age of Empire* (New York: Penguin, 2004), 195.

CHAPTER THREE

1. It is also worth mentioning, that Dilma Rouseff was also a leftist militant early in her career. Her activist past became an additional "sin" added to the long list of bogus reasons to impeach her.

2. Shannon Sims, "The Hilarious Feminist Backlash to Brazil's Impeachment Fallout," *Forbes*, April 20, 2016, https://www.forbes.com/sites/shannon-sims/2016/04/20/the-hilarious-feminist-backlash-to-brazils-impeachment-fallout/#24e4afc06573

3. Giaconda Belli's questions on the subject are right on point: "Argentina's Isabel Peron was the first woman to become president in the region in 1974, and between 1990 to 2014, a record number of women were elected as political leaders. After Violeta Chamorro in Nicaragua, Panama elected Mireya Moscoso in 1999; in Chile, Bachelet in 2006 and 2014; Argentina elected Cristina Fernández de Kirchner in 2007 and 2011; Brazil elected Dilma Rousseff in 2010 and, in the

same year, Costa Rica elected Laura Chinchilla. But how is it that in a region which is home to seven of the ten countries with the highest rate of female murder victims, a region that's all too known for its reigning machismo, where only less than half of the female population makes an income, women have access to a level of political representation second only to the Scandinavian countries?" "Why Has 'Macho' Latin America Elected More Female Leaders than the US?," *The Guardian*, November 7, 2016, https://www.theguardian.com/global-development-professionals-network/2016/nov/07/macho-latin-america-elected-more-female-leaders-than-us.

4. Jean Graham-Jones, *Evita, Inevitably: Performing Argentina's Female Icons before and after Eva Perón* (Ann Arbor: U of Michigan P, 2014), 175.

5. J. Jack Halberstam, *Gaga Feminism: Sex, Gender, and the End of Normal* (Boston: Beacon, 2012), 26.

6. Lucía Guerra, *La mujer fragmentada: Historia de un signo* (Santiago: Cuarto Propio, 1995), 31.

7. I would emphasize that gaga feminism, for which Halberstam found inspiration in the performance personae of Lady Gaga, has even older inspirations in Latin America and the Spanish-speaking world through the figure of Alaska. Alaska, a Mexican artist raised in Spain, first appeared in a film by Pedro Almodóvar (*Pepi, Luci, Bom,* 1980) and was one of the main characters of the *Movida Madrileña,* an important moment in post-Franco Spain that led to an explosion of cultural and social experimentation that impacted the development of new sexual and gender identity representations. Alaska started out in punk bands, but with her anthem "A quién le importa" (Who Cares) she became a pop-culture phenomenon who continues to exert great influence in the media while presenting a gender-questioning identity that provokes the norms of the status quo. At present she even has her own reality television show on MTV España.

8. Josefina Alcazar, "Performance art. El cuerpo freak de Rocío Boliver (La Congelada de Uva)," in *Freakish Encounters: Constructions of the Freak in Hispanic Cultures,* ed. Sara Muñoz and Analola Santana. Special issue of *Hispanic Issues Online* (forthcoming Spring 2018, no pagination available yet).

9. Although the performers in my case studies are of Latin American and Spanish descent, their pieces are created not to represent specific cultural or geographic manifestations of violence. Rather, these performances approach the topic of violence and discrimination against women utilizing a global perspective that acknowledges that these acts occur in various forms throughout the globe.

10. David Román, *Performance in America: Contemporary U.S. Culture and the Performing Arts* (Durham: Duke University Press, 2005), 80.

11. Halberstam, *Gaga Feminism,* 71.

12. Ibid., 67.

13. The title of the piece is not easily translatable. It points to the idea of someone able to face any challenge, as it combines the ancient name Geralda (from the German, meaning a warrior fighting with the spear of affection) with the *Avenca,* or maidenhair (a rare plant that fades easily, needs water, and does not tolerate direct sun), which represents someone who requires a lot of care.

14. Roger Bartra, *Territorios del terror y la otredad* (Valencia: Pre-Textos, 2007), 17.

15. Ibid., 17.

16. Suely Machado, interview with author. Belo Horizonte, July 2015. Unless otherwise noted, all statements by the artist are drawn from this interview.

17. The analysis of this piece is based on my viewing in October 2008 of the performance at the Festival Iberoamericano de Teatro in Cádiz, Spain. I also traveled to Belo Horizonte in July 2015 to spend three weeks with the company. I conducted several interviews with the artists and the director and was also provided with additional videos of the piece performed in other venues.

18. Baleiro is a renowned artist of Brazilian popular music (a post-bossa-nova urban popular sound that revisits typical Brazilian styles such as samba, samba-canção, baião, and other Brazilian regional music, combining those with foreign influences, such as jazz and rock).

19. An interesting example of defying the expected, standard body of the ballerina in the United States is Misty Copeland. In classical ballet, George Balanchine (considered the founder of American ballet) established a particular aesthetic for the ballerina: slender, taut, and very white, with long limbs, narrow hips, and visible sternums. For Balanchine, the female dancer is a glorified creature, though certainly subjugated to the male gaze and power. The Balanchine dancer embodied beauty and fragility. When Copeland became principal ballerina at the American Ballet Theater (ABT), there was much emphasis placed on her appearance across the media precisely because she did not fit this established aesthetic. Copeland is five feet two inches tall, and she has a woman's curves in an artistic tradition that glorifies prepubescent straight lines. And she is African American. Therefore, in a discipline in which young girls habitually mutilate their bodies in search of a rigid idea of perfection, Copeland's body aesthetics foreground a needed revision of what constitutes the construction of female bodies in the arts. This extends to many other examples of women who are expected to have specific types of bodies, such as gymnasts. In the Rio Olympics, another clear example was the case of Alexa Moreno, a Mexican gymnast who competed in the qualifying rounds. Most of the social media in Mexico focused on her body, poking fun at her for being "overweight." There was almost no notice of her accomplishments, which were overshadowed by the controversy surrounding her physical appearance.

20. Alicia del Campo, "Danza y género: Apuntes para una lectura de cuerpos en movimientos," in *Teatro en danza,* ed. Alicia del Campo (Cádiz: Fundación Municipal de Cultura de Cádiz, 2008), 13.

21. Diéguez, *Escenarios liminales,* 61–62.

22. Rosemarie Garland-Thomson, "Integrating Disability, Transforming Feminist Theory," in *The Disability Studies Reader,* Ed. Lennard J. Davis (New York: Routledge, 2013) 340.

23. This information comes from a 2014 episode of *All Things Considered* on National Public Radio, "In Brazil, Nips and Tucks Don't Raise an Eyebrow," http://www.npr.org/sections/parallels/2014/10/07/353270270/an-uplifting-story-brazils-obsession-with-plastic-surgery

24. The business of plastic surgery is so ubiquitous in Brazil that cosmetic

procedures have become a normalized aesthetic practice that is slowly trickling down to the less wealthy sectors of society. The Ivo Pitanguy Institute in Rio de Janeiro, named after a renowned plastic surgeon, is a teaching hospital that provides heavily subsidized cosmetic procedures in order to be affordable to more people. The hospital often represents its work as a form of altruism under the motto "The poor have the right to be beautiful too."

25. Rachel Adams, "An American Tail: Freaks, Gender, and the Incorporation of History in Katherine Dunn's *Geek Love,*" in *Freakery: Cultural Spectacles of the Extraordinary Body*, ed. Rosemary Garland-Thomson (New York: New York UP, 1996), 282.

26. This image of beauty, of course, decreases racial diversity. In a country that is primarily mixed race, models like Gisele Bündchen have become the standard of beauty: white, tall, and thin, with straight hair, large breasts, and few curves.

27. Ani Hao, "In Brazil, Women Are Fighting against the Sexist Impeachment of Dilma Rousseff," *The Guardian*, July 5, 2016, https://www.theguardian.com/global-development/2016/jul/05/in-brazil-women-are-fighting-against-the-sexist-impeachment-of-dilma-rousseff

28. Luce Irigaray, "Women on the Market," in *This Sex Which Is Not One.* Trans. Catherine Porter (Ithaca: Cornell UP, 1985), 181.

29. Preciado, *Testo Junkie,* 278.

30. Jean-Luc Nancy, *Noli me tangere: On the Raising of the Body*, trans. Sarah Clift, Pascale-Anne Brault, and Michael Nass (New York: Fordham UP, 2008), 48.

31. Suely Machado, quoted on the Primeiro Ato website, http://www.primeiroato.com.br/grupo.php#sobre.

32. Nancy Ruyter, "Dos ejemplares espectáculos de danza: Geraldas e Avencas y De cabeza," *Gestos Online,* http://www.humanities.uci.edu/gestos/GESTOS%20ONLINE/5-GESTOSONLINENancy%27s_dance_final.pdf

33. Jill Dolan, *Utopia in Performance: Finding Hope at the Theater* (Ann Arbor: U of Michigan P, 2008), 5.

34. Ibid., 19.

35. Katia Tirado, interview with the author. Mexico City, May 30, 2015. Unless otherwise noted, all statements by the artist are drawn from this interview.

36. The Ex-Teresa Arte Actual is a performance space, archive, and museum so named because it is located in the building that was formerly the Church of Santa Teresa la Antigua. The space focuses on the diffusion of contemporary art, mainly installation, performance, and multimedia.

37. Antonio Prieto-Stambaugh, "Wrestling the Phallus, Resisting Amnesia: The Body Politics of Chilanga Performance Artists," in *Holy Terrors: Latin American Women Perform*, ed. Diana Taylor and Roselyn Costantino (Durham: Duke UP, 2003), 251. PRI refers to the Partido Revolucionario Institucional (Institutional Revolutionary Party), Mexico's political ruling party, which held uninterrupted power in the country from 1929-2000, and once again in 2012. The UNAM is the national university in Mexico, Universidad Autónoma de México.

38. The performance at the CENART took place in May 2015 as part of the conference Encuentro Internacional Poética de la Acción. Tirado also presented

the piece at the Malta Theatre Festival in Poland in 2014. Here she went out into the streets on the days prior to the performance and asked people to tell her stories. She went to parks and bars and sat on street corners and let people come to her. She took these stories and worked with three tattoo artists during the performance, at one moment even asking for an image to be tattooed on her own back.

39. I am calling "program notes" what in reality was a fanzine that Tirado created with a collaborator (Baba de Lobo). It included photographs of the pig-skins with their tattoos from past performances and notes written by Tirado, including an essay titled "Variaciones sobre Xipetotec," where she explains the importance of this myth in the performance.

40. The quote is from Tirado's personal performance notes, which she provided to the author.

41. All the individuals' stories are part of Tirado's personal performance notes.

42. To be fair, Tirado invited the individuals in these stories to the performance. Most were there, those whose schedules would allow it, but their presence was not made evident.

43. Beatriz Sarlo, *Scenes from Postmodern Life*, trans. Jon Beasley-Murray (Minneapolis: U of Minnesota P, 2001), 21–22.

44. Chela Sandoval, *Methodology of the Oppressed* (Minneapolis: U of Minnesota P, 2000), 141.

45. Even though, as Tirado has clarified in her interview, this was the first time that she directly used tattooing in her performance, it is a practice that permeates her work because of her tattooed body, which includes parts of her head.

46. Andrea Stulman Dennet, *Weird and Wonderful: The Dime Museum in America* (New York: New York UP, 1997), 141. There has been much written about the art of tattooing as a cultural phenomenon. See, for example, Jane Caplan, ed., *Written on the Body: The Tattoo in European and American History* (Princeton: Princeton UP, 2000); and Margo DeMello, *Bodies of Inscription: A Cultural History of the Modern Tattoo Community* (Durham: Duke UP, 2000).

47. Karl Marx, *The Eighteenth Brumaire of Louis Bonaparte*, trans. Daniel de Leon, 63, published online by the Socialist Labor Party of America, accessed June 2017, http://www.slp.org/pdf/marx/eighteenth_brum.pdf

48. Bauman, *Wasted Lives*, 11–12.

49. Olivier Mongin, *Violencia y cine contemporáneo: Ensayo sobre ética e imagen* (Barcelona: Editorial Paidós, 1994), 141, 143.

50. Susan Sontag, *Regarding the Pain of Others* (New York: Picador, 2003), 111.

51. It is important to consider that the nature of human rights is curious, as it is often met with suspicion even as it enjoys the support of various groups across the world. This is largely due to concerns about western power, especially in societies that were ruled by colonial powers of the West. As Mark Hannam explains, "It has become a commonplace strategy to appeal to human rights in order to make legitimate the case for political change; such strategies are used not just by the leaders of popular movements against their own governments, but also by governments themselves seeking to justify their interfer-

ence in the domestic affairs of other states." [Mark Hannam, review of *On Human Rights*, by James Griffin, Democratiya 15 (2008): 115].This is especially the case because despite the human rights tradition having originated in the West and being based on Western values, it claims universality. Thus, the discourses of Human Rights are often found at the core of violent interventions upon "under-developed" and "non-Western" nations as a challenge to their sovereignty in the name of human rights violations—even as these challenges often lead to the death of large numbers of civilians.

52. Judith Butler, *Precarious Life: The Powers of Mourning and Violence* (New York: Verso, 2006), 46.

53. *Piedra* is the only piece in this book that I was not able to see live. I base my analysis on the two different videos that Galindo provided (both from the performance in São Paolo), as well as the multiple interviews and conversations I was able to conduct with her.

54. Saskia Sassen, "Global Cities and Survival Circuits," in *American Studies: An Anthology*, ed. Janice A. Radway et al. (Oxford: Wiley-Blackwell, 2009), 188.

55. The abuses of the coal-mining industry are present in various countries of Latin America, including Galindo's own nation of Guatemala. Since Galindo creates pieces based on the history of the country where she will perform them, she chose to focus on the exploitation of the mining industry in Brazil.

56. Soy una piedra
no siento los golpes
la humillación
las miradas lascivas
los cuerpos sobre el mío
el odio.
Soy una piedra
en mí
la historia del mundo

57. Hemispheric Institute Website: http://hemisphericinstitute.org/hemi/es/enc13-performances/item/2015-enc13-rjgalindo-piedra

58. From Regina José Galindo, interview with author. New Paltz, October 23, 2015. Unless otherwise noted, all statements by the artist are drawn from this interview.

59. From 1982 to 1996, the Guatemalan government, using the Guatemalan army and its counterinsurgency force (whose members defined themselves as "killing machines"), began a systematic campaign of repression and suppression against the Mayan Indians, whom they claimed were working toward a communist coup. General Efraín Ríos Montt came to power in Guatemala through a coup in March 1982. A month later he launched a "scorched earth" operation against the country's Ixil Maya population. Under Ríos Montt's dictatorship, the army and its paramilitary units systematically annihilated over six hundred villages. Armed forces cordoned off each village, rounded up the inhabitants, separated the men from the women and then killed them all. Those who managed to escape were hunted from the air by helicopter. The Ixil Maya faced extreme torture, mutilation, sexual violence, and violence against their

children. The Truth Commission in Guatemala acknowledged that the vast majority of raped women were indigenous.

60. Franco, *Cruel Modernity*, 77.

61. Rocío Silva Santiesteban, *El factor asco: Basurización simbólica y discursos autoritarios en el Perú contemporáneo* (Lima: Fondo Editorial Pontíficia Universidad Católica del Perú, 2008)

62. Caroline Rodrigues, "Performing Domination and Resistance between Body and Space: The Transversal Activism of Regina José Galindo," *Journal of Media Practice* 12.3 (2011): 301.

63. Enrique Dussel, *The Invention of the Americas: Eclipse of "the Other" and the Myth of Modernity* (New York: Continuum, 1995), 137.

64. Rosi Braidotti, "Signs of Wonder and Traces of Doubt: On Teratology and Embodied Difference," in *Feminist Theory and the Body: A Reader*, ed. Janet Price and Margrit Shildrick (New York: Routledge, 1999), 291.

65. Veena Das, *Critical Events: An Anthropological Perspective on Contemporary India* (Delhi: Oxford UP, 1995), 35.

66. Giorgio Agambem, *Remnants of Auschwitz: The Witness and the Archive* (New York: Zone, 1999), 39.

67. Ileana Diéguez, "*Communitas* of Pain: Performativities in Mourning," in *(Re)Positioning the Latina/o Americas: Theatrical Histories and Cartographies of Power*, ed. Jimmy Noriega and Analola Santana (Carbondale: Southern Illinois UP, 2018), 46.

68. Galindo insists that she was not able to learn the identity of this woman. She assumes that the woman must have been a participant in the conference, but she was unable to establish contact or obtain any information.

69. Garland-Thomson, *Staring*, 43.

70. Ibid., 75.

71. Diéguez, "*Communitas* of Pain."

72. Francine Masiello, *The Art of Transition: Latin American Culture and Neoliberal Crisis* (Durham: Duke UP, 2001), 231.

CHAPTER FOUR

1. Franco, *Cruel Modernity*, 2.

2. José Joaquín Brunner, "Notes on Modernity and Postmodernity in Latin American Culture," in *The Postmodernism Debate in Latin America*, ed. John Beverley, Michael Aronna, and José Oviedo (Durham: Duke UP, 1995), 42.

3. Ibid., 47.

4. Jorge Larraín, *Identity and Modernity in Latin America* (Cambridge: Polity, 2000), 172.

5. Ibid.

6. Foucault, "*Society Must Be Defended*," 257.

7. Ibid., 338.

8. Davis, "Introduction," 6.

9. Domingo Sarmiento's *Facundo: Civilización y Barbarie* (1845) is a well-

established example of the fear that the "savage indian" incited in the "civi-lized" white man. The central message of the text is very clear: Americanism was synonymous with barbarism. It was a primitive, cruel, tyrannical, and ret-rograde force. Sarmiento found these qualities to be endemic in the rural set-ting of vast uninhabited tracts of land, which should be eradicated and replaced with its antithesis: civilization. For Sarmiento, civilization meant urban indus-trialization, and he took as its example the ideas prevalent in the leading capi-tals of western Europe.

10. Franco, *Cruel Modernity*, 47.

11. Kruijt and Kooning, "Introduction," 7.

12. Franco, *Cruel Modernity*, 2.

13. Beatriz Sarlo, *Tiempo pasado: Cultura de la memoria y giro subjetivo una dis-cusión* (Mexico City: Siglo XXI Editores, 2005), 16.

14. Andreas Huyssen, *Twilight Memories: Marking Time in a Culture of Amne-sia* (New York: Routledge, 1995), 7.

15. Sandra Lorenzano, "Angels among Ruins," in *Telling Ruins in Latin Amer-ica*, ed. Michael J. Lazzara and Vicky Unruh (New York: Palgrave, 2009), 250–51.

16. Taylor, *The Archive and the Repertoire*, 2.

17. Ibid., 20.

18. Ibid., 24.

19. Brenda Werth, *Theatre, Performance, and Memory Politics in Argentina* (New York: Palgrave Macmillan, 2010), 2.

20. Marianne Hirsch, *Family Frames: Photography, Narrative, and Postmemory* (Cambridge: Harvard UP, 1997), 22.

21. Ibid., 8.

22. Ibid.

23. Ibid., 8–9.

24. Chimamanda Adichie, "Now is the Time to Talk About What We are Ac-tually Talking About," *New Yorker*, December 2, 2016,http://www.newyorker.com/culture/cultural-comment/now-is-the-time-to-talk-about-what-we-are-ac-tually-talking-about

25. The analysis of this play is based on a production I attended in Montreal in June 2014 during the Encuentro of the Hemispheric Institute of Performance and Politics at the Outremont Theatre, as well as a video of a performance in Chile in 2007 provided by the company.

26. This quote is taken from the Post-Performance Discussion of *Gemelos* in Montreal during the Hemispheric Institute's "Encuentro," June 21, 2014.

27. María de la Luz Hurtado, "*Gemelos*: Un prodigio de La Troppa," *Apuntes Teatro* 116.2 (1999): 10. This article provides a very complete analysis of the cre-ative process of the company.

28. Unless otherwise noted, this and other quotations from the play are from an unpublished text provided by the company. The translations are mine.

29. The father going to war signals the end of childhood for the twins. This is a very psychoanalytical moment: the loss of the father. According the Jung, the role of the father is to mediate the outer world for the child so as to build the child's self-confidence and hone his or her ability to function in life. The twins'

lack of a guiding figure in life can be associated with the violence of the Chilean military dictatorship, with Pinochet as the authoritarian father figure.

30. Paola S. Hernández, *El teatro de Argentina y Chile: Globalización, resistencia y desencanto* (Buenos Aires: Corregidor, 2009), 33.

31. Ibid., 34.

32. Juan Carlos Zagal, quoted in Hurtado, *"Gemelos,"* 11.

33. Ibid., 29.

34. The original score of the play was composed by Zagal.

35. Rosi Braidotti, "Mothers, Monsters, and Machines," in *Writing on the Body: Female Embodiment and Feminist Theory,* ed. Katie Conboy, Nadia Medina, and Sarah Stanbury (New York: Columbia UP, 1997), 64.

36. Hurtado, *"Gemelos,"* 4.

37. Mbembe, "Necropolitics," 39.

38. Antonin Artaud, *The Theater and Its Double* (New York: Grove, 1958), 102.

39. Norman Briski, interview with the author. Buenos Aires, May 2013. Unless otherwise noted, all statements by the artist are drawn from this interview.

40. *El barro se subleva* premiered in Buenos Aires in September 2012. I saw the performance in May 2013 and again in June 2015. The analysis in this section is based on these performances, as well as the published text: Norman Briski, *Nagasaki de memoria/El barro se subleva* (Buenos Aires: Editorial Dunken, 2011).

41. Jean Graham-Jones, *Exorcising History: Argentine Theater under Dictatorship* (Lewisburg: Bucknell UP, 2000), 16.

42. For a complete history of theatrical production during the military dictatorship, as well as a thorough study of this historical period, see: Jan Graham-Jones *Exorcising History*; Diana Taylor, *Theatre of Crisis: Drama and Politics in Latin America* (Lexington: UP of Kentucky, 1991); Taylor, *Disappearing Acts*; Paola Hernández, *El teatro de Argentina y Chile*; and Ana Elena Puga, *Memory, Allegory, and Testimony in South American Theatre* (New York: Routledge, 2008), to name a few.

43. The changes to a neoliberal model are prominent through the government of Néstor Kirchner, who launched his government on a firm critique of neoliberal policies, and Cristina Fernández de Kirchner. This turn to center left was short-lived, though, as the election of Mauricio Macri in 2015 demonstrates. Macri's government has been classified as a return to "classic" neoliberalism. I am over-simplifying a very complex period in Argentina. For more information please see: Francisco E. González, *Creative Destruction? Economic Crises and Democracy in Latin America* (Baltimore: The John Hopkins UP, 2012); Luis Daniel Vázquez Valencia, *Democracia y mercado: viejas disputas, nuevas soluciones. El caso argentino* (Mexico City: Flacso México, 2012)

44. Saskia Sassen, *Expulsions: Brutality and Complexity in the Global Economy* (Cambridge: Harvard UP, 2014), 10.

45. Umberto Eco, *Apocalípticos e integrados* (Mexico City: Tusquets Editores, 2005), 223.

46. Norman Briski, *Nagasaki de memoria/El barro se subleva* (Buenos Aires: Editorial Dunken, 2011), 73.

47. Eduardo Misch, interview with the author. Buenos Aires, June 2015. Unless otherwise noted, all statements by the artist are drawn from this interview.

48. Ibid., 75.

49. Ibid., 41.

50. Mikhail Bakhtin, *Rabelais and His World* (Bloomington: Indiana UP, 1984), 25.

51. Ibid., 27.

52. Ibid., 364.

53. Briski, *Nagasaki*, 70.

54. Ibid.

55. Ibid.

56. Jean Graham-Jones, "Rethinking Buenos Aires Theatre in the Wake of 2001 and Emerging Structures of Resistance and Resilience," *Theatre Journal* 66.1 (2014): 43.

57. Ibid., 40.

58. Briski, *Nagasaki/El barro*, 71.

59. Ibid., 77.

60. Ibid., 78.

61. Ibid., 79.

62. I originally watched this performance in Mexico City in July 2014 at the Centro Cultural del Bosque. The director also provided different video versions of the performance, which also inform this study.

63. The exact origins of the *ukuku* is unknown, although many stories say the main character represents a combination of a pre-Columbian trickster and a European devil. The *ukuku* dancer is dressed in a thick, stringy coat that resembles the fur of a wild animal, perhaps a bear. As a troublemaking figure, he brings disarray and confusion to otherwise highly choreographed dance routines. In recent times, *ukukus* have acquired a politicized role, often delivering messages that bring attention to contemporary social and economic issues in Peru.

64. Ana Correa, "The Flight of the Golden Falcon: A Road into War's Profound Sorrow" in *Theatre and Cartographies of Power: Repositioning the Latina/o Americas*, ed. Jimmy Noriega and Analola Santana (Carbondale: Southern Illinois UP, 2017), 200.

65. See chapter 1 for more about this company.

66. Apu is a Quechua name given to the sacred mountains. Kallahualla is the name of an indigenous community of traditional healers who live in the Andean mountains of Peru and Bolivia.

67. León Rozitchner, "Prologue," in *That Inferno: Conversations of Five Women Survivors of an Argentine Torture Camp*, ed. Manú Actis et al. (Nashville: Vanderbilt UP, 2006), xx.

68. Ana Correa, interview with the author. Lima, August 2012. Unless otherwise noted, all statements by the artist are drawn from this interview.

69. Correa, "The Flight," 201.

70. Franco, *Cruel Modernity*, 11.

71. Ibid., 55.

72. Primo Levi, *The Drowned and the Saved*, trans. Raymond Rosenthal (New York: Vintage 1989), 126.

73. Thomas Fahy, *Freak Shows and the Modern American Imagination: Constructing the Damaged Body from Willa Cather to Truman Capote* (New York: Palgrave Macmillan, 2006), 54.

74. Franco, *Cruel Modernity*, 57.

75. Mbembe, "Necropolitics," 11–12.

76. Ibid., 16.

77. Foucault, *"Society Must Be Defended,"* 17.

CONCLUSIONS

1. Helen Shaw, "The State of the Play: A Critic Addresses the Theatre Nation," *American Theatre,* October 2016, 31.

2. Ibid.

3. José Esteban Muñoz, *Disidentifications: Queers of Color and the Performance of Politics* (Minneapolis: U of Minnesota P, 1999), 4.

4. Bernal Díaz del Castillo, quoted in Bartra, *Wild Men,* 1–2.

Bibliography

Adams, Rachel. *Sideshow U.S.A.: Freaks and the American Cultural Imagination*. Chicago: U of Chicago P, 2001.

"An American Tail: Freaks, Gender, and the Incorporation of History in Katherine Dunn's *Geek Love*." *Freakery: Cultural Spectacles of the Extraordinary Body*. Ed. Rosemary Garland-Thomson. New York: New York UP, 1996. 277–90.

Agambem, Giorgio. *Remnants of Auschwitz: The Witness and the Archive*. New York: Zone, 1999.

Homo Sacer: Sovereign Power and Bare Life. Stanford: Stanford UP, 1998.

Alcazar, Josefina. "Performance Art: El cuerpo freak de Rocío Boliver (La Congelada de Uva)." *Freakish Encounters: Constructions of the Freak in Hispanic Cultures*. Ed. Sara Muñoz and Analola Santana. Special Issue of *Hispanic Issues Online* (forthcoming. Spring 2018).

Performance: Un arte del yo—Autobiografía, cuerpo e identidad. Mexico City: Siglo XXI Editores, 2014.

Altick, Richard D. *The Shows of London*. Cambridge: Belknap Press of Harvard UP, 1978.

A'ness, Francine. "Resisting Amnesia: Yuyachkani, Performance, and the Postwar Reconstruction of Peru." *Theatre Journal* 56.3 (2004): 395–414.

Antebi, Susan. *Carnal Inscriptions: Spanish American Narratives of Corporeal Difference and Disability*. New York: Palgrave Macmillan, 2009.

"Blindness and Freakishness." *Literal Magazine. Latin American Voices* 16 (Spring 2009): 27–28.

Arbus, Diane. *Diane Arbus*. New York: Millerton, 1972.

Arendt, Hannah. *The Human Condition*. 2nd ed. Chicago: U of Chicago P, 1998.

Aristotle. *Generation of Animals*. Trans. A. L. Peck. Cambridge: Harvard University Press, 1944.

Artaud, Antonin. *The Theater and Its Double*. New York: Grove, 1958.

Ávila Harper, Roxana. "Experiences from the Center of Abya Yala." *(Re)Positioning the Latina/o Americas: Theatrical Histories and Cartographies of Power*. Ed. Jimmy Noriega and Analola Santana. Carbondale: Southern Illinois UP, 2018. 186-190.

Bacon, Francis. "Novum Organum." *Francis Bacon: Advancement of Learning, Novum Organum, New Atlantis*. Great Books of the Western World, vol. 30. Chicago: Encyclopaedia Britannica, 1952.

Bakhtin, Mikhail. *Rabelais and His World*. Bloomington: Indiana UP, 1984.

Bartra, Roger. "El trágico viaje de una mujer salvaje mexicana al mundo civilizado." *Freakish Encounters: Constructions of the Freak in Hispanic Cultures*. Ed.

Sara Muñoz and Analola Santana. Special Issue of *Hispanic Issues Online* (forthcoming Spring 2018).

Territorios del terror y la otredad. Valencia: Pre-Textos, 2007.

The Artificial Savage. Modern Myths of the Wild Man. Trans. Christopher Follett. Ann Arbor: U Michigan P, 1997.

Wild Men in the Looking Glass: The Mythic Origin of European Otherness. Trans. Carl T. Berrisford. Ann Arbor: U of Michigan P, 1994.

Bauman, Zygmunt. *Wasted Lives: Modernity and Its Outcasts*. New York: Blackwell, 2004.

Baxandall, Michael. *Painting and Experience in Fifteenth-Century Italy*. Oxford: Oxford UP, 1072.

Becerra, Marina. "Maternidad y ciudadanía en la Argentina de principios del siglo XX: Un análisis de la autobiografía de María Rosa Oliver." *Contracorriente: A Journal of Social History and Literature in Latin America* 10.2 (2013): 202–18.

Benjamin, Walter. "The Work of Art in the Age of Mechanical Reproduction." *Illuminations*, ed. Hannah Arendt, trans. Harry Zohn. New York: Schocken, 1969. 217–52.

Bhabha, Homi K. "Postcolonial Authority and Postmodern Guilt." *Cultural Studies*. Ed. Lawrence Grossberg, Cary Nelson, and Paula A. Treichler. New York: Routledge, 1992. 56–68.

Bly, Mark. "Introduction." *The Production Notebooks*. Vol. 1. New York: Theatre Communications Group, 1996.

Bogdan, Robert. "The Social Construction of Freaks." *Freakery: Cultural Spectacles of the Extraordinary Body*. Ed. Rosemary Garland-Thomson. New York: New York UP, 1996. 23–37.

Freak Show: Presenting Human Oddities for Amusement and Profit. Chicago: U of Chicago P, 1988.

Braidotti, Rosi. "Signs of Wonder and Traces of Doubt: On Teratology and Embodied Difference." *Feminist Theory and the Body: A Reader*. Ed. Janet Price and Margrit Shildrick. New York: Routledge, 1999. 290–301.

"Mothers, Monsters, and Machines." *Writing on the Body: Female Embodiment and Feminist Theory*. Ed. Katie Conboy, Nadia Medina, and Sarah Stanbury. New York: Columbia UP, 1997. 59–79.

Briski, Norman. *Nagasaki de memoria/El barro se subleva*. Buenos Aires: Editorial Dunken, 2011.

Brunner, José Joaquín. "Traditionalism and Modernity in Latin American Culture." *Latin America Writes Back: Postmodernity in the Periphery*. Ed. Emil Volek. New York: Routledge, 2002. 3–31.

"Notes on Modernity and Postmodernity in Latin American Culture." *The Postmodernism Debate in Latin America*. Ed. John Beverley, Michael Aronna, and José Oviedo. Durham: Duke UP, 1995. 34–54.

Buenaventura, Enrique. "El Método de Creación Colectiva." *Creación Colectiva: El legado de Enrique Buenaventura*. Ed. Beatriz Rizk. Buenos Aires: Atuel, 2008. 127–83.

Butler, Judith. *Precarious Life: The Powers of Mourning and Violence*. New York: Verso, 2006.

Bodies That Matter: On the Discursive Limits of "Sex." New York: Routledge, 1993.

Caplan, Jane, ed. *Written on the Body: The Tattoo in European and American History.* Princeton: Princeton UP, 2000.

Canguilhem, Georges. *The Normal and the Pathological.* New York: Zone, 1989.

Cassuto, Leonard. "Freak." *Keywords for Disability Studies.* Ed. Rachel Adams, Benjamin Reiss, and David Serlin. New York: New York UP, 2015. 85–88.

Cayo Córdoba, Percy. *Perú y Ecuador: Antecedentes de un largo conflicto.* Lima: Universidad del Pacífico, 1997.

Chemers, Michael. *Staging Stigma: A Critical Examination of the American Freak Show.* New York: Palgrave Macmillan, 2008.

"Le Freak, C'est Chic: The Twenty-First Century Freak Show as Theatre of Transgression." *Modern Drama* 46.2 (2003): 285–304.

Chomsky, Noam. "Chiapas: Symbol of Resistance." Foreword to *Ya basta! Ten Years of the Zapatista Uprising,* by Subcomandante Insurgente Marcos. Oakland: AK Press, 2004. 13-14.

Cixous, Hélène. "The Laugh of the Medusa." Trans. Keith Cohen and Paula Cohen. *Signs* 1.4 (Summer 1976): 875–93.

Cohen, Ed. *A Body Worth Defending: Immunity, Biopolitics, and the Apotheosis of the Modern Body.* Durham: Duke UP, 2009.

Comisión de Derechos Humanos (COMISEDH). *Memoria para los ausentes desaparecidos en el Perú (1982–1996).* Lima: COMISEDH, 2001.

Condit, Celeste Michelle. *The Meaning of the Gene: Public Debates about Human Heredity.* Madison: U of Wisconsin P, 1999.

Cooper, Evan. "Looking at the Latin 'Freak': Audience Reception of John Leguizamo's Culturally Intimate Humor." *Latino Studies* 6 (2008): 436–55.

Correa, Ana. "The Flight of the Golden Falcon: A Road into War's Profound Sorrow." *Theatre and Cartographies of Power: Repositioning the Latina/o Americas.* Ed. Jimmy Noriega and Analola Santana. Carbondale: Southern Illinois UP, 2018. 199–207.

Creed, Barbara. *The Monstrous-Feminine: Film, Feminism, Psychoanalysis.* London: Routledge, 1993.

Daley, Susan. "Guatemalan Women's Claims Put Focus on Canadian Firms' Conduct Abroad." *New York Times,* April 2, 2016.

Das, Veena. *Critical Events: An Anthropological Perspective on Contemporary India.* Delhi: Oxford UP, 1995.

Daston, Lorraine, and Katharine Park. *Wonders and the Order of Nature, 1150–1750.* New York: Zone, 1998.

Davis, Lennard. "Introduction: Normality, Power, and Culture." *The Disability Studies Reader.* Ed. Lennard Davis. New York: Routledge, 2013. 1–14.

Debord, Guy. *Society of the Spectacle.* Detroit: Black & Red, 2010.

DeMello, Margo. *Bodies of Inscription: A Cultural History of the Modern Tattoo Community.* Durham: Duke UP, 2000.

De Giorgi, Alessandro. *Re-thinking the Political Economy of Punishment.* Burlington: Ashgate, 2006.

del Campo, Alicia. "Danza y género: Apuntes para una lectura de cuerpos en movimientos." *Teatro en danza.* Ed. Alicia del Campo. Cádiz: Fundación Municipal de Cultura de Cádiz, 2008. 11–24.

Diamond, Larry, Jonathan Hartlyn, Juan J. Linz, and Seymour Martin Lipset, eds. *Democracy in Developing Countries: Latin America*. Boulder: Lynne Rienner, 1999.

Diéguez, Ileana. "*Communitas* of Pain: Performativities in Mourning." *(Re)Positioning the Latina/o Americas: Theatrical Histories and Cartographies of Power*. Ed. Jimmy Noriega and Analola Santana. Carbondale: Southern Illinois UP, 2018. 46–55.

Escenarios Liminales: Teatralidades, performatividades, políticas. Mexico City: Toma, Ediciones y Producciones Escénicas y Cinematográficas, 2014.

Dolan, Jill. *Utopia in Performance: Finding Hope at the Theater*. Ann Arbor: U of Michigan P, 2008.

Douglas, Mary. *Purity and Danger: An Analysis of Concepts of Pollution and Taboo*. New York: Routledge, 2003.

Durbach, Nadja. *The Spectacle of Deformity: Freak Shows and Modern British Culture*. Berkeley: U of California P, 2010.

Dussel, Enrique. *The Invention of the Americas: Eclipse of "the Other" and the Myth of Modernity*. New York: Continuum, 1995.

Eagleton, Terry. "Bakhtin, Schopenhauer, Kundera." *Bakhtin and Cultural Theory*. Ed. Ken Hirschkop and David Shepherd. Manchester: Manchester UP, 2001. 229–40.

Eco, Umberto. *Apocalípticos e integrados*. Mexico City: Tusquets Editores, 2005.

History of Beauty. New York: Rizzoli, 2004.

Esslin, Martin. *The Theatre of the Absurd*, 3rd Edition. New York: Vintage Books, 2004.

Fahy, Thomas. *Freak Shows and the Modern American Imagination: Constructing the Damaged Body from Willa Cather to Truman Capote*. New York: Palgrave Macmillan, 2006.

Fernández Retamar, Roberto. *Caliban and Other Essays*. Minneapolis: U of Minnesota P, 1989.

Fiedler, Leslie. *Freaks: Myths and Images of the Secret Self*. New York: Simon and Schuster, 1978.

Foucault, Michel. *Abnormal: Lectures at the College de France (1974–1975)*. Ed. Valerio Marchetti and Antonella Salomoni. Trans. Graham Burchell. New York: Picador, 2003.

"Society Must Be Defended": Lectures at the College de France, 1975–1976. Trans. David Macey. New York: Picador, 2003.

Discipline and Punish: The Birth of the Prison. Trans. Alan Sheridan. 2nd ed. New York: Vintage, 1995.

"The Masked Philosopher." *Politics, Philosophy, Culture: Interviews and Other Writings, 1977–1984*. Ed. Lawrence D. Kritzman. New York: Routledge 1988. 323–30.

Franco, Jean. *Cruel Modernity*. Durham: Duke UP, 2013.

Friedman, John Block. *The Monstrous Races in Medieval Art and Thought*. Cambridge: Harvard UP, 1981.

Galeano, Eduardo. *Genesis*. New York: Norton, 1998.

García Canclini, Néstor. *Consumers and Citizens: Globalization and Multicultural Conflicts*. Trans. George Yúdice. Minneapolis: U of Minnesota P, 2001.

García Menéndez, José Ramón. *Política económica y deuda externa en América Latina.* Santiago de Compostela: Iepala, 1986.

Garland-Thomson, Rosemarie. "Integrating Disability, Transforming Feminist Theory." *The Disability Studies Reader.* Ed. Lennard J. Davis. New York: Routledge, 2013. 333–53.

Staring: How We Look. Oxford: Oxford UP, 2009.

"Feminist Disability Studies." *Signs* 30.2 (2005): 1557–87.

Extraordinary Bodies: Figuring Physical Disability in American Culture and Literature. New York: Columbia UP, 1997.

"Introduction." *Freakery: Cultural Spectacles of the Extraordinary Body.* Ed. Rosemarie Garland-Thomson. New York: New York UP, 1996. 1–21.

Gerber, David. "The 'Careers' of People Exhibited in Freak Shows: The Problem of Volition and Valorization." *Freakery: Cultural Spectacles of the Extraordinary Body.* Ed. Rosemary Garland-Thomson. New York: New York UP, 1996. 38–54.

Germani, Gino. "Democracia y autoritarismo en la sociedad moderna." *Los límites de la democracia.* Ed. Fernando Calderón. Buenos Aires: Consejo Latinoamericano de Ciencias Sociales (CLACSO), 1985. 13–52.

Giorgi, Gabriel and Fermín Rodríguez, ed. "Prólogo." *Ensayos sobre biopolítica: Excesos de vida.* Buenos Aires: Paidós, 2009. 9–33.

Girard, René. "From Mimetic Desire to the Monstrous Double." *Mimesis, Masochism, and Mime: The Politics of Theatricality in Contemporary French Thought.* Ed. Timothy Murray. Ann Arbor: U of Michigan P, 1997. 87–109.

Goffman, Erving. *Stigma: Notes on the Management of a Spoiled Identity.* New York: Simon and Schuster, 1963.

Graham-Jones, Jean. *Evita, Inevitably: Performing Argentina's Female Icons before and after Eva Perón.* Ann Arbor: U of Michigan P, 2014.

"Rethinking Buenos Aires Theatre in the Wake of 2001 and Emerging Structures of Resistance and Resilience." *Theatre Journal* 66.1 (2014): 37–54.

Exorcising History: Argentine Theater under Dictatorship. Lewisburg: Bucknell UP, 2000.

Greer, Margaret, Walter D. Mignolo, and Maureen Quilligan. "Introduction." *Rereading the Black Legend: The Discourses of Religious and Racial Difference in the Renaissance Empires.* Ed. Margaret R. Greer, Walter D. Mignolo, and Maureen Quilligan. Chicago: U of Chicago P, 2007. 1–24.

Grosz, Elizabeth. "Intolerable Ambiguity: Freaks as/at the Limit." *Freakery: Cultural Spectacles of the Extraordinary Body.* Ed. Rosemarie Garland-Thomson. New York: New York UP, 1996. 55–66.

Guerra, Lucía. *La mujer fragmentada: Historia de un signo.* Santiago: Cuarto Propio, 1995.

Habermas, Jürgen. *The Inclusion of the Other: Studies in Political Theory.* Ed. Ciaran Cronin and Pablo De Greiff. Cambridge: MIT P, 1998.

Halberstam, J. Jack. *Gaga Feminism: Sex, Gender, and the End of Normal.* Boston: Beacon, 2012.

Handelsman, Michael. "El teatro contemporáneo del Ecuador entre dos milenios: Resistencia y representatividad." *Antología del Teatro Ecuatoriano de fin de siglo.* Ed. Lola Proaño Gómez. Quito: Casa de la Cultura Ecuatoriana "Benjamín Carrión," 2003. 27–55.

Haraway, Donna. "The Promises of Monsters: A Regenerative Politics for Inappropriate/d Others." *Cultural Studies.* Ed. Lawrence Grossberg, Cary Nelson, and Paula A. Treichler. New York: Routledge, 1992. 295–337.

"A Cyborg Manifesto: Science, Technology, and Socialist-Feminism in the Late Twentieth Century." *The Transgender Studies Reader.* Eds. Susan Stryker and Stephen Whittle (New York: Routledge, 2006): 103–18.

Hardt, Michael, and Antonio Negri. *Multitude: War and Democracy in the Age of Empire.* New York: Penguin, 2004.

Harvey, David. *A Brief History of Neoliberalism.* New York: Oxford UP, 2005.

Hao, Ani. "In Brazil, Women Are Fighting against the Sexist Impeachment of Dilma Rousseff." *The Guardian,* July 5, 2016, https://www.theguardian.com/global-development/2016/jul/05/in-brazil-women-are-fighting-against-the-sexist-impeachment-of-dilma-rousseff

Hayles, N. Katherine. *How we Became Posthuman :Virtual Bodies in Cybernetics, Literature, and Informatics.* Chicago: U of Chicago P, 1999.

Hernández, Paola S. *El teatro de Argentina y Chile: Globalización, resistencia y desencanto.* Buenos Aires: Corregidor, 2009.

Hevey, David. *The Creatures Time Forgot: Photography and Disability Imagery.* London: Routledge, 1992.

Hirsch, Marianne. "Surviving Images: Holocaust Photography and the Work of Postmemory." *Yale Journal of Criticism* 14.1 (2001): 5–37.

Family Frames: Photography, Narrative, and Postmemory. Cambridge: Harvard UP, 1997.

Huber, Evelyne, and Fred Solt. "Success and Failures of Neoliberalism." *Latin American Research Review* 39.3 (2004): 149–64.

Hurtado, María de la Luz. "*Gemelos*: Un prodigio de La Troppa." *Apuntes Teatro* 116.2 (1999): 7–15.

Huyssen, Andreas. *Twilight Memories: Marking Time in a Culture of Amnesia.* New York: Routledge, 1995.

Irigaray, Luce. *To Speak Is Never Neutral.* Trans. Gail Schwab. New York: Routledge, 2002.

"Women on the Market." *This Sex Which Is Not One.* Trans. Catherine Porter. Ithaca: Cornell UP, 1985. 170–91.

Jáuregui, Carlos. *Canibalia: Canibalismo, calibanismo, antropofagia cultural, y consume en América Latina.* Madrid: Iberoamericana, 2008.

Jáuregui, Carlos, and Paola Uparela Reyes. "La vagina-ojo y otros monstruos gineco- escópicos." *Freakish Encounters: Constructions of the Freak in Hispanic Cultures.* Ed. Sara Muñoz and Analola Santana. Special issue of *Hispanic Issues Online* (forthcoming Spring 2018).

Karl, Terry Lynn. "Dilemmas of Democratization in Latin America," *Comparative Politics* 23.1 (1990): 1–21.

Klein, Naomi. *Shock Doctrine: The Rise of Disaster Capitalism.* New York: Picador, 2007.

Kristeva, Julia. *Powers of Horror: An Essay on Abjection.* Trans. Leon S. Roudiez. New York: Columbia UP, 1982.

Kruijt, Dirk, and Kees Kooning. "Introduction." *Societies of Fear: The Legacy of Civil War, Violence, and Terror in Latin America*. Ed. Dirk Kruijt and Kees Kooning. London: Zed, 1999. 1–30.

Kuppers, Petra. *The Scar of Visibility: Medical Performances and Contemporary Art*. Minneapolis: U of Minnesota P, 2007.

"Bodies, Hysteria, Pain: Staging the Invisible." *Bodies in Commotion: Disability and Performance*. Ed. Carrie Sandahl and Philip Auslander. Ann Arbor: U of Michigan P, 2005. 147–62.

Kuri, Jorge, and Claudio Valdés Kuri. "De monstruos y prodigios: La historia de los castrati." *Gestos* 16.31 (2001): 116–56.

Larraín, Jorge. *Identity and Modernity in Latin America*. Cambridge: Polity, 2000.

Leroi, Armand Marie. *Mutants: On Genetic Variety and the Human Body*. New York: Penguin, 2003.

Levi, Primo. *The Drowned and the Saved*. Trans. Raymond Rosenthal. New York: Vintage 1989.

Lorenzano, Sandra. "Angels among Ruins." *Telling Ruins in Latin America*. Ed. Michael J. Lazzara and Vicky Unruh. New York: Palgrave, 2009. 249–59.

Ludmer, Josefina. "El Coloquio de Yale: Máquinas de leer 'fin de siglo.'" *Las culturas de fin de siglo en América Latina*. Buenos Aires: Beatriz Viterbo Editora, 1994. 7–24.

Marcos, Beatriz. "Memoria y dramatización del daño." Accessed June 1, 2017. https://beatrizmarcos.wordpress.com/2012/07/07/memoria-y-dramatizacion-del-dano-estoy-pensando-estoy-recordando-el-grupo-de-teatro-peruano-yuyachkani/

Marín, Paola. "Performance e hibridez: *NK 603* de Violeta Luna." *Gestos* 50 (2010): 196–200.

Martí, José. "Two Views of Coney Island." *Inside the Monster by José Martí: Writings on the United States and American Imperialism*. Trans. Elinor Randall. New York: Monthly Review Press, 1975. 165–75.

Martín-Barbero, Jesús. "Globalización y multiculturalidad: Notas para una agenda de investigación." *Nuevas Perspectivas desde/sobre América Latina: El desafío de los estudios culturales*. Ed. Mabel Moraña. Pittsburgh: Instituto Internacional de Literatura Iberoamericana, 2002. 17–29.

Martínez, América Luna. "Maternidad y escritura femenina: Una experiencia perturbadora." *La otredad: Los discursos de la cultura hoy*. Ed. Silvia Elguea Véjar. Mexico City: Universidad Autónoma Metropolitana, 1997. 45–52.

Marx, Karl. *The Eighteenth Brumaire of Louis Bonaparte*. Trans. Daniel de Leon. Published online by the Socialist Labor Party of America. Accessed June 2017. http://www.slp.org/pdf/marx/eighteenth_brum.pdf

Masiello, Francine. *The Art of Transition: Latin American Culture and Neoliberal Crisis*. Durham: Duke UP, 2001.

Mbembe, Achille. "Necropolitics." *Public Culture* 15.1 (2003): 11–40.

Mendieta, Eduardo. *Global Fragments: Globalization, Latinoamericanisms, and Critical Theory*. New York: State U of NY Press, 2007.

Mignolo, Walter. *The Idea of Latin America*. Malden: Blackwell, 2005.

Mongin, Olivier. *Violencia y cine contemporáneo: Ensayo sobre ética e imagen*. Barcelona: Editorial, 1994.

Mora, Denise. "Fauna: Una indagación sobre cómo el arte puede representar la vida." *Revista Telon de Fondo* 20 (2014): 241–48.

Moulián, Tomás. *Chile actual: Anatomía de un mito*. Santiago: LOM, 2002.

Muñoz, José Esteban. *Disidentifications: Queers of Color and the Performance of Politics*. Minneapolis: U of Minnesota P, 1999.

Nancy, Jean-Luc. *Noli me tangere: On the Raising of the Body*. Trans. Sarah Clift, Pascale-Anne Brault, and Michael Nass. New York: Fordham UP, 2008.

Negrón-Muntaner, Frances. "Poetry of Filth: The (Post) Reggaetonic Lyrics of Calle 13." *Reggaeton*. Eds. Raquel Z. Rivera, Wayne Marshall, and Deborah Pacini Hernández. Durham: Duke UP, 2009. 327–40.

Nelkin, Dorothy, and M. Susan Lindee. *The DNA Mystique: The Gene as a Cultural Icon*. New York: Freeman, 1995.

Nelson, Alondra. *The Social Life of DNA: Race, Reparations, and Reconciliation after the Genome*. Boston: Beacon, 2016.

Nielsen, Lara. "Introduction: Heterotopic Transformations, the (Il)Liberal Neoliberal." *Neoliberalism and Global Theatres: Performance Permutations*. Ed. Lara Nielsen and Patricia Ybarra. New York: Palgrave Macmillan, 2012. 1–21.

Noguerol Jiménez, Francisca. "Driven up the Wall: Maternity and Literature in Contemporary Latin American Women Writers." *Review: Literature and Arts of the Americas* 86.46 (2013): 13–19.

Noriega, Jimmy. "Teatro Travieso and *creación colectiva*: Devising Intercultural Performance in Lima, Peru." *Theatre Topics* 26.2 (2016): 207–19.

Olea, Raquel. "Feminism: Modern or Postmodern?" *The Postmodernism Debate in Latin America*. Ed. John Beverly, José Oviedo, and Michael Aronna. Durham: Duke UP, 1995. 192–200.

Paula, Romina. *Fauna. Tres obras*. Buenos Aires: Editorial Entropía, 2013. 9–59.

Perales, Rosalina. "El mundo al revés: Inversión y carnavalización de la historia." *Discursos teatrales en los albores del siglo XXI*. Ed. Juan Villegas and Alicia del Campo y Mario Rojas. Irvine: Gestos, 2001. 173–85.

Pérez Laborde, Elga. *A Questão Teórica do Esperpento e sua Projeção Estética: Variações Esperpênticas da Idade Média ao Século XXI*. Brasília: Department de Teoria Literária, Universidade de Brasília, 2004.

Phaik Lin Goh, Janice. "Deterritorialized Women in the Global City: An Analysis of Sex Trafficking in Dubai, Tokyo and New York." *intersection* 10.2 (2009): 271–324.

Preciado, Beatriz. *Testo Junkie: Sex, Drugs, and Biopolitics in the Pharmacopornographic Era*. Trans. Bruce Benderson. New York: Feminist Press at the City University of New York, 2013.

Prieto-Stambaugh, Antonio. "Wrestling the Phallus, Resisting Amnesia: The Body Politics of Chilanga Performance Artists." *Holy Terrors: Latin American Women Perform*. Ed. Diana Taylor and Roselyn Costantino. Durham: Duke UP, 2003. 245–73.

Proaño Gómez, Lola. *Teatro y estética comunitaria: Miradas desde la filosofía y la política*. Buenos Aires: Editorial Biblos, 2013.

Poéticas de la globalización en el teatro Latinoamericano. Irvine: Gestos, 2007.

Puga, Ana Elena. *Memory, Allegory, and Testimony in South American Theatre*. New York: Routledge, 2008.

Quijano, Aníbal. "Coloniality and Modernity/Rationality." *Cultural Studies* 21.2–3 (2007): 168–78.

Rama, Ángel. "José Martí en el eje de la modernización poética: Whitman, Lautréamont, Rimbaud." *Nueva Revista de Filología Hispánica (NRFH)* 32.1 (1983): 95–135.

Ramos-García, Luis. "Las Notas de Miguel Rubio: Teatralización en el imaginario social peruano." *Notas sobre teatro*, Miguel Rubio Zapata. Lima: Grupo Cultural Yuyachkani, 2001. vii–xxxviii.

Rancière, Jacques. *The Emancipated Spectator*. New York: Verso, 2009.

Remmer, Karen L. "Democracy and Economic Crisis: The Latin American Experience." *World Politics* 42.3 (1990): 315–35.

Rizk, Beatriz. *Imaginando un continente: Utopía, democracia, y neoliberalismo en el teatro latinoamericano.* Vol. 1. Lawrence: Latin American Theatre Review Books, 2010.

Rodrigues, Caroline. "Performing Domination and Resistance between Body and Space: The Transversal Activism of Regina José Galindo." *Journal of Media Practice* 12.3 (2011): 292–303.

Román, David. *Performance in America: Contemporary U.S. Culture and the Performing Arts.* Durham: Duke UP, 2005.

Rosenzvaig, Marcos. *El teatro de la enfermedad.* Buenos Aires: Editorial Biblos, 2009.

Rozitchner, León. "Prologue." *That Inferno: Conversations of Five Women Survivors of an Argentine Torture Camp.* Ed. Manú Actis, Cristina Aldini, Liliana Gardella, and Miriam Lewin. Nashville: Vanderbilt UP, 2006. xix–xxiv.

Rubin, Gayle. "The Traffic in Women: Notes on the 'Political Economy' of Sex." *Towards an Anthropology of Women.* Ed. Reyna Reiter. New York: Monthly Review Press, 1975. 157–210.

Rubio Zapata, Miguel. *El cuerpo ausente (performance política).* Lima: Grupo Cultural Yuyachkani, 2008.

Ruyter, Nancy. "Dos ejemplares espectáculos de danza: Geraldas e Avencas y de cabeza." *Gestos Online,* http://www.humanities.uci.edu/gestos/GESTOS%20ONLINE/5-GESTOSONLINENancy%27s_dance_final.pdf

Salazar del Alcázar, Hugo. *Teatro y violencia: Una aproximación al teatro peruano de los '80.* Lima: Centro de Documentación y Video Teatral Jaime Campodónico, 1990.

Salessi, Jorge. *Médicos maleantes y maricas: Higiene, criminología, y homosexualidad en la construcción de la nación argentina* (Buenos Aires, 1871–1914). Buenos Aires: Editorial Beatriz Viterbo, 1995.

Sandhal, Carrie, and Philip Auslander, eds. *Bodies in Commotion: Disability and Performance.* Ann Arbor: U of Michigan P, 2005.

"Introduction." *Bodies in Commotion: Disability and Performance.* Ed. Carrie Sandhal and Philip Auslander. Ann Arbor: U of Michigan P, 2005. 1–12.

Sandoval, Chela. *Methodology of the Oppressed.* Minneapolis: U of Minnesota P, 2000.

Sandoval-Sánchez, Alberto. "Nuyorican Fairy Tales: Allegories of Existence and Bare Survival in Migdalia Cruz and Eddie Sánchez's Theatre." *Freakish Encounters: Constructions of the Freak in Hispanic Cultures.* Ed. Sara Muñoz and Analola Santana. Special Issue of *Hispanic Issues Online* (forthcoming Spring 2018).

Santana, Analola. "Vida del proyecto." *De monstruos y prodigios: La historia de los castrati, recuento de un proyecto teatral inclasificable*. Ed. Leonel Sagahón. Mexico City: CONACULTA/Tintable, 2014. 45–57.

Teatro y cultura de masas: Encuentros y debates. Mexico City: Escenología, 2010.

Sarlo, Beatriz. *Tiempo pasado: Cultura de la memoria y giro subjetivo, una discusión*. Mexico City: Siglo XXI Editores, 2005.

Scenes from Postmodern Life. Trans. Jon Beasley-Murray. Minneapolis: U of Minnesota P, 2001.

Sassen, Saskia. *Expulsions: Brutality and Complexity in the Global Economy*. Cambridge: Harvard UP, 2014.

"Global Cities and Survival Circuits." *American Studies: An Anthology*. Ed. Janice A. Radway, Kevin K. Gaines, Barry Shank, and Penny Von Eschen. Oxford: Wiley-Blackwell, 2009. 185–93.

Schatan, Jacobo. *El saqueo de América Latina: Deuda externa, neoliberalismo, globalización*. Santiago: LOM, 1998.

Shaw, Helen. "The State of the Play: A Critic Addresses the Theatre Nation." *American Theatre*, October 2016. http://www.americantheatre.org/2016/09/21/the-state-of-the-play-a-critic-addresses-the-theatre-nation/.

Siebers, Tobin. *Disability Theory*. Ann Arbor: U of Michigan P, 2008.

"Disability in Theory: From Social Constructionism to the New Reality of the Body." *The Disability Studies Reader*. Ed. Lennard Davies. 2nd ed. Hoboken: Routledge, 2006. 173–84.

Silva Santiesteban, Rocío. *El factor asco: Basurización simbólica y discursos autoritarios en el Perú contemporáneo*. Lima: Fondo Editorial Pontificia Universidad Católica del Perú, 2008.

Sims, Shannon. "The Hilarious Feminist Backlash to Brazil's Impeachment Fallout." *Forbes*, April 20, 2016, https://www.forbes.com/sites/shannonsims/2016/04/20/the-hilarious-feminist-backlash-to-brazils-impeachment-fallout/#24e4afc06573

Sontag, Susan. *Regarding the Pain of Others*. New York: Picador, 2003.

Stiglitz, Joseph E. *Making Globalization Work*. New York: Norton, 2007.

Stulman Dennet, Andrea. *Weird and Wonderful: The Dime Museum in America*. New York: New York UP, 1997.

Taylor, Diana. *The Archive and the Repertoire: Performing Cultural Memory in the Americas*. Durham: Duke UP, 2003.

Disappearing Acts: Spectacles of Gender in Argentina's "Dirty War." Durham: Duke UP, 1997.

Theatre of Crisis: Drama and Politics in Latin America. Lexington: UP of Kentucky, 1991.

Valdés Kuri, Claudio. "Genealogía de monstruos: Concepción y proceso de creación." *De monstruos y prodigios: La historia de los castrati, recuento de un proyecto teatral inclasificable*. Ed. Leonel Sagahón. Mexico City: CONACULTA/Tintable, 2014. 13–31.

"Del director sobre la puesta en escena," *Gestos* 16.31 (2001): 115.

Valle-Inclán, Ramón del. *Bohemian Lights*. Trans. Anthony N. Zahareas and Gerard Gillespie. Austin: U of Texas P, 1976.

Van Dijck, Jose. *Imagenation: Popular Images of Genetics*. New York: New York UP, 1998.

Vargas, Arístides. "Texto Negro." *Revista Teatro/CELCIT* 35–36 (2009): 26–29.

Vich, Víctor. *El cannibal es el Otro: Violencia y cultura en el Perú contemporáneo*. Lima: Intituto de Estudios Peruanos Ediciones, 2002.

Villegas, Juan. "De monstruos y prodigios: La historia de los castrati y la decadencia de la cultura y la estética de occidente." *TEATRO/CELCIT* 19–20 (2002): n.p.

Weiss, Judith. *Latin American Popular Theatre*. Albuquerque: U of New Mexico P, 1993.

Werth, Brenda. *Theatre, Performance, and Memory Politics in Argentina*. New York: Palgrave Macmillan, 2010.

Williams, Gareth. *The Mexican Exception: Sovereignty, Police, and Democracy*. New York: Palgrave Macmillan, 2011.

Wilson, Philip K. "Eighteenth-Century 'Monsters' and Nineteenth-Century 'Freaks': Reading the Maternally Marked Child." *Literature and Medicine* 21.1 (2002): 1–25.

Worthen, Hana. "For a Skeptical Dramaturgy." *Theatre Topics* 24.3 (2014): 175–86.

Woynarski, Lisa. "Snapshot—Ecological Health in Violeta Luna's NK603: Action for Performance & e-Maiz." *Performing Health and Wellbeing*. Ed. Veronica Baxter and Katharine Low. London: Bloomsbury Methuen Drama, 2017. 230–34.

Yúdice, George. "Postmodernism on the Periphery." *South Atlantic Quarterly* 92.3 (1993): 543–56.

Zien, Katherine. "Troubling Multiculturalisms: Staging Trans/National Identities in Teatro de Ciertos Habitantes's *El Gallo*." *Theatre Survey* 55.3 (2014): 343–61.

Žižek, Slavoj. *The Plague of Fantasies*. London: Verso, 2008.

Index